Robert Browning

The Later Poetry

Nandita Sinha

PRESTIGE

Published by
Prestige Books International
New Delhi 110 060

ISBN: 81-85218-72-2
1994

Phototypesetting by
Pivot Computers
Delhi 110 006

Printed at
Mehra Offset Press
New Delhi 110 002

CONTENTS

For
my respected teacher
Professor O.P. Govil
my revered father-in-law
Dr. H.P. Sinha
and
my dearest sister
Mrs. Aloka Ghosh
of Thorold, Ontario, Canada

in grateful acknowledgement
of help and encouragement
generously given

INTRODUCTION

In 1875, Browning wrote to a correspondent about the manner in which critics approached his works:

> The notice had (to my apprehension) the usual fault of beginning at the very beginning of my somewhat lengthy series of works, and criticizing those on a scale which, presently, the writer finds it impossible to sustain, and so he finds it convenient to dismiss the product of half my life with a summary sentence or two – which, in the nature of things, must needs be a condemnatory one, for there is no calling a thing simply 'good' without advancing some proof of its goodness; whereas, if you call it indifferent or bad, readers will gladly dispense with a further sample. I myself have always liked to read a man's *collected* works, of any kind, *backwards,* and what I once thought a fancy I incline now to consider an eminently rational procedure.[1]

The implication is that a correct appraisal of any literary development needs to take into account all its phases. This procedure has, unfortunately, not been applied to Browning's own works, the critical examination of which generally tends to end with *The Ring and the Book* (1868), on the premise that all the writing that followed was essentially minor. This neglect is surprising when we consider, on the one hand, Browning's personal opinions on the course of his later poetic development, and on the other, the evidence of the later poems themselves.

In a letter to Carlyle dated January 23, 1856, Browning wrote: "As I believe no man a real poet or genius of any sort who does not go on improving till eighty and over, I shall begin again and again as often as you set me right."[2] Again, on December 19, 1864, he wrote to Isa Blagden: "On the other hand, I feel such comfort and delight in doing the best I can with my own object of life, – poetry, – which, I think, I never *could* have seen the good of before, . . . I hope to do much more yet."[3]

In the twenty-one years that spanned the period between *The Ring and the Book* (1868) and *Asolando* (1889) Browning kept up a steady output of poetry that intellectually and formally bear witness to his astonishing versatility. Relentlessly experimenting with new forms in which to express his ideas and seeking fresh perspectives to interpret a world in the throes of change, Browning in his later period can never be accused of stagnation.

Nevertheless, the significance of this period has generally escaped notice. The contemporary reviewers were puzzled by what they regarded as Browning's increasing eccentricity. Henry James, writing in *The Nation* of January 20, 1876, remarked:

> Nothing that Mr. Browning writes, of course, can be vapid; if this were possible, it would be a much simpler affair. If it were a case of a writer running thin, as the phrase is, there would be no need for criticism, ... But it may be said of Mr. Browning that he runs thick rather than thin, and he need claim none of the tenderness granted to those who have used themselves up in the service of their admirers. He is robust and vigorous; more so now, even, than heretofore, and he is more prolific than in the earlier part of his career. But his wantonness, his wilfulness, his crudity, his inexplicable want of secondary thought, as we may call it, on the stage of reflection that follows upon the first outburst of an idea, and smooths, shapes and adjusts it – all this alloy of his great genius is more sensible now than ever.[4]

When twentieth century criticism censured Browning's poetry on the twin counts of form and content, the later poetry became its main target of hostility. A characteristic evaluation runs as follows: "Here, in the sequence of works following *The Ring and the Book*, appears the figure of the Ancient Sage, the Browning who tiresomely reiterated his cherished beliefs with a boisterous optimism which has become positively offensive."[5]

Another estimate dismisses the later poetry as being enveloped in "a dense smog of verbal pollution."[6]

But these misconceptions stem from the habit of judging Browning's poetry by standards alien to his art. What is urgently needed is a revaluation that views the later poetry as an integral part of the "whole" Browning. While the earlier period was experimental and as such formed a prelude to the period of the great dramatic monologues, the later period was one of diversification, when ideas and techniques were expanded to suit a temperament that had undergone change with the years.

Recent Browning criticism has viewed the later poetry with sympathetic attention. The development may be traced to an awareness of the importance of Browning's literary influence on the modernists. The foundations were laid by William Clyde DeVane's pioneering research into the sources and background of these poems[8] as well as his meticulous study of a significant later poem – the *Parleyings with Certain People of Importance in Their Day* (1885).[9] Books by scholars like Roma A. King,[10] Philip Drew,[11] and Clyde de L. Ryals,[12] as well as individual studies of the later poems by

John Hintner, Mark Siegchrist, Charlotte Watkins and others,[13] have brought home to us the importance of Browning's later phase. But apart from Ryals's work, no comprehensive attempt has hitherto been made to deal exclusively with the later poetry as representative of Browning's maturity. Ryals' method of examining the poems in the chronological order, illuminating as it is with regard to the form and content of these poems needs, however, to be supplemented with an examination of the later poems as groups having markedly similar structural and thematic characteristics, so that the salient features of Browning's mind and art during this period may be more easily assessed. This is the approach adopted in the present study, an approach that allows for an evaluation of characteristic features within the group and facilitates comparison with earlier poems of the same kind so that Browning's later poetic development is clearly traced.

Six recurrent preoccupations in Browning's poetry – philosophy, love, casuistry, satire, aesthetic theory and Greek themes – are examined through the later poetry, in order to assess Browning's mode of treating them in his maturity and to place them in relation to his earlier poetry. This approach serves two related purposes. First, it enables us to discern in the poetry of the later period a continuation of interests initiated in the earlier. Secondly, it gives a view of this poetry, not as mirroring Browning's decline, but as a culmination in practice of Browning's theory of the poet's development.

It has generally been held that Browning was a dramatic and objective poet, and that he rejected the Romantic tradition of subjective poetry. But in his *Essay on Shelley* (1852), after a discussion of the role of the poet as fashioner and seer respectively, Browning goes on to describe "a time when the general eye has, so to speak, absorbed its fill of the phenomena around it, whether spiritual or material, and desires rather to learn the exacter significance of what it possesses, than to receive any augmentation of what is possessed. Then is the opportunity for the poet of loftier vision, to lift his fellows, with their half-apprehensions, up to his own sphere, by intensifying the import of details and rounding the universal meaning."[14] Sufficient attention has not been paid to the fact that, in his later period, Browning attempted to take his verse in this very direction. It was not enough for him at this later stage to present points of view as he had hitherto done; his work needed to be more explicitly meaningful. Possibly he now felt impelled to comply with his dead wife's desire that he express truths more overtly:

> I do not think with all the music in you, only your own personality should be dumb, nor that having thought so much and deeply on life and its ends, you should not teach what you have learnt, in the directest

> and most impressive way, the mask thrown off however moist with the breath. And it is not, I believe, by the dramatic medium, that poets teach most impressively. . . . I have seemed to observe *that*! . . . It is too difficult for the common reader to analyse, and to discern between the vivid and the earnest. . . . Therefore I do want you to do this with your surpassing power – it will be so easy for you to speak, and so noble, when spoken.[15]

But along with this desire to fuse the inner and the outer worlds, the "spiritual comprehension" and the "raw material" that he had spoken of in the *Essay on Shelley*, was Browning's keener awareness of the difficulties of attaining to the absolute truth amidst the limited perceptions vouchsafed to man in this finite world. It is this tension betwen the desire to unequivocally express the truth and the realisation that this expression can, at best, be partial, that permeates the later poetry and gives it its particular shape. Once this is understood and accepted, all the difficulties of Browning's later poetry may be seen as inescapable adjuncts to a poetry of search.

For Browning is led to present truth as he saw it, not dogmatically, but as an exploration of the process of attaining to that truth. Over and over again he insists that his assumptions hold good for his own self alone. This exploration demands the wider framework that is so noticeable in the later poetry, and even its unattractive features, argumentativeness, prolixity, may be traced to this desire to present as many perspectives as possible within a poem. An emphasis on this aspect of the later poetry is, therefore, necessary in order to refute the fallacies that have been most detrimental to a true appreciation of the later work – the impression that these poems are merely versified argumentation and full of a blustering yea-saying. A detailed study of various themes in the poetry of this period will help to define the complexity of Browning's mind and art and to expose the hollowness of these charges.

Clyde de L. Ryals points out in the introduction to his book on Browning's later poetry that with the composition of *The Ring and the Book*, Browning came to discover that "what man is left with finally in his determination of truth is himself: in his search for 'objective reality' he discovers that he always confronts himself alone."[16] But Ryals fails to develop this crucial point further, and it will be the object of this study to show that the next step in Browning's growth as a poet was taken in the poetry that followed, when he evolved his theory of the imaginative vision, a theory that replaced the Incarnation as Browning's source of value in the later period and became his primary aid in the task of putting the infinite within the finite.

Browning's later narrative art is, an aspect of his poetry that, in the mass of critical attention devoted to the dramatic monologue as a form most characteristic of Browning, has generally been neglected. The contemporary critics who noted the "prose effect" in Browning's verse, did so disparagingly. Henry James, however, saw a novel in *The Ring and the Book*,[17] while R.L. Stevenson noted of *The Inn Album* (1875): "It bears a remarkable resemblance to some of Balzac's shorter tales... it has the same purely human import."18 Oscar Wilde said: "Yes, Browning was great. And as what will he be remembered? As a poet? Ah, not as a poet! He will be remembered as a writer of fiction, as the most supreme writer of fiction, it may be, that we have ever had."[19] More recently, Hugh Sykes Davies asked:

> But when we read Browning are we reading poetry? Or are we reading him primarily because it is poetry? Those are the really dubious points, for it must be granted at once that with many of his young readers the real attraction is in the incident, the character, the gusto of the monologue. And this, after all, is an attraction by no means special or proper to poetry, for it is shared with prose fiction, and also with drama.

He further suggested Browning's affinities with the novel, pointing out that "he was the Victorian poet who most completely fell in with – surrendered to, if you like – this new and overwhelming literary impetus."[20] Philip Drew is of the opinion that *Prince Hohenstiel-Schwangau* (1871), *Fifine at the Fair* (1872), *Red Cotton Night-Cap Country* (1873) and *The Inn Album* (1875) "show a progressively greater affinity with the novels of the mid-century."[21] But no critic has so far examined the links between Browning's techniques in his narrative poems of the later period and the techniques that have been used by "modern" novelists, such as Henry James' rendering rather than reporting, and Conrad's putting the narrator inside the story to refract and interpret it. In fact, Browning himself faced a problem that was a major preoccupation with the modern novelists – the problem of approaching the subject through a point of view that was not the author's own. The interior monologue that is a feature of modern fiction bears a close resemblance to the dramatic monologue and many studies have looked into this area in recent years.[22] The present study, however, proposes to show that in the longer narrative poems of his later phase, Browning sought to enlarge the range of the dramatic monologue in directions reminiscent of the point-of-view novel, in order to create, by juxtaposition of multiple perspectives, his sense of the manifold complexity of ideas, feelings and motives in individual minds.

All quotations from Browning's poetry from *The Ring and the Book* (1868) and onwards are from the second volume of *The Poetical Works of Robert Browning*, 2 Vols., London: Smith Elder, 1904, with the exception of quotations from *Balaustion's Adventure* (1871) and *Aristophanes' Apology* (1875) for which *The Poems and Plays of Robert Browning*, New York: The Modern Library, 1934, has been used. Line numbers have been added for the shorter poems, while page numbers or stanza numbers have been cited for the longer poems. All references to poems prior to *The Ring and the Book* are from *Browning: Poetical Works, 1833-1864,* ed. Ian Jack, London: Oxford University Press, 1970.

NOTES

1. *Letters of Robert Browning Collected by Thomas J. Wise,* ed. Thurman L. Hood (London: John Murray, 1933), p. 165. Hereafter cited as *Letters*, ed. Hood.
2. *Ibid.*, p. 44.
3. *Dearest Isa: Robert Browning's Letters to Isabella Blagden*, ed. Edward C. McAleer (Austin: University of Texas Press, 1951), p. 201.
4. Quoted in *Browning: The Critical Heritage*, ed. Boyd Litzinger and Donald Smalley (London: Routledge and Kegan Paul, 1970), p. 415.
5. J.W. Harper, "'Eternity Our Due': Time in the Poetry of Robert Browning" in *Stratford-upon-Avon Studies, 15, Victorian Poetry,* ed. Malcolm Bradbury and David Palmer (London: Edward Arnold, 1972), p. 59.
6. Ian Jack, *Browning's Major Poetry* (Oxford: Clarendon Press, 1973), p. 272.
7. George Bornstein, *Poetic Remaking: The Art of Browning, Yeats and Pound* (Pennsylvania State Univ. Press, 1988).
8. William Clyde DeVane, *A Browning Handbook,* 2nd edition (New York: Appleton Century Crofts, 1955).
9. William Clyde DeVane, *Browning's Parleyings: The Autobiography of a Mind* (New Haven: Yale University Press, 1927).
10. Roma A. King, *The Focusing Artifice* (Athens: Ohio University Press, 1968).
11. Philip Drew, *The Poetry of Browning: A Critical Introduction* (London: Methuen, 1970). Hereafter cited as Drew, *The Poetry of Browning.*
12. Clyde de L. Ryals, *Browning's Later Poetry* (1871-1889) (Ithaca: Conrnell University Press, 1975).
13. See Select Bibliography.
14. *Essay on Shelley,* in *Browning: Poetry and Prose,* selected by Simon Nowell-Smith (London: Rupert Hart-Davis, 1967), p. 675.
15. *The Letters of Robert Browning and Elizabeth Barrett 1845-1846,* ed. Elvan Kintner (Cambridge, Mass.: The Belknap Press of Harvard University Press, 1969), II, p. 732. Hereafter cited as *Letters of RB and EBB.*
16. *Browning's Later Poetry*, p. 23.

17. "The Novel in *The Ring and the Book*" in *Notes on Novelists with Some Other Notes* (London: Dent, 1914), pp. 306-26.
18. Quoted in *Browning: The Critical Heritage*, p. 412.
19. *Ibid.*, pp. 525-26.
20. Hugh Sykes Davies, "Browning" in *Robert Browning: A Collection of Critical Essays,* ed. Philip Drew (London: Methuen, 1966), p. 62.
21. *The Poetry of Browning,* p. 336.
22. For example, Loy D. Martin, *Browning's Dramatic Monologues and the Post-Romantic Subject* (John Hopkins Univ. Press, 1985). Also, E. Warwick Slim, *Browning and the Fictions of Identity* (Macmillan Press, 1982), and Ross Posnock, *Henry James and the Problem of Robert Browning* (University of Georgia Press, 1985).

PHILOSOPHICAL THOUGHT IN THE LATER POETRY

With the founding of the Browning Society in 1881 and the publication of Mrs. Sutherland Orr's *Handbook*[1] (1836), where she noted that "much of Mr. Browning's moral influence lies in the hopeful religious spirit which his works reveal" the adulation of Browning's so-called moral fervour reached its height. Sir Henry Jones in his book *Browning as a Philosophical and Religious Teacher*, 1891, specifically called Carlyle and Browning "the prophets of our age."[2] In fact, Bernard Shaw was led to remark wryly of the Browning Society--"No matter what paper they had before them, in the discussion they always got into Browning's optimistic theology."[3]

It was this emphasis on Browning as a philosopher, teacher and religious thinker, and the impression created of a hearty, blustering optimist that proved so unpalatable to twentieth century opinion. The general consensus was: "From being a comfort to his century, a stay against confusion, he has become an irritant to ours."[4]

The increasingly direct philosophic burden of the later poetry appeared in response to the atmosphere of religious uncertainty in the latter half of the nineteenth century. It was also the result of Browning's increasing need to voice what he felt was the truth, as evinced by his letter to Isa Blagden, "but I look on everything in this world with altered eyes, and can no more take interest in anything I see there but the proof of certain great principles, strewn in the booths at a fair."[5] Between the barren intellectual despair of an Empedocles and a passive non-involvement (both totally alien to Browning's nature), lay his own choice of intellectual search supplemented by intuitive guidelines. Having rejected Romantic idealism and historical dogma, Browning in his later poetry embarks on a hard quest to go beyond traditional solutions towards a view that is experiential and not doctrinaire. The basis of this quest is the belief that solutions have to be evolved by man himself in response to his own personal needs.

The philosophy in the later poetry is thus not didacticism, but an exploration of meaning and values. A central feature of these poems is the intellectual pattern of enquiry followed by an assertion of the necessity for the imaginative apprehension of truth. This apprehension is of necessity partial, tentative, subjective. It is often neither logical nor consistent, not a formulated idea that dispels the problem, but an advancement in perception. To point out the illogicality of the process and its imprecision, as critics like Henry Jones have done, is to miss the point that Browning is not advocating a system. As Roma A. King points out: "We ask rather if it provides the motive and means by which man may act out his being and achieve a sense of wholeness. Its validity rests upon the quality of life which it makes possible."[6]

Recent studies, assessing Browning's poetry anew, have found in him "a spirit which ached with longing and uncertainty"[7] and "a probing, questioning mind"[8] behind the deceptively confident exterior. Poems like *La Saisiaz* and the "Epilogue" to *Ferishtah's Fancies* reveal Browning's sensitive awareness of the ambiguities and complexities that surround human life. His resolutions at this later stage waver between incisiveness and an awareness of the tentative nature of all judgements. Even as he presents man's imaginative perception and loving faith as the means of apprehending the infinite and as antidotes to the meaninglessness that is consequent upon man's realization of his imperfections, he stresses its validity for his own self alone. The later Browning is much less strident than he is generally held out to be; and the "thought" in the later poetry is best approached not in terms of theological doctrine but in terms of the felt experience of a man seeking truths by which to live.

In 1877, the year in which *La Saisiaz* was written, Browning was 65 years old, and the reality of death appears to have impinged on his consciousness with forceful immediacy with the sudden death of his close friend, Miss Annie Egerton Smith, at the chalet "La Saisiaz" near Geneva, where they were spending a summer holiday together. The emotional upheaval engendered by this event may have set Browning upon a course of elucidation of the problem of personal salvation and life after death. In "Bishop Blougram's Apology," he had voiced his awareness of the uncertainties that underlie human existence with lyrical sincerity:

> Just when we are safest, there's a sunset-touch,
> A fancy from a flower-bell, someone's death,
> A chorus-ending from Euripides--
> And that's enough for fifty hopes and fears
> As old and new at once as nature's self,
> To rap and knock and enter in our soul,
> Take hands and dance there, a fantastic ring,
> Round the ancient idol, on his base again-
> The grand Perhaps! (ll. 182-90)

In *La Saisiaz*, Browning takes up the same problem of faith and belief and examines it, not as a vehicle to explore its psychological ramifications in a dramatized character (as he had done in "An Epistle of Karshish" and "Cleon"), but as a personal question which demands an agonizing debate of the mind with the self.

Browning's assault on the possibility and nature of the after-life is characteristically a vigorous one, devoid of either pessimism or despairing apathy. While profound grief made Tennyson lyrically poignant,[9] it makes Browning all the more tortuously argumentative as he seeks to come to grips with that grief. His exploration is based on the belief that though man is a limited finite creature, he holds infinity within him and demands infinity as an end. Whether this instinctive demand can have a rational basis is the problem that engages Browning in *La Saisiaz*.

The dedication lyrically presents the main theme of the poem--death and the consequent release of the soul from earthly bondage. The sudden realization of the barrier between the living and the dead gives intensity to the first part of the poem which describes the climb up Mount Saleve, a climb originally planned by Miss Smith, but now attempted by Browning alone. Browning's playful rejoinder to Miss Smith at the end of an initial reconnoitre--"With yourself it rests to have a month of tomorrows like today" (l.58)--becomes painfully ironic in retrospect. With a quick description of the hours of pleasant companionship, Miss Smith's shy nature, the suddenness of her passing away, the first part ends with "Climbing--here I stand; but you--where?" (l. 139)

The personal mode of utterance in the poem serves to emphasize the depth of the emotion that is at the base of the poem and to off-set the aridity of the analytical argument that forms its structure. Yet, the argument is not always a "mere grey" one. As Geoffrey Tillotson remarks: "It is always vigorous and better still always breaking into pictures."[10]

One example will suffice to illustrate Browning's firm hold on the concrete even amidst the most abstruse philosophising. Browning talks of the five days since Miss Smith's death:

> Five short days, sufficient hardly
> to entice from its den
> Splintered in the slab, this pink
> perfection of the cyclamen;
> Scarce enough to heal and coat with
> amber gum the sloe-tree's gash,
> Bronze the clustered wilding apple,
> redden the mountain ash. (ll. 15-18)

The debate in *The Nineteenth Century* conducted on the subject of "The Soul and Future Life," which had been followed with keen interest by both Miss Smith and Browning, provided the basic premises on which Browning grounded his arguments on immortality. DeVane notes that these arguments "like those of most of the contributors to the Symposium deliberately left on one side the question of the authority of the Christian revelation."[11] While on the one hand the ideas have a familiar echo from *Easter-Day* (1850) and "A Death in the Desert" (*Dramatic Personae*, 1864), on the other, *La Saisiaz* marks a change in the direction of Browning's thought. For if, as T.J. Collins says, "In *Christmas-Eve and Easter-Day* Browning moves from the God-centred non-doctrinal Christianity of his early poetry to an equally liberal, but more specifically doctrinal mode of belief,"[12] then *La Saisiaz* shows him reverting to his former position and adopting a freer, more exploratory point of view.

A recurrent motif in Browning's poetry--the antithesis between Power and Love is in this poem transposed into specific questions, "Does the soul survive the body? Is there God's self, no or yes?" (l.145), and into personal terms--"Was ending once and always, when you died?" (l. 173), Browning rigidly imposes control on his emotions by establishing the precise pattern of the question-and-answer debate with which to examine his beliefs. Since he cannot know but can only surmise he acknowledges his willingness to accept the truth, however unpalatable, as also to accept the fact, as F.E.L. Priestley states it, that "the truth arrived at will be limited by man's finitude: it will be truth for 'truth is truth in each degree," but will not be the ultimate truth as God sees it."[13]

A famous philosopher once said, "Only the feeble resign themselves to final death and substitute some other desire for the longing for personal immortality."[14] For Browning, the first possibility in the face of this longing is the transcendentalist concept of a cosmic continuity. But the idea of a consciousness ceasing to be its unique self is repugnant to the ego. What remains is the feeling that without the certainty of continued existence after death, life itself is a cruel mockery. Having rejected a scientific hypothesis, Browning's next step in his exploration of the "controverted doctrine" (l. 211) is based on intuitive belief, his personal belief in the "soul's eclipse" (l. 213) and not the "Soul's extinction"[15] (l. 214). He finds corroboration in Dante's lines: "I believe and I declare--/ Certain I am--from this life I pass into a better, there/ Where that lady lives of whom enamoured was my soul" (ll. 214-16).

But this also is temporarily set aside, for instinctive feeling has no place in Browning's scheme for this debate. What he sets out to prove has to be gleaned through rationally acceptable facts. Therefore, he begins again with two of the very basic facts--the existence of God and the soul. What lies beyond these Browning terms "conjecture styled belief." (l. 234) Various arguments in favour of immortality--God is wise and good, He seems potent, Anyhow we want it--are propounded and demolished as inapplicable to the argument because hypothetical. For the poet is determined to go only on facts, and the one fact of which he can be absolutely sure is the fact of his own experience: "Knowledge stands on my own experience" (l. 273).[16] So now his course of action is this: "From thine apprehended scheme of things, deduce/Praise or blame of its contriver" (ll. 288-89).

Browning's own apprehension of the scheme of things results in a struggle within him between the intellect searching for the certainties of life on the basis of reason alone, and the heart intuitively reaching out for something which defies logical explanation but which is emotionally a reality.

When he attempts to solve his problem on a purely intellectual level, pushing his speculations as far as they would go, his efforts are doomed to failure. For reason shows him on all sides a world of evil and despair and darkness, which then confronts him with the dilemma--" did He lack power or was the will at fault." (l. 304). Reason by itself can only lead man to pessimism, for everywhere he is faced with evidence of Power but not of Love. In the poems of the earlier period, this duality is reconciled by recourse to the concept of the Incarnation, through the belief that in sending Christ, His son, to suffer and die for man, God revealed his infinite love. In "A Death in the Desert," John says--"I say, the acknowledgement of God in Christ/Accepted by thy reason, solves for thee/All questions in the earth and out of it." (ll. 474-76). In *The Ring and the Book*, the Pope's response is similar:

> An isoscele deficient in the base.
> What lacks, then, of perfection fit for God
> But just the instance which this tale supplies
> Of love without a limit? (X, 1366-69)

In *La Saisiaz* the solution is sought to be attained through reason alone, but Browning cannot for long maintain this position. In fact, he is led to some jugglery at this point in order to justify his carrying over the argument into the realms of the emotions. Having already prepared the ground by stating that his personal experience is the "fact" on which he bases his assumptions, he can now safely assert that since his own experience corroborates it, he is sure of the presence of love in his heart, and that this love includes hope and faith in the future life, where all the imperfections of this earth are made perfect. The inference is clear that the approach which leads to hope is to be preferred to that which is conducive to despair. Without the certainty of the after-life, the burden of this life is meaningless. It is this certainty that provides him "solid, standing place" amidst the "wash and welter of doubts," as he would say later in the "Parleying with Francis Furini" (section X).

Taking a stand similar to that of the peasant who, when told by the philosopher that there might be God in the form of an universal consciousness but that man's soul might not be immortal, replied, "Then wherefore God?" Browning can find no explanation for the obvious limitations of the goodness, wisdom and power of the Divine Being on earth, if it is not linked with Love in ordaining man immortality after death. He is brought to a point similar to Cleon's situation, a point at which he feels that life would be meaningless without Divine concern and Divine intervention:

> Only grant a second life; I acquiesce
> In this present life as failure, count misfortune's worst assaults
> Triumph, not defeat, assured that loss so much the more exalts
> Gain about to be. (ll. 359-62)

At this point, Browning again changes his vantage-point to view his problem from the other side. He realizes that his belief in the after-life has not been proved as fact through the ratiocinative process, but neither is he willing to acknowledge that it is merely a fancy that he cherishes so dearly. Now, in the face of his dominant need to believe, categorical imperatives become unimportant. The train of his thoughts ranges from doubt to will-to-believe to uncertainty. Only one option remains open. If the realm of fact can offer no hope, then perhaps conjecture and surmise, hitherto rejected, may be made use of. The tension is thus delicately sustained between the inter-play of opposing forces--the intuitive belief and the analytical propensity to discard all but the proven facts.

Following the sudden realization that he has been straying into just the territory that he had stipulated to exclude, Browning once again avows: "Ay, well and best, if fact's self I may force the answer from" (l. 396). To this end, as Clyde de L. Ryals observes, he "reverts to interior dialogue such as characterized *Prince Hohenstiel-Schwangau*, dividing himself into two persons to do battle with each other."[18] Fancy is now allowed to take as proven fact the existence of the soul after death. The focus of the argument is thus reversed and at once becomes more complex, for now it is no longer the fact that he is to be examined, but the consequences and suppositions that may be drawn from it.

Both Fancy and Reason begin with the accepted premise that "O'er this life the next presents advantage much and manifold" (l. 428). Reason goes on to argue that if death is so desirable, shouldn't man choose death "at suspicion of first cloud athwart his sky/Flower's departure, frost's arrival?" (ll. 457-58). Fancy then adds another proviso--suicide is prohibited. Reason counters with the philosophy of passive acceptance of life on earth, whether for good or evil, because all shall be righted in the next life. This again is inadmissible, with Fancy demanding that "man become aware/Life has worth incalculable, every moment that he spends/So much gain or loss for that next life." (ll. 480-82) Reason proceeds to pinpoint the flaw in this line of reasoning. Fixed laws regarding reward and punishment will make man's moral nature of no significance, "Prior to this announcement, earth was man's probation place/Liberty of doing evil gave his good a grace" (ll. 495-96). The debate between Fancy and Reason thus reaches, as Philip Drew points out "an equally unacceptable terminus."[19] The inference is that it is not possible for the mind to prove anything with certainty, for whether one begins with the hypothetical possibility of the after-life, or whether one accepts it as fact and then analyzes the effect of this knowledge on man, all lines of argument end in uncertainty. The emphasis is on the essential incommunicability of faith. What remains is hope, but, for Browning, this is once again a personally held belief: "Hope the arrowy, just as constant, comes to pierce its gloom, compelled/ By a power and a purpose which, if no one else beheld,/ I behold in Life, so--hope!" (ll. 547-49). Philip Drew is correct in his conclusion that for Browning "an act of trust was an essential element of faith: this meant believing even when the reason withheld its assent."[20] Bishop Blougram expresses a similar idea:

> All's doubt in me, where's break of faith in this?
> It is the idea, the feeling and the love,
> God means mankind should strive for and show forth
> Whatever be the process to that end,--
> And not historic knowledge, logic sound
> And metaphysical acumen, sure! (ll. 620-25)

In *La Saisiaz*, Browning expresses his awareness that the conclusion reached is not unassailable, but just about the best that can be done under the circumstances. If the doctrine of hope is but the "Sad summing up of all to say" (l. 550), it is nevertheless the only alternative to spiritual despair. This message of despair had been preached by Rousseau: "All's that's good is gone and past;/ Bad and worse grows the present, and worst of all comes last" (ll. 566-67); and also by Byron: "Of all objects found on earth/ Man is meanest" (l. 573-74). Men acquiesced because "the famous bard believed" (l. 577) and also because they found "significance in fire-works" (l. 605). F.E.L. Priestley rightly points to the irony behind these lines,[21] which highlight Browning's contempt for men who passively accept formulated doctrines without testing them against their own experience. In fact, the whole process in *La Saisiaz* is directed to showing how men may shape own belief in a way that would be true to their individuality. The doctrines of pessimism are entirely opposed to Browning's belief in man's essential nobility and his unceasing progress towards goodness. In a fine frenzy of indignation, he yearns for fame, the "coruscating marvel" (l. 600), and with a prolonged metaphor suggestive of fire and light and energy--Beacon-like, dazzling, flashed, sparkled, kindled, effulgence, brand flamboyant--he gives voice to his own message as a man who "at least believed in Soul, was very sure of God" (l. 609).

Browning's argument may thus be summed up: that while objective certitude is not possible or even desirable (because it would destroy the freedom of man's ethical choices), still, since believing is first an act of will or desire, since faith in the thing helps to create the thing itself, the final test of truth lies in the consequences which it produces. For Browning himself, it results in a hopeful stance with which to face the world. His final position is thus a return to his initial one of belief in the two unshakeable certainties of self and God. The rest is personal conviction, frankly admitted as such, though none the less important for being based on his own experience. Like Tennyson in *In Memoriam* he can "trust,/ With faith that comes of self-control,/The truths that never can be proved" (CXXXI).

After the breathless urgency of the passage on fame, the movement of the poem slides down to a muted phase of emotion recollected in tranquillity. The poet admits his failure in conducting the enquiry on the purely intellectual level. His thoughts are the linked chain whose arguments are valid only until they encounter that unfathomable entity, death. Like a root that is transplanted at a congenial time most suited to its flowering, he has carried the memory of the climb and the thoughts there evoked, to London, where he has "link by link, unravelled any tangle of the chain" (l. 616). But those memories whose awakening would cause greater emotional upheaval still lay dormant within him. The reticence that had briefly been pushed aside in the lyrical assertion of his wife's immortality now descends again to veil his deepest thoughts and emotions about her. His argument as represented by the poem is but the "least part" (l. 623) of his total feelings. We remember Browning's disgust for the mawkish, sentimental poetry of self-revelation. So even in such a personal utterance as *La Saisiaz* there is the imposition of an intellectual pattern that helps to objectify and distance the emotion, while in its turn, the personal note serves to lend sincerity and credibility to the philosophy.

La Saisiaz represents an attempt by Browning to approach the problem of faith, salvation and immortality from an intellectual standpoint. His failure to do so is his answer Harrison essayists who, as has been pointed out, insisted on "knowledge not feeling, on fact not fancy, on evidence and proof not surmise, on law not hypothesis, on prose, not poetry as a serious and effective medium."[22] Browning's own conclusion is that reason is ineffectual without the wider apprehensions of the intuitions. A comparison with "Cleon" is illuminating. In the figure of Cleon, Browning combines the rationalistic philosopher with the imaginative poet, and shows how inability to reconcile these two aspects leads to despair. Cleon's intellectual pride blinds him to the very apprehension that he desires and that would save him.

Both John in "A Death in the Desert" and the Pope in *The Ring and the Book* recognize the need in man for an indication of love along with his awareness of will and might. Just as man's instinctive need for love makes him respond to the Christian story, so, in *La Saisiaz*, Browning argues that man's instinctive need for life after death is the most powerful evidence of its truth. No scientific evidence can provide certain proof. But to reject the partial revelations of God's love on earth is to invite despair and negation.

In a letter to Julia Wedgewood in 1864, Browning tells her that "though his temper is inclined to dispute both authoritative tradition and mere wishes of the mind, he reasons upon 'the rare flashes of momentary conviction that come and go in the habitual dusk and doubt of life' and so, taking the result of all this to be indisputable, believes in re-union after death."[23] His plea, in *La Saisiaz*, is a plea for the acknowledgement of the validity of the imaginative and the intuitive along with the rational and the intellectual, and is characteristic of the later poetry in general, reiterated in various guises in *Ferishtah's Fancies* and in the *Parleyings*.

"Pisgah Sights I and II" (*Pacchiarotto and How He Worked in Distemper: With Other Poems*, 1876) present a recurrent theme in Browning's poetry, the mixed nature of man's existence on earth, with good and evil coexisting side by side, and the necessity of accepting this state as a challenge. The speaker realizes that there is more to be gained in experiencing all the aspects of life than in unwisely attempting to change any particular one.

In "Jochanan Hakkadosh," the longest poem of the *Jocoseria* volume (1883), Browning carries out another exploration of the nature and the implications of man's awareness of the existence of the other world. The philosophical content is only superficially dramatized. DeVane remarks: "Browning's main intention in the poem is to expound the favourite metaphysical doctrines of his old age--the superiority of the intuitive faculties over the intellectual ones in giving man a knowledge of God."[24]

The old and wise Hakkadosh is granted an extension to his life by periods of three months at a time, the gifts of a lover, a soldier, a statesman, a poet and a young boy. Jochanan finds "Love, war, song, statesmanship--no gain, all loss." (l. 427) These make man aware of his body, not his soul. It is only in the period of his last gift that he finds himself "Absurdly happy." (l.468) He has attained to the "calm struck by encountering opposites,/Each enullifying either." (ll. 476-77) Speaking from the vantage point of an enlarged consciousness, Hakkadosh finds that the opposites of right and wrong, false and true, dream and reality only appear irreconciliable to man because of his limited perceptions. Even man's reason cannot help him to perceive truths in their "primal clarity" (l. 526) for reason which "sees light half shine half shade,/ Because of flesh, the medium that adjusts/ Purity to his visuals" (ll. 519-31) is both "an aid/And hindrance." (ll. 531-32) Only to a man freed from the bondage of the bounded self does life appear as "Waves brackish, in a mixture, sweet with brine,/That's neither sea nor river but taste of both--so meet the earthly and the divine." (ll. 580-82) From the juxtaposition of faith and doubt and of hopes and fears, Hakkadosh discovers that this life is as a winepress, blending both good and evil. The idea of the relativity of knowledge as a necessary condition of finite existence receives similar attention in the Pope's monologue in *The Ring and the Book*:

> Absolute, abstract, independent truth,
> Historic, not reduced to suit man's mind,--
> Or only truth reverberate, changed, made pass
> A spectrum into mind, the narrow eye,--
> The same and not the same, else unconceived--
> Though quite conceivable to the next grade
> Above it in intelligence,--as truth. (X,1389-95)

The story in the sonnets that follow the main body of the poem is "pure mystification,"[25] according to DeVane, but the last lines merit attention. The axe that keeps falling without reaching the bottom of what appears to be a shallow rivulet is man's understanding of God which can never encompass the total reality. The poem thus illustrates Browning's belief that the intimations of the divine in this world are necessarily unsatisfactory, but that man must strive to attain that larger perspective that can fuse the actual and the ideal.

Most of the poetry immediately following *La Saisiaz* is narrative in form, the impression they give being that of a story telling itself. But Browning's intellectual and moral seriousness impelled him in a contrary direction. His desire to give fuller expression to his understanding of human nature caused him to turn to poetry that was frankly an embodiment of his personally held beliefs. To put it differently, he used his poetry as a vehicle for exploring the validity of his beliefs. In *Ferishtah's Fancies* (1884), the dramatic tension is reduced to sundry philosophical reflections and speculations. But though the sense of taking part in an actual, living experience is missing, Browning's thought rarely veers into the abstract. His method of using homely, everyday analogies to illustrate his concepts firmly establishes his philosophy as an integral part of human personality.

The quotation from *King Lear* in the epigraph is revealing; the garments are ostensibly Ferishtah's, but they can be "changed" i.e. transferred to somebody else (in this case to the poet himself). As Philip Drew notes, "the resultant discourse is so much in accord with Browning's own temper that there is little pretence at dramatic distancing of poet and speaker."[26]

The form of the poem is whimsically explained in the "Prologue" in terms of the Italian style preparation of ortolans--toasted bread, followed by a pungent sage-leaf and then by the roasted bird. So the poem will have "sense, sight and song," i.e. the meaning or the philosophy, its exposition through a parable and a lyric embodying the theme in concrete terms. Clyde de L. Ryals describes it thus: "The structure of *Ferishtah's Fancies* manifests Browning's belief that all philosophical questions can be answered only by reference to human love; or, to put it another way, the form reflects the poet's philosophy that the counsels of the intellect which form the dialectic of the fancies, are authenticated by man's ability to love."[27]

The "Prologue" presents the context for the arguments that follow, acceptance of God's will on earth and faith in the beneficence of what is to come hereafter.

The Fancies, may, for convenience, be divided into three broad groups. The first group of poems deals with man's duties towards God and humanity at large. "The Eagle" narrates the incident which prompted Ferishtah towards dervishhood--the sight of the eagle feeding the helpless raven fledgelings inspires him to the thought that man's duty is to acquire "helpful strength" (l.28) for the benefit of mankind. And yet, since one should (in the words of Festus in *Paracelsus*) "Presume not to serve God apart from such/ Appointed channels as wills shall gather/ Imperfect tributes" (l.306-8), the lover in the lyric abjures isolation for the pressing throngs of the world.

"Two Camels" illustrates the point that wholesome joy is to be preferred to righteous misery. Asceticism is to be condemned because it does not contribute to the joys of others. Man exists to serve God and he can do so only when he accepts thankfully the pleasures that God provides, not when he mortifies himself by rejecting them. The lyric enlarges upon a theme touched upon very frequently in Browning's poetry--that of acceptance of man's finite conception of God's infinitude. Yet, in the fact of human love lies our best evidence of divine beatitude. Once again, there is a characteristic idea that recurs over and over again in the later poetry--life on earth is not be disdained because it is imperfect:

> . . . how should I conceive
> What a heaven there may be? Let it but resemble
> Earth myself have known! No bliss that's finer, fuller,
> Only--bliss that lasts, they say, and fain would I believe.

"Cherries" carries forward an idea that Ferishtah had initially propounded in "Two Camels," namely that man must render gratitude to God for his gifts and work to multiply his talents. But though man's means are limited, though his good will meets obstacles at every step, his loving gratitude for the simple pleasures of life is dear to the Giver. The idea is transposed into concrete terms in the lyric. Even if the little that can be accomplished falls short of man's aspirations, it is better than nothing at all. The speaker asserts that he has carried on with verse-making and love-making, if not with transcendental effect, but at least to the best of his ability. Waiting for great blessings for which to render gratitude in larger measures is undesirable. Neither is man to doubt the worth of his least gifts of gratitude. Another parable in the same poem illustrates the necessity of paying thanks for the present pleasures and not probing unwisely into what is essentially unknowable.

"Plot-Culture" discusses the validity of the gratification of the senses, Ferishtah's position is that man has been apportioned his plot on earth to use as he deems fit, provided he "remember doomsday" (l. 46) when he must account to God. The lyric affirms the importance of sense as well as soul in a love-relationship. The duality that Browning had established in earlier love poems is reaffirmed.[28] DeVane reads this poem as "Browning's protest, as in the lyric attached to 'The Family' in *Ferishtah* against a Platonic infatuation."[29] The memories that intrude, which DeVane believes to be those of Mrs. Browning may be more logically attributed to those of Lady Ashburton, so that, viewed in this light, the lyric becomes an assertion on Browning's part of his hopes of reunion with his wife in a fully integrated relationship.

The second group of poems in *Ferishtah's Fancies* concerns itself with the theme of acceptance of God's will on earth and trust in his ultimate beneficence.

Both good and evil are part of God's dispensation in "The Melon-Seller," but, while some may find prayer to be an imposition on God's will, Ferishtah would rather believe that prayer serves to express the vital emotions of pity, sympathy, fear and love, with the ultimate decision left trustingly to God's wisdom.

An important theme in this group of poems is the problem of evil. The question had engaged Browning from his earliest poetry. In *Paracelsus*, the faculty of love enhances that of knowledge, leading man to see "a good in evil, and a hope/In ill-success." (V.875-76) The idea is present in *Easter-Day*:

> Mere misery under human schemes,
> Becomes, regarded by the light
> Of love, as very near, or quite
> As good a gift as joy before. (ll.218-21)

A further corollary to the idea is given by the Pope in *The Ring and the Book*, who believes that "this dread machinery/Of sin and sorrow" (X,1375-76) has been devised "To evolve/By new machinery in counterpart/The moral qualities of man." (X.1378-80) *In Fifine at the Fair*, evil and falsehood are the means by which truth is attained. *La Saisiaz* acknowledges the immense burden which evil in this world poses to a consciousness that would come to terms with the conception of a loving God. The reality of evil is accepted, because, when seen in the light of the possibility of an after-life for man, it becomes virtually a necessity for this life of probation.

In "Mihrab Shah," pain becomes the bond of sympathy between man and man, and also the means for giving thanks to God for escape from it. The conclusion is that without gratitude to God and loving sympathy towards fellowmen, man's life would not be a worthy one. Browning's manner of explaining the presence of evil and pain in this world centres on his characteristic belief that man's finite perceptions are limited while "In the eye of God/ Pain may have a purpose and be justified." (ll. 136-37)[30] The approach in *La Saisiaz* seems, however, to be less open to criticism, when he justifies the evil in this world as being necessary for the exercise of man's moral faculty and his freedom of choice.

The most extended examination of the question of evil is conducted in the twelfth Fancy, entitled "A Bean-Stripe: also Apple-Eating." The problem as posed by Ferishtah's disciple is, "A good thing or a bad thing--Life is which?" (1.5) The solution is again a characteristic of Browning's later thought--since certainty is not possible, man must of necessity accept ignorance of God's plan. Evil can serve to increase man's joy in goodness and to act as a testing ground for faith. Ferishtah concludes with the assertion that life is a mixture of both joy and sorrow. Thus for him, the appropriate colour to assign to the world is neither black nor white, but grey. But in order to achieve this view, man must widen his perspective. "Pass from such obvious power to powers unseen," (l. 384)[31] and thus attain to a wholeness of vision in which he realizes that "Deepest in black means white most imminent." (l. 112) As in *La Saisiaz*, however, this affirmation is qualified with a proviso, that what he speaks of is "my own appointed patch o' the ground." (l. 168) If he is an optimist, he is also aware, in Blougram's words of "a thousand diamond weights between." (l.406) Ferishtah admits that while he has not seen life as "all-subduing black," (l. 205) yet

> . . . such may wreck
> My life and ruin my philosophy
> Tomorrow doubtless: hence the constant shade
> Cast on life's shine,--the tremor that intrudes
> When firmest seems my faith in white. (ll.207-11)

Yet his response, he feels, is more honest than that of the "sourly-Sage" (l.256) who proclaimed "Life's best was that it led to death" (l.261) and who yet "Lived out his seventy years, laughed loud,/ liked--above all--his dinner." (ll.275-76) DeVane points to these lines as a reference to Thomas Carlyle, whom Browning would again accost in the "Parleying with Bernard de Mandeville."[32]

In the second part of the fancy, the doubting disciple wants "truth at any cost." (l.295) But Ferishtah points out that absolute conviction is untenable. If the conditions of life do not meet our desires and expectations, it is because our conceptions are bounded and finite and distinct from God's. What man needs is the imaginative vision to "Blend the quality of man/ With the quality of God, and so assist/Mere human sight to understand." (ll.358-60) For if absolute knowledge is denied to man, the mind can infer immensity. Ferishtah illustrates the point with the analogy of fire:

> Yet since to think and know fire through and through
> Exceeds man, is the warmth of fire unknown,
> Its uses--are they so unthinkable?
> Pass from such obvious power to powers unseen,
> Undreamed of save in their sure consequence. (ll. 382-86)

From his examination of the scheme of life, Ferishtah reaches to the conception of a beneficent giver: "The sense within me that I owe a debt/Assures me--somewhere must be somebody/ Ready to take his due." (ll.422-24) Thus he eats his apple, relishes, praises, admires and thanks, not the apple, but the creator, "but for whose work, the orchard's wealth/ Might prove so many gall-nuts." (ll.485-86) The lyric postulates the idea of not caring for the world's reactions, for man has his rewards in the after-life to look forward to. The world might be unappreciative, but the poet for his own part has "looked beyond the world for truth and beauty."

The problem of belief, faith and knowledge is the central theme of the third group of fancies.

In "Shah Abbas," Ferishtah argues with the disciple who asks: "Did beauty live in deed as well as in word,/ Was this life lived, was this death died--not dreamed?" (ll.13-14) Thus at this late stage, Browning once more takes up the discussion of the authenticity of the story of Christ. As DeVane has shown, the three analogies or fables used in the argument illustrate varieties of belief[33]--the belief in historical fact (as revealed by the story of Shah Abbas); the belief in fiction (as exemplified by the tale of Thamasp who saw his beloved Zurah devoured by a nine-headed snake), a belief which appeals to the emotions even while the intellect doubts its validity; and thirdly, the kind of belief that is prompted by love (as shown by the story of the return of Ishak to his sons). The inference is that it is the last kind of belief that man needs to respond to Christ. The validity of the instinctive will to believe had been propounded in *La Saisiaz*. As Caponsacchi's brave act demonstrates, the instinct stands surer than the intellect. Browning's firm conviction that in matters of faith and belief the intuition achieves more positive results, is very evident here. The lyric embodies the idea of loving faith as a means of illuminating the heart's darkness.

In "The Sun," the question discussed is once again that of faith in the historic fact of the Incarnation. An angry man confronts Ferishtah with the statement that someone had dared to say "God once assumed on earth a human shape." (l.10) Ferishtah's arguments follow the line of John's in "A Death in the Desert," "Man apprehends Him newly at each stage." (l.432) The sun was, formerly, worshipped as the giver of light and life, but step by step man attained to the conception of "purpose with power." (l.100) For a homelier example, he takes the case of a man eating a tasty fig, who gives thanks to the gardener. But since "gift claims gift's return," (l.74) man can only love what gives love. Thus man desires some evidence of God's love operating on earth. So, says Ferishtah, to meet the yearnings of man, the legend arose that God once took human shape and came down to earth. The proper response to such a revelation should not be one of disbelief, but the feeling--"I stand appalled before/Conception unattainable by me/Who need it most." (ll.175-77) The accompanying lyric traces man's heavenly origins, reminiscent of Wordsworth's "Our birth is a sleep and a forgetting" in the "Immortality Ode."

DeVane calls "A Pillar at Sebzevar" "perhaps the bluntest and clearest statement of Browning's doctrine of the inefficacy of human knowledge."[34] In *Easter-Day* the narrator discards knowledge in favour of love and so wins God's approval. In *La Saisiaz* Browning asserted the superiority of intuitive faith and love to rational, intellectual analysis. In the present fancy, the idea is stated much more dogmatically: "Wholly distrust thy knowledge, then, and trust/ As wholly to love allied to ignorance." (ll.64-65) This seems anomalous in a poet who placed so much emphasis on the processes of the mind. But Philip Drew correctly points out that knowledge does not mean Reason itself, but "that kind of unreal ratiocination which tries to replace the experience of the individual by an abstract generalization."[35] One feels that Browning formulated this particular theory to counter the negativism engendered by rationalistic criticism of religion. Browning's solution to the problem of belief rests not in historic, external truth, but in the truth within man himself, tested by his personal experience. In "Epilogue" to *Dramatis Personae* (1864) he had propounded the same idea, that God is actually present in the universe and in all mankind, so that man need not look beyond his own world to find God. In the present fancy, the analogy that Ferishtah uses is that of water, the drop of water that man finds when he scoops up sand should be enough for him if it quenches his thirst. What need further digging fifty fathoms deep:

> Thy soul's environment of things perceived,
> Things visible and things invisible,
> Fact, fancy--all was purposed to evolve
> This and this only--was thy wit of worth
> To recognize the drop's use, love the same,
> And loyally declare against mirage
> Though all the world asseverated dust
> Was good to drink? Say, "What made moist my lip,
> That I acknowledge moisture": thou art saved! (ll.124-32)

But even as he lauds the method of personal choice based on individual experience, Browning cannot be said to be unaware of its dangers. Earlier in "A Death in the Desert," John had said, "Truth, deadened of its absolute blaze/ Might need love's eye to pierce the o'erstretched doubt." (ll.320-21) But he also warns of the dangers of the misapplication of one's reasoning powers, as when a man is led to say, "Since love is everywhere,/ And since ourselves can love and would be loved,/ We ourselves make the love, and Christ was not." (ll.505-7) The lyric appended to "A Pillar at Sebzevar" sings of unspoken love. Words of praise cannot do justice to intuitive appreciation.

As "A Camel-Driver" shows, Browning does not discard wholly the reasoning faculty, for that would be advocating mindlessness:

> Reason aims to raise
> Some make-shift scaffold-vantage midway, whence
> Man dares, for life's brief moment, peer below:
> But ape omniscience? Nay! (ll.71-74)

When man attempts by his reason to overleap the bounds of life, then this quality is to be denigrated. In this poem, Ferishtah advocates the necessity for man to chart out his own beliefs based on his own inner promptings: "Ask thy lone soul what laws are plain to thee,--/ Thee and no other,-- stand or fall by them." (ll.99-100)

The "Epilogue" to *Ferishtah's Fancies* is both an affirmation of the major ideas presented in the *Fancies* and a sober questioning of their worth. In fact, the whole import of the poem is changed by the "Epilogue." If the tone of the main body of the poem has been optimistic, the conclusion presents a mood of troubled uncertainty. If Browning had earlier presented man's intuitive promptings as the basis of his belief, he now points out the dangers that accompany subjectivism. David Shaw observes that "Browning dramatizes the dark foundations of belief, the voids beneath the affirmations of theology,"[36] and further remarks that "The poet who grants that his central faith may be in error lives from a great depth of being". The speaker is very clearly the poet himself. He has been a "happy one" (1.4) for whom appeared "bright-edged the blackest shroud." (1.8) He achieves a vision of the glorious souls who battled valiantly in life without thought of reward, but only of duty, and comes to realize the worth of their endeavour. It is a vision of "All the good and beauty, wonder crowning wonder,/ Till my heart and soul applaud perfection, nothing less." (ll.23-24) Yet this enchantment becomes suddenly fraught with terror at the thought that his hopeful view of life may be only a reflection of his own happiness in love, and may not be a true interpretation of the scheme of things in the universe at large. The "Epilogue" may thus be cited as a rejoinder to Leavis who felt that "Browning was unaware of disharmonies because for him there were none, or rather, only such as were enough to exhilarate, to give him a joyous sense of physical vitality."[37] It provides the evidence to refute the conventional view of the later Browning as a hearty optimist, who conveniently shut his eyes to unpleasant realities.

In the "Parleying with Bernard de Mandeville" (*Parleyings With Certain People of Importance in Their* Day, 1887), Browning elaborates his discussion of the problem of evil by arguing with Carlyle about the necessity of accepting evil in this world without undue pessimism. Carlyle said of Browning: "But there's a great contrast between him and me. He seems very content with life, and takes much satisfaction in the world. It's a very strange and curious spectacle to behold a man in these days so confidently cheerful."[38] The parleying provides Browning's explanation for his hopeful attitude.

As already noted, the problem of evil had engaged Browning from his earliest poetry. To the Pope in *The Ring and the Book*, the presence of evil is an indication for man to struggle valiantly towards goodness and truth. Even Guido's unmitigated evil has its uses--it becomes a means for the revelation of goodness in Pompilia and Caponsacchi. In this poem, man's confrontation with evil is seen as a matter of instinctive responses:

> See how this mere chance-sown, cleft-nursed seed,
> That sprang up by the wayside 'neath the foot
> Of the enemy, this breaks all into blaze,
> Spreads itself, one wide glory of desire
> To incorporate the whole great sun it loves (X, 1041-4)

as well as of conscious choices: "White shall not neutralize the black, nor the good/Compensate bad in man, absolve him so: Life's business being just the terrible choice." (X, 1236-38)

In all his poems treating this theme, Browning does not deny evil and suffering, but puts forward the belief that love in a man's heart is an indication of God's love, and an indication of God's ultimately beneficent purpose for man. In *Ferishtah's Fancies*, as we have seen, Browning asserts that the quest for the unknowable through the medium of the intellect can only lead to pessimism and despair. It is only through love and trust that man can come to terms with the existence of pain and sorrow. Love gives man the wisdom to see that evil may serve some definite purpose.

In the *Parleying*, Browning reproaches Carlyle for wanting certain knowledge of the goodness, in spite of existent evil, of God's plan for man. Mandeville had, according to Browning, shown how men could accept the evil of this world in a realistic and positive way. He had believed that "Every growth of good/Sprang consequent on evil's neighbourhood" (V) and that both together were products of a "Primal law." (V) The Biblical parallel of the story of the wheat and the tares gives depth to the argument. On the one side is presented the contention that the "Gardener of Man" plants both wheat and tares "for a purpose," (V) on the other is the inability to understand and accept this intermingling: "Why grant tares leave to thus o'erstep, o'ertower/ Their field-mate, boast the stalk and flaunt the flower/ Triumph one sunny minute?" (VI)

Browning's explanation repeats an idea already presented in *Ferishtah's Fancies*, namely that man's perceptions are finite and limited, and so can never encompass the infinitude of God. Paracelsus comes to learn that absolutes are not within man's reach and man must ever be content with the "uncertain fruit of an enchancing toil" (V, 697) and the "weakness" (V, 699) of human love.

Yet even in the midst of his limitations man can aspire. As early as *Paracelsus* Browning uses the sun as the image for something vast, desirable and essentially unknowable: "Like plants in mines which never saw the sun,/But dream of him, and guess where he may be,/and do their best to climb and get to him." (V, 882-84) In *The Ring and the Book* the Pope insists on the need for clouds to shade man's eye, which "Sun-suffused" (X, 1645) may be made "blind by blaze." (X, 1646) In a passage which anticipates Browning's arguments in "Mandeville," the Pope refers to the need for man to accept a knowledge of God that best suits his finite nature:

> O Thou,--as represented here to me
> In such conception as my soul allows,--
> Under Thy measureless my atom width!--
> Man's mind--what is it but a convex glass
> Wherein are gathered all the scattered points
> Picked out of the immensity of sky,
> To reunite thee, be our heaven on earth,
> Our known unknown, our God revealed to man?
> Existent somewhere, somehow, as a whole,
> Here, as a whole proportioned to our sense,--
> There, (which is nowhere, speech must babble thus!)
> In the absolute immensity, the whole
> Appreciable solely by Thyself,--
> Here, by the little mind of man, reduced
> To littleness that suits his faculty,
> Appreciable too in the degree. (X, 1308-23)

In "A Bean-Stripe: Also Apple Eating," as already mentioned, Ferishtah uses the image of fire to describe the limited yet inescapable nature of man's conception of infinity. In "Mandeville," the same idea is expressed in "Look through the sign to the thing signified." (VII) Countering Carlyle's imagined assertion (as described by DeVane) that "Spiritual things are not to be comprehended in human terms,"[39] Browning shows the means whereby the infinite may be apprehended by the finite. The fiction which makes fact alive is fact too, as he had explained in *The Ring and the Book*. (ll.461-472) Thus the sign or the symbol assumes great importance in man's attempts to understand the nature of God. As W.O. Raymond puts it: "Browning uses the imagery of the Sun as representative of God's absolute being, and the myth of Prometheus bringing fire from heaven in a hollow tube as the symbol of a revelation of the Divine nature which is adapted to the lowliness and imperfect faculties of man. It is true that the fire thus won is 'glass-conglobed' and narrowed to a 'pin-point circle.' Nevertheless it is 'the very Sun in little' sharing its elemental nature."[40]

Man's imagination, operating through symbolic representations, lifts him from the darkness of meaninglessness and into the light of hope and faith in the beneficence of God. The fervour, almost religious though non-doctrinal, of Browning's belief is emphasized by the concluding imagery of light and warmth (sun, fire). As Park Honan points out, light images combine with those involving fire and seeing in "A Death in the Desert" to reveal the spiritual nature of an experience.[41] Browning's stress on the symbol is in keeping with his belief that it is through the finite that the infinite manifests itself.

Ultimately, Browning's arguments serve not to discount the reality of evil, but to point to a way in which this evil may have positive implications. Browning derives hope from the fact that God is not a remote being indifferent to man's agonizing, for man's emotional and moral consciousness in itself is an evidence of a God of Love. In the poems of the earlier period the Incarnation provided the fact that man needed to prove God's love for man. Now in the last major poem, embodying his mature views, Browning's emphasis shifts from the historic fact of the Incarnation to its significance as a symbol of the communion between the divine and the human. God's love and concern for man is further evinced in the love that exists in the human heart. As Browning would affirm in the later parleyings also, man's own experience is sufficient for apprehending God. And thus he proves Carlyle's pessimism as uncalled-for.

In the ninth and tenth sections of the "Parleying with Francis Furini", Browning moves from a discussion of Art to Science, and makes his criticism of the evolutionists a vehicle for his characteristic philosophical thought.

Browning was not against the theory of Evolution as such, for in many ways the theory accorded well with his faith in progress.[42] But what he set himself against was those interpretations of the theory that made negative all positive assertions about humanity. Ultimately, his stand against the Evolutionists may be summed up by the concepts Abstraction versus Experience, Knowledge (ratiocination) which leads to sterility and a loving Ignorance (acceptance) which leads to faith and hope. The parleying asserts that no matter how far the speculations of the scientists take them, ultimately "You drop to where the atoms somehow think/Feel, know themselves to be." (ll.282-83)

Browning attempts to combat the feelings of despair and pessimism that the evolutionary theories might give rise to. For it had been contended that, as a facet of organic nature subject to mechanistic laws, man no longer was such a splendid figure. Browning's argument runs thus: "Where began/ righteousness, moral sense except in Man?" (IX) and concludes: "Accept in Man advanced to this degree,/The Prime Mind, therefore." (IX) He puts his belief in the moral consciousness that is symbolic of God in man. It is true that both power and knowledge are sharply limited in man, that everywhere he finds "faults to mend/Omissions to supply." (IX) Yet he "stands/Confessed supreme--the monarch whose commands/Could he enforce, how bettered were the world!" (IX)

To Browning it was unthinkable that the evolutionist concept of the mechanical weeding out of individuals for their physical survival value should set at nought all human aspiration and striving. Unthinkable too was the idea that no evidence existed of a loving Creator. Once again, Browning is on familiar ground arguing that self-knowledge is just about the only thing that man can be sure of on earth. The rest is a "profound/ Of ignorance I tell you surges round/ My rock-spit of self-knowledge." (X) This is a repetition of what he had already made clear in *La Saisiaz*--"Knowledge stands on my experience." (l.273)[43] In the present parleying, the glorious raptures of the soul point to a "consummator sealing up the sum of all things past and present and to come--/Perfection? No, I have no doubt at all" (X). On the other hand, man's experience forces him to acknowledge the reality of evil. Browning's position in this respect is familiar: "...still must needs wrong/To do right's service, prove men weak or strong/Choosers of evil or good." (X)

Browning then proceeds to use Furini's painting of Andromeda as an illustration of how pain and sorrow, whether as reality or illusion (as in a painting) serve to inspire nobility in man. It is not desirable for man to be passive, but to struggle to overcome evil. DeVane points out that at this point, "Andromeda represents Browning's own faith, standing precariously upon the rock of consciousness amidst the growing darkness of the sky and the waters waste and wild, and awaiting destruction from the monster of new scientific thought, or rescue from heaven."[44] And according to Douglas Bush: "Andromeda on the rocks awaiting the serpent becomes the poet himself, standing on the firm ledge of his individual consciousness amid the wash and welter of ignorance, facing the monster evil; needless to say, the all-wise deliverer is God."[45]

Orr points out that this "constant assertion of the necessity of evil would land Mr. Browning in a dilemma, if the axiom were presented by him in any character of dogmatic truth. . . . But the anomaly disappears in the more floating outlines of a poetic experience."[46] Therefore, Browning insists that his belief in a Supreme Cause--"Strong, wise, good" (X) is a very personal belief: "All--for myself--seems ordered, wise and well/Inside it,--what reigns outside, who can tell?" (X)

Philip Drew points out that by the time Browning came to write the *Parleyings* he had moved away from dogma, the Church and traditional philosophy, so that "even the idea of God's love of man being made manifest in the incarnation of Christ, which had animated so many of his poems, is found rarely in his later works."[47] Hence, Browning is led more and more to stress individual responsibility and individual consciousness. In the "Parleying with Francis Furini," Browning once again focuses on individual experience as the source of an innate perception of higher reality made manifest through the appearances of the world: "Though Master keep aloof,/Signs of his presence multiply from roof/To basement of the building." (X) Therefore, it behoves man to "Look around,/ Learn thoroughly." (X) Browning firmly places the burden of creating value on man himself.

The *Asolando* volume (1889), though predominantly lyrical and narrative in content, contains two poems which are embodiments of Browning's philosophical thought. "Rephan" is the story of a human being who remembers a previous life when his home was "the Star of my God Rephan." (l.3) It was a realm of absolute perfection and bliss, "Nowhere deficiency nor excess" (l.24). Unlike this world where, as Don Juan discovers in *Fifine at the Fair*, "nowhere things abide,/ And everywhere we strain that things would stay," (LXXXIV) in "Rephan" there is "no fear nor hope, no growth, no change, everything is faultlessly exact." (l.54) Yet, perfection becomes irksome. It is the challenge to aspire, if not to attain, to suffer for love's sake, to wring knowledge from ignorance, that is desirable, all the more so because of the hopeful assurance that life hereafter will right all wrongs.[48] That this striving is valuable for its own sake had been expressed by Browning in "Life in a Love." (*Men and Women*, Vol. I, 1855)

But what if I fail of my purpose here?
It is but to keep the nerves at strain,
To dry one's eyes and laugh at a fall,
And baffled, get up and begin again,--
So the chase takes up one's life, that's all. (ll.11-15)

The Chorus of the Fates in the "Prologue" to the *Parleyings* sings: "What is? No, what may be--sing! That's man's essential." (l.239) As in "Jochannan Hakkadosh," the present poem, too, describes life on earth as one of striving and effort that does not always bring fulfilment, and the after-life as one of harmony and completion. But perfection can mean stagnation. The vitality of the challenge to realize the infinite gives man the deepest sense of his own being, and the speaker yearns to exchange his neutral, uniform state for the conditions of earthly life--with its hopes, fears, loves, hates and doubts.

The acknowledgement of the imperfections of this world and the necessity of reconciling it with the idea of a just and loving God is, once again the theme of "Reverie." DeVane observes: "The old antithesis of power and love which he had first propounded in *Paracelsus* (1835) appears here again as the central problem."[49] The poem is an amalgam of Browning's characteristic ideas: a veil lies between man and the ultimate truth, which man cannot attain in totality in this world, man's attempts to gain knowledge of the infinite should begin with the finite--"How but from near to far/Should knowledge proceed, increase/ Try the clod ere test the star!" (ll.36-38) Evil exists, but men should regard it "haply as cloud across/ Good's orb, no orb itself." (76-77) Life on earth is beset by "chance, change, death's alarm," (l.135) but its effect is to create faith in man.

To Karshish, the idea that "The All-Great were the All-Loving too," (l.305) is a conception that almost defies belief. What is lacking in this world is the evidence of Love as obvious as that of Power. But for Browning, this veil of ignorance as to the true purposes of the Creator is a necessity for engineering faith. As in *La Saisiaz* the sorrows of this life lead to the hope in the after-life where wrongs are righted. It is faith which elevates man's mind, burdened with knowledge which can never be complete and hence is always unsatisfying: So life on earth becomes a process of endless questing and striving (ll.105-9) to reconcile the power and love of God, a reconciliation brought about by man's personal, imaginative reconstruction of the facts of his experience. As Roma A. King writes: "Browning's awareness of man's situation, his alienation, his impotency, his unfulfilled frustrated desires, and his transformation of external structures from sources of values into hypothetical constructs which enable man to create values provides the basic reality that underlies his creative efforts. What is implicit in the earlier poems becomes increasingly explicit in the later ones."[50]

Structurally, the later poems which embody Browning's philosophical thought use different forms. In *La Saisiaz*, for example, he speaks in his own voice, but contrives to mask the personal with impersonal argumentation. In *Ferishtah's Fancies* he uses the form of the parable spoken by a scholarly dervish, but by using everyday analogies and appending love-lyrics, contrives to infuse warmth and emotions into what would otherwise be mere argumentation. The pattern of the debate, with its various lines of argument raised through the persons of imaginary objectors and interlocutors, or as in *La Saisiaz*, through two aspects of the poet's own personality and the three-layered argument in the *Parleyings*, is a pattern which best conveys Browning's speculative, inquiring, exploratory approach to philosophical questions.

In the later poems Browning evolves a mode of belief based on personal experiences and feeling, that he sets forth, very tentatively, as a means of withstanding onslaughts on the foundations of faith. Love, being the central feature of man's personal experience, is an inseparable adjunct to Browning's philosophy of life, and the next chapter proposes to examine this theme in the later poetry.

NOTES

1. Sutherland Orr, *A Handbook to the Works of Robert Browning,* 6th Edition (London: George Bell and Sons, 1892), p. 7.
2. Sir Henry Jones, *Browning as a Philosophical and Religious Teacher* (London: Macmillan, 1899), p. xi.
3. Quoted in Philip Drew, *The Poetry of Robert Browning,* p. 1.
4. *Browning: 'Men and Women' and other Poems. A Casebook*, ed. J.R. Watson (London: Macmillan, 1974) p. 21.
5. *Dearest Isa,* ed. Edward McAleer (Austin: University of Texas Press, 1951), p. 201; Letter of December 19, 1864.
6. Roma A. King, "The Necessary Surmise: The Shaping Spirit of Robert Browning's Poetry" in *Romantic and Victorian: Studies in Memory of William H. Marshall,* ed. W. Paul Elledge and Richard L. Hoffman (Rutherford: Fairleigh Dickinson University Press, 1971), p. 359.
7. *Browning: A Casebook,* p. 21.
8. *Ibid,* p. 22.
9. Cf. *In Memoriam,* XLIX.

   Beneath all fancied hopes and fears
   Ay me, the sorrow deepens down,
   Whose muffled motions blindly drown
   The bases of my life in tears.

10. Geoffrey Tillotson, "Browning" in *Browning's Mind and Art*, ed. Clarence Tracy (London: Oliver and Boyd, 1968), p. 208.
11. DeVane, p. 422.
12. T.J. Collins, *Browning's Moral-Aesthetic Theory, 1833-1855* (Nebraska: University of Nebraska Press, 1967), p. 112.
13. F.E.L. Priestley, "A Reading of *La Saisiaz*," *University of Toronto Quarterly*, Vol. XXV, I (1955), pp. 48-49.
14. Quoted in Alan Harrington, *The Immortalist* (St. Albans: Panther, 1973), p. 121.
15. Browning's belief in reunion after death, as a sign of both God's Power and Love was a constant one. In a letter to Isa Blagden on December 19, 1864, he wrote: "I sometimes see a light at the end of this dark tunnel of life, which was one blackness at the beginning. It won't last forever. In many ways I can see with my human eyes why this has been right and good for me as I never doubted it was for her and if we do but re-join any day the break will be better than forgotten, remembered for its uses." (*Dearest Isa,* ed. McAleer, pp. 200-1) And again, to a correspondent, on May 11, 1876: "It is a great thing, the greatest, that a human being should have passed the probation of life, and sum up its experience in a witness to the power and love of God. . . . I see ever *more* reason to hold by the same hope and that by no means in ignorance of what has been advanced to the contrary; and for your sake I would wish it to be true that I had so much of 'genius' as to permit the testimony of an especially privileged insight to come in aid of the ordinary argument. For I know I, myself, have been aware of the communication of something more subtle than a ratiocinating process, when the convictions of 'genius' have thrilled my soul to its depths. . . . as when Dante wrote what I will transcribe from my wife's Testament wherein I recorded it fourteen years ago, 'Thus I believe, thus I affirm, thus I am certain it is, that from this life I shall pass to another better, where that lady lives of whom my soul was enamoured." (*Letters*. ed. Hood, pp. 171-72)
16. Browning treats this idea again in "A Pillar at Sebzevar" (*Ferishtah's Fancies*): "Were knowledge all thy faculty, then God/Must be ignored" (ll.135-36).
17. It is easy to see why critics have expressed dissatisfaction with Browning's line of reasoning. But both the reviewer in *The Athenaeum*. May 1878, who wrote "his answer if weak is worse than worthless; for, as Bacon has told us, the worst enemies of truth are its weak defendersF and the critic in *The Saturday Review,* June 15, 1878, who wrote "the argument is written in a shorthand of crabbed and condensed phrases, which seem designed rather to remind the poet of his own process of reflection than to communicate his conclusions to others," miss the point that Browning is not aiming at "conclusions" but attempting to enact the process of a personal exploration. Quoted from *Browning: The Critical Heritage,* p. 448 and p. 451.
18. *Browning's Later Poetry, 1871-1889,* p. 153.
19. *The Poetry of Browning,* p. 159.
20. *Ibid*., p. 194.
21. A Reading of *La Saisiaz* , p. 56.

22. Cory Biemann Davis, "From Knowledge to Belief in *La Saisiaz: The Two Poets of Croisic*," *Studies in Browning and His Circle,* Vol. 6. No. 1, Spring, 1978, p. 10
23. Quoted from H.C. Duffin, *Amphibian: A Reconsideration of Browning* (London: Bowes and Bowes, 1965), p. 39.
24. DeVane, *Handbook*, p. 472.
25. *Ibid.*
26. *The Poetry of Browning*, p. 449.
27. *Browning's Later Poetry,* p. 193.
28. See "By the Fireside," stanza XLIV.
29. DeVane, *Handbook*, p. 487.
30. In "A Death in the Desert", John echoes a similar idea: "And as I saw sin and death, even so/See I need yet the transiency of both", (ll.218-19).
31. cf. "Parleying with Bernard de Mandeville," X. and XII.
32. DeVane, *Handbook,* p. 489.
33. *Ibid,* pp. 480-81.
34. *Ibid,* p. 485.
35. *The Poetry of Browning,* p. 189.
37. Quoted in Philip Drew, *The Poetry of Browning,* p. 422.
38. Quoted in Maisie Ward, *Robert Browning and His World: Two Robert Brownings?* (1861-1889) (London: Cassell, 1969), p. 229. Chapter 14 of this book is an excellent summary of Browning's later relationship with Carlyle.
39. W.C. DeVane, *Browning's Parleyings,* p. 43.
40. W.O. Raymond. *The Infinite Moment and Other Essays in Robert Browning,* 2nd ed. (Toronto: University of Toronto Press, 1965), p. 205.
41. Park Honan, *Browning's Characters: A Study in Poetic Technique* (New Haven: Yale University Press, 1961), p. 198.
42. In a letter to Furnivall on October 11, 1881, Browning wrote: "In reality, all that seems proved in Darwin's scheme was a conception familiar to me from the beginning: see in *Paracelsus* the progressive development from senseless matter to organized, until man's appearance (Part V). Also in "Cleon," see the order of 'life's mechanics', and I daresay in many passages of my poetry: for how can one look at Nature as a whole and doubt that, wherever there is a gap, a "link" must be "missing" through the limited power and opportunity of the looker? But go back and back as you please, at the back, as Mr Sludge is made to insist, you find (my faith is as constant) creative intelligence, acting as matter but not resulting from it. Once set balls rolling, and ball may hit ball and send any number in any direction over the table; but I believe in the cue pushed by a hand." (*Letters*, ed. Hood, p. 199)
43. In *La Saisiaz,* his personal experience had led him to base all his speculations on two basic facts: the thing perceiving and "the thing perceived outside itself" (l.220), which he terms soul and God. But in *Paracelsus,* he had presented a reverse idea that God was to be found in the soul itself, "There is an inmost centre in us all,/Where truth abides in fullness," (I, 728-29)
44. DeVane, "The Virgin and the Dragon" in *Browning: A Collection of Critical*

Essays, ed, Philip Drew (London: Methuen, 1966), p. 99.

45. Douglas Bush. *Mythology and the Romantic Tradition in English Poetry* (Cambridge: Harvard University Press, 1937, Re-issued with new Preface, 1969), p. 381.
46. Orr, *Handbook*, pp. 354-55.
47. *The Poetry of Browning*, p. 226.
48. cf. "Rabbi Ben Ezra," XXVI.
49. DeVane, *Handbook*, p. 552.
50. Roma A. King, "The Necessary Surmise: The Shaping Spirit of Robert Browning's Poetry" in *Romantic and Victorian: Studies in Memory of William H. Marshall*, p. 346.

THE THEME OF LOVE

Browning's assertion of the supreme importance of love is based on his belief that it is a means of communicating with the infinite, that, as one critic puts it, "in their imperfection created things can serve as instruments which ultimately lead, through human love, to a fuller appreciation of spiritual perfection."[1] The magnificent love poems of the earlier period had been written under the glowing aura of a happy marriage. The death of Elizabeth Browning was the major influence that operated in the love poetry of the later years. The concept of re-union after death, first postulated in "Evelyn Hope" (*Men and Women* 1855) took hold of Browning in a significant way after Elizabeth's death,[2] so that the later love poetry encompasses such ideas as love as the supreme reality amidst change and impermanence,[3] its power to transform and complete what is incomplete, and the hope of reunion of lovers after death. Love in the later poetry becomes a means of transcending the temporal and of becoming one with the eternal.[4]

In *Balaustion's Adventure* (1871), the power of love conquers death itself. In *Fifine at the Fair*, (1872) Don Juan asserts: "Beneath the veriest ash, there hides a spark of soul/Which, quickened by love's breath, may yet pervade the whole/O' the gray, and, free again, be fire?" (XLIII) He formulates "love's law" – " each soul lives, longs and works/For itself, by itself, because a lodestar lurks,/An other than itself." (LIX) In the end he comes to realize that inconstancy to the truth of love is to deny oneself anchorage in the flux of life. In *Red Cotton Night-Cap Country* (1873), love as mere selfish passion is condemned:

> Love bids touch truth, endure truth, and embrace
> Truth, though, embracing truth, love crush itself.
> "Worship not me but God!"
> The angels urge:
> That is love's grandeur. (p. 423).

In "The Inn Album" (1875) love is a saving power, of which "one drop saves – sends to flower and fruit at last/The laggard virtue in the soul which else/Cumbers the ground" (p. 453).

The "Epilogue" to *Fifine at the Fair* depicts the householder being reunited by death to his wife. The complex emotions that the occasion arouses are deliberately underplayed by means of the conversational tone of the poem. The staccato rhythms in the early lines are evocative of the turbulence of the poet's mood, intensifying to a climax with "When, in a moment, just a knock, call, cry,/Half a pang and all a rapture, there again were we!" (ll.5-6) The poem ends with the triumphant assertion "'Love is all, and Death is nought:' quoth She." (1.32) It is this hope of the invincibility of love that can support lovers in the midst of despair and disappointment.[5]

For the speaker in the "Prologue" to *Pacchiarotto and How He Worked in Distemper* (1676), reunion is not yet an accomplished fact. He sees himself as a "prison-bird," (l.19) separated by the barriers of the world from his beloved. For him, the only thing to do is to soar free in the imagination to the final reunion of souls. The deep emotion of longing is expressed through the precise and denotative imagery of segregation – wall, prison-bird, cloister. But here, as in all Browning's poetry, the world is desirable in its own way:

> And lush and lithe do the creepers clothe
> Yon wall I watch, with a wealth of green:
> Its bald red bricks draped, nothing loth,
> In lappets of tangle they laugh between (l.4-8)

As with other sensitive lovers in Browning, the speaker here finds the world alive with intimations from the world of the spirit.

The ability of love to breathe life and beauty into emptiness is the theme of "Natural Magic." What is required is imagination and a sensitive receptivity. Yet, if bareness becomes "embowered/With – who knows that verdure, o'erfruited,, o'erflowered?" (ll.7-8) it can, at best, remain a purely personal experience. In love as well as in philosophical thought, Browning's affirmations are always undercut by tentativeness.

In "Magical Nature," Browning reverses the conventional mataphor for a loved one. Instead of a flower which is at the mercy of time, his beloved is a jewel, which, though "Dim to sight and rough to touch," (1.4) defies the onslaught of Time.

"Bifurcation" is structured on the tension created by the opposing concepts of love and duty. The poem is, in fact, shaped by these antitheses, and imitates the ultimately tragic structure of reality. The reason for the failure of the lovers in this poem to achieve harmony is because the woman chooses the dictates of conventional behaviour. The poem begins on a casual, narrative tone, and proceeds to build up by a series of antitheses the dichotomy between the flower-strewn path and the pavement, heaven and earth, light and darkness, truth and falsehood, sinner and saint. The disappointed lover chooses the "darkling half" (l.19) but finds the going rough.

In words reminiscent of Pompilia's dying speech – "In heaven we have the real and true and sure," (VII, 1026) he awaits "the new world where light and darkness fuse." (l.20) Browning's mastery over characterization reveals itself through telling phrases which tell us all we need to know of the false mistress, the patent falsity of whose words, "How I loath a flower/How prize a pavement!" (l.9-10) "caressed" "the deafish friend's ear" who "laughed (coughing)." (ll.10-12) The reader is left in no doubt as to which character is to be praised and which condemned. As E.D.H. Johnson points out, "Browning holds that undue reliance on the intellect with its ulterior motivations makes for failure in affairs of the heart."[6] In "Bifurcation", self-deluding conformity to conventions turns truth into falsehood. The poem echoes "Youth and Art" in *Dramatis Personae* with the further addition of hope of completion in the hereafter.

Browning called "Numpholeptos" "an allegory of an impossible ideal of love."[7] DeVane agrees with Mrs. Miller in her interpretation of the poem as "an allegory of Browning's mood in 1876, his feeling that his lot is harder than that of his dead wife's – since he has to live through all the temptations of a passionate nature, while she is immune from such experience – his momentary rebellion from his bondage to a memory, and his capitulation to his fate."[8] But while the predominant moon-symbolism, which Browning invariably uses with reference to his wife would seem to support this interpretation of the poem as an expression of Browning's depressed state of mind after the Lady Ashburton affair, the emotion is much more complex than that of mere self-pity. On the one hand, the feeling that his infidelity to his wife's memory had created a rift between them and in the invisible harmony that still linked them results in an emphasis on pardon and forgiveness. On the other hand, there is the feeling of rebellion, for his failure is consequent of the conditions of finite life. As other dejected lovers in Browning's poetry do, the speaker vows to resume his quest, hoping against hope for the final rewards. The strength of passion straining at the leash is vividly presented through a riot of prismatic hues – purple, yellow, scarlet, crimson, saffron, orange. "Numpholeptos" emphasizes Browning's conception of manhood as a state of striving for the ultimately unrealizable, of love on this earth as a process of suffering which nevertheless liberates and exhilarates. The joy of perfect union, as expressed by Don Juan in *Fifine*, is fleeting:

> What joy, when each may supplement
> The other, changing each, as changed, till, wholly, blent,
> Our old things shall be new, and, what we both ignite,
> Fuse, lose the varicolor in a chromatic white. (LIX)

"Numpholeptos" presents the obverse side of perfect communion between lovers. It gives expression to the poet's perception of the fate of love in a world of time, of the gulf between lover and the object of love, a gulf that can but rarely be completely bridged.

The falsity and deceptiveness of appearances which had been a major theme in *Fifine*, re emerges in the lyric "Appearances," where the main idea is the power of love to transform what is insignificant. The "poor dull/Dark" (ll.1-2) attains significance from the love it has been witness to, while the rich room is associated with deceit, the place where "The other word was spoken." (l.11) The bare simplicity of the language heightens the complex evocations produced by the phrase "dropped the mask." (l.12)

Like the lover in "Two in the Campagna" (*Men and Women*) who can discern only "infinite passion and the pain/Of finite hearts that yearn," (ll.59-60) the lover in "St. Martin's Summer" is aware of the fickleness of Time and the changeableness of human nature. Hence he would "weave a bower" (l.8) instead of building "durable mansionary," (l.58) prefer the fluid instead of the rigid in human relationships, because the former may prove the more lasting and rewarding because less restricting. Yet, he has a past of his own to contend with, a past that extends its insistent claims on the present. Though he protests his innocence, he is aware that "Love's ghost plays truant" (l.56) and that "dead loves are the potent" (l.91) The memories of past love infuse the present. The present appears to be a "mere semblance," (l.93) it is the past that has substance.[9] To be bereft of past memories of love is to be left anchorless. We have a similar insistence in *Fifing* on constancy in love as a bulwark against negation. Critics have pointed out the biographical significance of "St. Martin's Summer"[10] Beyond this, however, is Browning's awareness of the complexities embodied in a love-relationship, and the mysterious ways in which this relationship can continue to operate between the living and the dead.

In the introductory poem to *The Two Poets of Croisic* (1878), human love is equated with divine love that can make violets grow in a "starved bank of moss" (l.1) or cause a star to be revealed in "a scowl of cloud." (l.5) The emphasis is on the creative power of love. "Starved," "scowl," "walled," suggest the insistent claims of man's mortal nature, reminiscent of the "flapping door" and "echoing roof" of the "Epilogue" to *Fifine*.

The "Epilogue" to *The Two Poets of Croisic*, a delightful story of a musician who was helped to win a prize despite a broken lyre by a cicada, affirms the power of love to aid man in times of adversity.

The prologue to Jocoseria (1883), "Wanting is—what?" reveals what DeVane calls "The delightful faculty that still existed in the old poet in spite of much mere grey argument." It re-affirms the idea of love as the power which makes "complete incompletion," (1.9) which breathes life into what was till then only a framework. Individual growth, indeed salvation itself, depends on the wholeness of a soul's union in love with another soul.[12]

"Mary Wollstonecraft and Fuseli" joins the rank of pieces like "James Lee's Wife" and "In a Year" as a poem of unrequited love. Like other Browning women, the heroine of this piece has an appealing humility. It is Browning's tribute to the depth in love that a woman is capable of, that we are made to feel of this group of poems that the woman "suffers not because of any innate unworthiness, but rather because of some flaw in her lover."[13] In this poem, however, the lack of images which act as objective correlatives to the emotion lessons the emotive force that characterized earlier poems with similar themes.

In "Adam, Lilith and Eve" Browning uses a Biblical analogy in the title to emphasize the universality of the experience portrayed and thus to intensify its meaning. As a dramatization of deception and unfulfilment in love, it is a companion piece to the preceding poem, revealing the diverse facets of disillusionment. The two poems together form an ironical comment on the fallacy of ideal love.

"Never the Time and the Place" presents feeling that is genuinely realized, for its theme gives rise to emotions that are deeply felt by the poet. The speaker affirms his hope that the future will be as the past, and that the grave will reunite him with his beloved – "Oh, close, safe, warm sleep I and she,/I and she." (ll.20-21) The repetition of the last phrase functions importantly to stress the main idea of "completeness." The passage of time, with all its temptations, becomes the arch – enemy that the poet has to contend with, and the only armour is the invincibility of his love. One can discern an undercurrent of distress in the early lines of the poem, the feeling that perfect union is hardly possible in this hostile temporal world. Thus the awareness of frustration and pain is never far away in these later love poems. The "rough world's busy thrust" is an ever-present reality. The antidote to the "hostile eye," (1.10) the "furtive ear," (1.9) the "malice that marks each word, each sign" (1.11) is the true love between two souls, a love that continues beyond the grave. The vivid, supple, concentrated presentation of the idea, with its emotional intensity and depth of suggestion, makes this poem one of the finest lyrics in the later poems.

The *Asolando* volume (1889) shows the poet in a mellow mood of reminiscence. In "Dubiety," he reiterates the sustaining powers of the memories of love, which alone is "Truth ever, truth only the excellent!"(1.24)

But the very precariousness of the love-relationship leads to an emphasis not only on future completion but on present fulfilment. The lover in "Now" sweeps away time past and time future in the wholeness of his response to the present. He realizes that the moments of perfect communion are as rare and fleeting as they are precious.[14] The physical here is the pathway to the spiritual; sense is the means by which the soul can express itself.

The lover in "Humility" recognizes the value even of unreciprocated love. In love nothing is insignificant, for love is not an end in itself but a process of finding realization in life. This spirit of humility and self-sacrifice is the counterpart to the spirit of aspiration which is so important in Browning's poetry.

The fantasizing extravagance of conventional metaphor in love will not do justice to "Her human self."(l.8) In "Poetics" Browning makes a case for realism in love, as opposed to abstract idealism, for the former helps to achieve a truer sense of identity.

In "Summum Bonum" Browning once again speaks of subjective experience as being the base for all value perceptions. "Truth" is that which enhances a man's awareness of self, and enlarges his consciousness in relation to the universe. In this poem, as in "Dubiety", the brightest truth is "In the kiss of one girl." (l.8)

The imperfections of the finite are transformed through the transcendental power of love in "A Pearl, A Girl." Once again, the love that is celebrated is pre-eminently human.

"Speculative" boldly reverses a recurrent theme in Browning's poetry, that of heaven as the place where the incompletion of effort is made complete as achievement. Here the lover eschews renewed possibilities in the next life and opts for the pleasures and pains of earthly life, with the one qualification that he and his beloved remain together for ever. The poem reveals a characteristic tension between Browning's desire for the perfection of a world beyond time and the invigorating challenges posed by experience within time.

"Which" and "Beatrice Signorini" deal with single minded purposefulness in love which brings its reward in terms of a prize to the woman who chooses her man for love alone in the first poem, and the return of an errant husband "Past power to change" in the latter poem.

"Inapprehensiveness" and "Flute Music with an Accompaniment" are written as dialogues between lovers who have not attained that ultimate awareness of each other when two souls are fused. In the former poem, the woman is absorbed in her fancies, yet oblivious to the fact of the man's "dormant passion" (l.23) needing but a look to break into a "rush of life."(l.24) In "Flute Music" the fanciful speculations belong to the man, whom the snatches of music set musing on "Passion insupressive." (l.9) But though the woman coldly dampens his enthusiasm, he protests:

What if all's appearance?
Is not outside seeming
Real as substance inside?
Both are facts, so leave me dreaming. (ll.185-88)

These two poems embody an ideal that occurs frequently in Browning's poetry – that if the significant moment in a relationship is not recognized, the chances of spiritual growth and integration may be lost. Unimaginativeness, as much as timidity, may result in a sterile relationship,[15] just as the attempt to substitute "knowing" for "being" can destroy harmony.

The four poems entitled "Bad Dreams" use the unconscious levels of our dream-life to dramatize the complexities inherent in any love-relationship, the terror of the void that exists just beneath the surface of the conventional. The inner life is glimpsed by a series of nightmarish images – the huge hall with chained dancers, the chapel with its dark spirit, the forest and the city devouring each other – ending in the last poem with the tombstone representing death. The compression and the suggestiveness of the sequence is remarkable. As in "Childe Roland" the nightmare quality is emphasized by the way in which events emerge without apparent logic. The images of horror become a portrayal of the upheaval within the souls of unhappy lovers. The idea of the passing of time as an instrument of reconciliation and as a means of union after death is an idea characteristic of the later love poetry. Along with "Numpholeptos" and "St. Martin's Summer," "Bad Dreams" is a portrayal of the darker side of love.

The love-lyrics in *Ferishtah's Fancies* celebrate love that can lead to wholeness of being, in contrast to knowledge that at best can only bring partial fulfilment. The lyrics may be regarded as an extension of the awareness reached in *Paracelsus* of love not as an abstract quest for an ideal of perfection, but a reconciling of the claims of the world and the spirit. In these lyrics, we may discern the sharply "descendental" thrust in Browning's vision in the later period, his conviction that heavenly or spiritual love is not superior to earthly love, and that love is as much a matter of sense as of soul. These poems cherish man's humanity with all its changeableness and imperfections. The experiences of human love are not less valuable because less perfect than transcendental love. If infinite, perfect love is an ideal unattainable on this earth, man can be content with what he can achieve with his limited means. This is not the passive acceptance of a "Meaner spirit" but the acceptance of one "Clothed/In humbler guise" as Aprile puts it in *Paracelsus*. (II, 567, and 568-69) Further, love in these lyrics is not only an aid in finding universal harmony. It is also the power that *creates* harmony out of discord and sees the flaws in the object of love as a source of fresh affection.

The "Parleying with Daniel Bartoli" (1887) is important as a gathering point for all Browning's characteristic idea on love.

Browning here takes up a story from the past, not as an emotional sentimentalist, but as a dramatic realist, once again affirming his belief that poetic interest and moral truth could reside in ordinary human circumstance. The story of the druggist's daughter who sacrificed her happiness for the sake of the man she loved becomes the focal point for many of the ideas that had been embodied in Browning's poetry from the earliest phases. Marianne Pajot stands representative of that admirable class of women who "Would waive, when need were, all but love—from pelf/To potency." (X) She refuses to compromise with honour and pleads with her husband-to-be (risking her own security) not to compromise either: "Never dare alienate God's gift you hold/Simply in trust for him! Choose muck for gold?"(X) In the magnificence of her moral stature she is as far above the Duke as was Alcestis above her husband Admetos. Her action in deliberately renouncing the duchess-ship is all the more remarkable because she lived at a time when "to be duchess was to dance the hays/Up, down, across the heaven amid its host:" (XV) and also "to be hailed the sun's self almost." (XV) The lady's sacrifice in this poem is similar to Alcestis' because both recognize the weakness in their men, yet calmly continue with their planned course of action. Their magnanimity is the other side of Browning's belief that self-interest is love's greatest enemy.

Browning's treatment of the story is in keeping with the theme of the *Parleyings*—loving imagination and intuition as superior to reason, the former as a more infallible means of reaching the central truths of life than the latter. In glorifying the nobility of a woman's sacrifice, he is transposing into the story the flesh-spirit dichotomy that is a major theme in his poetry. It is for those who are true in spirit in spite of loss as regards worldly success and ambition that Browning has the highest regard. Thus, in ""Bifurcation," Browning holds as a sinner the woman who turns truth into falsehood by faint-heartedly choosing the conventional path of duty to the more challenging one of love. The decisiveness of the lady in the *Parleying* also reinforces a recurrent theme in Browning's poetry—weakness and cowardice in love irretrievably mar the lives of the lovers. She exemplifies the kind of character whom Browning admires, those who, as E.D.H. Johnson puts it, "are all exceptionally clearsighted in their confrontation of actuality. They see through the false shows at which society connives, preferring to meet life on its own terms rather than to indulge in fanciful self-delusion."[16]

Further, in depicting the wide-ranging ramifications of a single act of moral struggle and decision, Browning also draws on his theory of the conflict of good and evil. Each successful confrontation with evil in this world makes man stronger and benefits him in some way. Thus, for the lady, there is mental peace and well-being of a kind denied to the Duke, as it had been denied to the false DeLorge in "The Glove" and to the remorseful lover in "Dis Aliter Visum."

W.O. Raymond says in his chapter on "The Statue and the Bust": "The worth of the moral conflict cannot be confined to the mere process of subjective experience. Its motivation and goal have an ethical and spiritual objective value and reality."[17] Because Browning grounds the lady's choice on an instinct that is almost spiritual in nature, he lets us see the transforming effects on all those concerned: the young man, who recognized her greatness and was given a taste of the "exquisite deliciousness" (XIV) of joy; the Duke who, entranced by a dancer, too late recognized that what he had taken for the moon was merely a cloud that "moon-suffused, plays moon perhaps," (XVII) and so was willing to have the "brisk-marching, bold she-shape" (XVIII) conquer him. For what she asserted her power over was his ghost: "he died since left and lorn,/As needs must Samson when his hair is shorn." (XVIII) The Biblical image is powerfully evocative.

As with the artists whose work increases in value in proportion as they scorn worldly success and conformity, so with the lovers. The true banner of love is upheld by those who refuse to compromise: salvation is granted to those who opt for the lonely integrity of the spirit.

Thus Browning stresses the folly of looking for the miraculous in legends. The divine is manifested in the human. Modern man has his miracles in the infinite capacity for love that exists in the human heart. Browning re-affirms his belief in love as the link between the finite and the infinite.[18] Characteristic of the love poetry of the later period is the insistence, at the end, of a reunion of lovers in the hereafter. "Some day, and soon, be sure himself will rise,/Called into life by her who long ago/Left his soul whiling time in flesh disguise." (XVIII) This is strongly reminiscent of the "Epilogue" to *Fifine at the Fair,* and thus lends credence to the view that Browning saw himself both as the young man who married the lady and at the duke who betrayed her. The later love poems very often have this markedly autobiographical ring.

Love, as represented by Browning, has many aspects. In *Paracelsus*, the love that is a corrective to Paracelsus' overweening desire for supreme knowledge is in the nature of sympathy and fellowship with human kind and with all finite manifestations of life. The romantic and transcendental characteristics of love that Aprile represents, are as imperfect as Paracelsus' hunger for knowledge, for ultimately love answers to the claims not only of the spirit but also of the flesh.

In *Easter-Day*, the concept of love has Christian overtones. Love is now seen as a manifestation of God and its value proved by the fact that through his love for man, God came down to earth and suffered for man. Similarly, in "Saul" *(Men and Women)* love is the medium by which man is linked to the divine – "a man like to me,/Thou shall love and be loved by, for ever!" (ll.310-11)

In the poems of *Men and Women*, the emphasis is on various aspects of human love, whether harmonious or unfulfilled. The fulfilled lovers are those who have used love to overcome the barriers of the flesh and attained to a true fusion of the spirit. The unfulfilled are those who have let wordly considerations, sheer faint-heartedness or intellectual pride destroy the delicate link. In these poems, true love leads to an enlargement of consciousness which enables lovers to see "New depths of the divine." ("By the Fire-Side," l.140)

In the later poems on love, as we have seen, the theme of time, death and eternity become a new adjunct to Browning's treatment of love. Few love poems in the earlier phase had a reference to death; "Evelyn Hope" (*Men and Women)* affirms the immortality and invincibility of love. Less specifically, "A Lover's Quarrel" in the same volume refers to the emptiness that is in the heart of the disappointed lover as a "bare-walled crypt," (l.140) and describes true love as means to "thrill/Back to life" (ll.144-45) his dead heart. In "Prospice" (*Dramatis Personae*), death is welcomed because it means reunion.

Death, now, is a reality that separates lovers in the flesh. The hostility of the world is an ever present feature to be contended with, while another insidious enemy is the passing of time. Thus, Browning is led to emphasize the importance of all aspects of love, physical as well as spiritual, imperfect as well as ideal. In the later love poetry, love is not only intrinsically valuable in itself, it becomes a mode for discovering meaning and value in man's limited world.

But just as love leads man to a perception of truth, its negation through the inordinate exercise of ratiocination can pervert the truth and lead to falsehood. The casuistry in the poems that will be examined in the following chapter illustrates what W.O. Raymond calls "the cleavage between man's faculties of love and reason."[19]

NOTES

1. T.J. Collins, *Browning's Moral-Aesthetic Theory, 1833-1855* (Nebraska: University of Nebraska Press, 1967), p.136.
2. See "Prospice" (*Dramatis Personae,* 1864), ll.21-28.
3. See Browning's letter to Isa Blagden, July 2, 1870: "Nine years ago, completed on the 29th. The years they come and go The roses drop in the grave But never the love doth so." (*Dearest Isa*, ed. McAleer, p. 338).
4. In "Dis Aliter Visum" (*Dramatis Personae,* 1864), love involves "gaining a share/O' the sole spark from God's life at strife/With death."(ll.26-28).
5. For a fuller discussion, see the next chapter.
6. E.D.H. Johnson, "Authority and the Rebellious Heart" in *Browning: "Men and Women" and Other Poems: A Casebook,* p. 105.
7. See DeVane, *Handbook,* p. 405.
8. *Loc. cit.*
9. See *Letters*, ed. Hood, p. 267.
10. See Maisie Ward, *Robert Browning and His World: "Two Brownings? 1861-1889."*
11. *Handbook,* p. 461.
12. See "By The Fire-side" (*Men and Women*) XXVII and LI. Also *Fifine at the Fair,* XXXIX and XLIV.
13. E.D.H. Johnson, p. 105.
14. See "Two in the Campagna," (*Men and Women,* Stanza X).
15. cf. "The Statue and the Bust," (*Men and Women)*, "Youth and Art" and "Dis Aliter Visum, Le Byron De Nos Jours" (*Dramatis Personae*).
16. *The Alien Vison of Victorian Poetry,* p. 99.
17. *The Infinite Moment*, pp. 225-26.
18. cf. "A Death in the Desert," "Himself conceives of life as love,/Conceived of love as what must enter in,/Fill up, make one with His each soul He loved." (ll.670-72)
19. *The Infinite Moment,* p. 130.

THE CASUISTICAL MONOLOGUES

A characteristic feature of Browning's poetry is its penchant for special pleading, and in the later period, three long poems have their protagonists making a case for positions which are not entirely justifiable: *Prince Hohenstiel-Schwangau, Saviour of Society* (1871), *Fifine at the Fair* (1872), and *Aristophanes' Apology* (1875).

The most striking feature in these poems, when compared to the earlier casuistical poems like "Bishop Blougram's Apology" and "Mr.Sludge, 'The Medium'," is the significant enlargement of range. *Prince Hohenstiel-Schwangau,* DeVane remarks, discusses "almost every conceivable topic of interest in 1871."[1] *Fifine at the Fair* touches upon the poetic controversy between Rossetti and Buchanan,[2] and includes a wide range of metaphysical subjects like the nature of perception and the existence of absolute values. *Aristophanes' Apology* is a reaction against the current attacks on Euripides, and as Douglas Bush points out – "it is not a mere academic dispute on the merits of Aristophanes and Euripides, of comedy and tragedy, it embodies all that Browning passionately thought and felt about the ethical function of poetry and the conflict between flesh and spirit, sense and soul."[3]

The forms in which Browning shapes these poems emerge from his belief that since moral judgements are a complex, difficult matter, a more comprehensive range of evidence must be provided on which to base those judgements. Thus, in order to establish an even balance between sympathy and judgement, Browning experiments with techniques to enlarge the scope of the dramatic monologue, so that these poems explore not just a single, limited point of view, but create a number of different perspectives which throw light on that particular viewpoint. Thus, we have in *Prince Hohenstiel*, the effect of a number of voices interacting with the voice of the speaker, while *Fifine* uses an almost cinematic technique of multifarious perspectives fading into each other. In *Aristophanes' Apology*, the auditor plays a more definite role than in any other dramatic monologue, so that the poem is really two monologues, representing the two sides of the debate between Balaustion and Aristophanes.

In *Prince Hohenstial-Schwangau*, Browning puts forward his own estimate of Napoleon III of France, dramatized within the framework of an imaginary apology for his career by the Emperor. That career had been followed with great interest both by Browning and his wife. DeVane points out that "the Brownings scarcely wrote a letter during the fifties in which Louis Napoleon does not figure."[4] But while Mrs Browning's admiration for the French Emperor remained constant, Browning's feelings underwent considerable fluctuations. In contrast to her "fanatically strident offensives for Louis Napoleon"[5] Browning's judgements of the Prince revealed a "typical tendency to reduce every problem in human affairs to the problem of character."[6] Mainly, his reaction was one pitying contempt for a man who, because of a vacillating and temporizing attitude had lost valuable chances.

On August 19, 1870, Browning wrote to Isa Blagden: "morally everybody from the highest to the lowest is as blameable as he."[7] On August 22, 1870, he was more critical: "Not one human being could venture to approve the conduct of the Emperor – for what was ever more palpably indefensible."[8] On October 29, 1870, the indignant tone continued: "but with respect to Napoleon, – he should simply be blotted out of the world as the greatest failure on record. The 'benefits of his reign' are just the extravagant interest which a knavish banker pays you for some time till he, one fine day, decamps with the principal, – and then where are you? But there has been no knavery, only the decline and fall of the faculties corporeal and mental", and further on in the same letter, in gentler tones: " – but who can control his fate? – and his was only to be nearly a great man."[9] On January 23, 1871, he again wrote to Isa: "we all, in our various degrees, took the man on trust, believed in his will far too long after the deed was miserably inadequate to what we supposed the will; but when the mask fell and we found a lazy old and worn-out voluptuary had neglected every duty, ignored every necessity."[10] On April 25, 1871; "...no more bitterness about the dear man, who, if France likes, may try and do what he can once more at the 'edifice' with all the advantages of old age and decayed faculty. The poor country seems properly to belong to the devil – and he is not, nor ever was a devil – only a weaker mortal than one's respect for human nature thought conceivable, when given such splendid opportunities for good."[11]

On December 29, 1871, he wrote to Miss Blagden about the poem: "I think in the main, he meant to do what I say, and, but for the weakness-grown more apparent in these last years than formerly, would have done what I say he did not. I thought badly of him at the beginning of his career, et pour cause, better afterwards, on the strength of the promises he made, and gave indications of intending to redeem--I think him very weak in the last miserable year."[12] Browning's ambivalence is best revealed in the letter he wrote to Edith Story on January 1, 1872: "I don't think, when you have read more, you will find I have 'taken the man for any Hero' – I rather made him confess he was the opposite, though I put forward what excuses I thought he was likely to make for himself, if inclined to try. I never at any time thought much better of him than now; and I don't think so much worse of the character as shown in the last few years, because I suppose there to be a physical and intellectual decline of faculty, brought about by the man's own faults, no doubt – but I think he struggles against these; and when that is the case, depend upon it, in a soliloquy, a man makes the most of his good intentions, and sees great excuse in them – far beyond what our optics discover."[13]

Thus, Browning's ambiguous attitude to his protagonist colours the poem, in which the mixture of sympathy and judgement is more pronounced than in any other dramatic monologue. For if, as Leo A.Hetzler suggests,[14] Browning revived this poem in 1871 – a poem originally conceived in Rome in 1860 – because, in reaction to his impulsive proposal of marriage to Lady Ashburton, he turned to a subject dear to his wife, he may also have been motivated by an impulse to make amends for his difference of opinion with her on this issue by making a case for Napoleon that would present both the good and the bad aspects of his career.

The structure of the poem is unique among Browning's dramatic monologues for what purports to be a self-defence before a silent, but nevertheless implicity questioning interlocutor, turns out ultimately to be a dream-reverie. Prince Hohenstiel-Schwangau is really in his Residenz, relieving the tension of making a crucial decision by imagining himself in exile, explaining his life's work to a "bud-mouthed arbitress" (p. 318) in a "pork-pie hat and crinoline" (p. 292) in Leicester Square. The fact that he is not really in exile is not revealed till the very end, when the sudden reversal comes as a shock, heightening the dramatic impact. Hetzler remarks that possibly Browning was experimenting with this complex structure in an effort to comply with Carlyle's advice to the biographer not to portray each phase of a man's earlier life in the light of his final destiny, but to report each phase as it really was, when the future was only an "unwound skein of possibilities, of apprehensions, attemptabilities, vague looming hopes." (p. 348) The form of the dream-reverie enables Browning to present a case without committing himself to specific judgements. It also helps to present multiple perspectives, for past, present and the future coalesce in the mind of the speaker. Browning's technique here is what Auerbach calls "a method which dissolves reality into multiples and multivalent reflections of consciousness."[15] It allows explorations into what Roma A.King calls a "semi-rationalized, semi-verbalized consciousness."[16]

A further level of complexity is provided by the introduction of a debate between the Head Servant and Sagacity, in which the latter assumes the role of an alter-ego. At this point there is a shift from autobiography to biography. Hetzler points out that this device enables Browning to present all that was good about the Emperor, and also, by contrasting the right decisions made by the idealized prince but not by the real Napoleon, enables Browning to present his criticism of a man whose indecisiveness brought about the frustration of good intentions and the failure of correctly conceived plans. Thus, the conflicting nature of the speaker and his contradictory impulses are dramatized by the structure of the poem.

As Irvine and Honan note, "Deeply, Robert's political quarrels with Elizabeth proceeded not so much from a conviction that she was politically wrong, as from a conviction that politics disguises the real facts of human behaviour."[17] And it was in human behaviour that Browning's own interests lay; so that his treatment of the Prince in *Prince Hohenstiel-Schwangau* is "less topical and satirical than exploratory and psychological."[18]

The monologue does not use the crisis moment as a means of character revealment, because the Prince is shown (ostensibly) as surveying the political vista of his reign from a comparatively uninvolved perspective. What is of greater importance is the "significant historical crisis"[19] which Park Honan finds operating in the case of Mr. Sludge, Bishop Blougram, Caliban and the Prince, "Browning's nineteenth century figures who have all been forcibly altered in some way by an historical situation. In each case, the personality which the speaker has been compelled to adopt is very different from the personality he once had, or would have but for his historical context; in each case there is a special contrast between these two personalities."[20]

The prince reveals an acute self-consciousness when he acknowledges the divergence between his ideals and his course of action. In fact, his casuistry lies in his attempts to justify a course of action which he very well realizes is not quite justifiable. As he says in the beginning of the poem – "Fitter to do than let alone, I hold," (p. 293) and then proceeds for the rest of the poem to exonerate his let-alone policies. His whole arguments revolves round this awarenesss of the duality of the actual and the potential, the flesh and the spirit. In Hohenstiel-Schwangau's attempt to justify his subjugation of the one (his ideals) in favour of the other (worldly expedience) lies his sophistry, and a further irony is introduced by his awareness that it is a finer thing to "Live in the luminous circle that surrounds/The planet, not the leaden orb itself." (p. 303) This awareness makes his most persuasive argument suspect, for we realize that we are dealing with a man who is untrue to his own ideals.

Prince Hohenstiel-Schwangau begins his monologue with a tenet characteristic of Browning – God's infinitude as opposed to man's finite nature and the inter-relationship between the two:

> I only know
> That varied modes of creatureship abound,
> Implying just as varied intercourse
> For each with the creator of them all. (p. 294)

Starting with this hypothesis, he argues that the particular course of action adopted by him is in consonance with God's plan; to interfere by chopping and changing things would be presumptuous. Therefore, "a conservator, call me, if your please,/Not a creator nor destroyer: one/Who keeps the world safe." (p. 296) He claims that if it is not his mission to light up the darkness, his helping that light to do fuller service is as worthy a task as the other, if less dramatic. The Prince makes much of this argument in order to prove that he did not thwart God's purpose in creation. But his casuistry becomes evident when he asserts that since evil is the means by which good is brought about, to tamper with evil would be an act of impunity against God's divine plan. We see here Browning's characteristic method in the casuistical monologues of giving the speaker one of his own favourite doctrines and then allowing him to reveal his sophistical character by the particular interpretation he (the speaker) gives to the doctrine. Prince Hohenstiel-Schwangau twists Browning's theory of the necessity of accepting the limitations of this finite world into an excuse for apathy and expedience. He feels that he is not to blame for his timorous, time-serving policies, even though his opponents may wish that his vision were less of an owl's and more of an eagle's. His excuse is that since his aim was to "save" society, he has refused to risk the gains and stability of what had been accomplished, and that this was the best he could have done with the capacities granted to him.[21]

The Prince rationalizes his reactionary policies by arguing that idealism can never accomplish anything concrete in this imperfect world. His arguments on this point are very much like Bishop Blougram's, who, as W.O.Raymond says, "bases part of his defence on the contrast between the futility of abstract idealism and the success of a prudential and practical adaptation of one's talent and outlook to the environment and capacities of a workaday world."[22]

As we will see later, Aristophanes uses a similar argument to justify the compromises he makes.

Pulled in opposite directions by the conflicting claims of "least wants first" and "Exceptionally noble causes," (p. 305) the Prince vacillates. He justifies his narrow policies by arguing that a man's life is too short for grand experiments. Yet he is forced to recognize the grandeur of the "brave thinkers", who are worth "All that our world's worth, flower and fruit of man!" (p. 306) He acknowledges:

> 'Tis part of life, a property to prize,
> That those o'the higher sort engaged i'the world,
> Should fancy they can change its ill to good,
> Wrong to right, ugliness to beauty: (p. 306)

and admits to have had ideals and dreams of his own. This is reminiscent of Bishop Bougram's "Enthusiasm is the best thing, I repeat."(l.556) Like Blougram, the Prince is condemned as a casuist because he has allowed his inner truths to be deflected. Both passively accept the situations in which they find themselves, even though they are aware of the deficiencies therein. This is entirely antithetical to Browning's belief that value lies in energy, vitality and honest confrontation of life's problems. For the limitations of the finite world are not as incompatible with aspiration as Hohenstiel-Schwangau would have us believe. While man must of necessity accept the compromises demanded by reality, it does not preclude lofty aims and ambitions. Man must pursue the infinite even if it is inaccessible. And above all, he must be loyal to his conception of truth.

That Hohenstiel-Schwangau is subconsciously aware of the unsoundness of his arguments is revealed by his assertion: "Change life, in me shall follow change to match!" (p. 306) Philip Drew points out that the two alternatives envisaged by the Prince – keeping his subjects alive and giving them democratic freedoms – are not really "mutually exclusive, and that the Prince is simply inventing a powerful reason for breaking his promise."[23] Like Chiappino *in* A *Soul's Tragedy*, the Prince has compromised at the expense of truth. He is a lazy opportunist, not a principled revolutionary, and is revealed as such, in spite of his claim that his opponents accuse him of indolence, apathy and vacillation merely because they have made an error in interpreting his policies.

There is bitter irony in the fact that despite his ostensible high-mindedness, the Prince has few compunctions as to the ways of silencing opposition. To his opponent's charge that he

> Leave the illogical touch now here now there
> I'the way of work, the tantalising help
> First to this, then the other opposite:

The blowing hot and cold, sham policy,
Sure ague of the mind and nothing more,
Disease of the perception or the will,
That fain would hide in a fine name! (p. 302)

the Prince retaliates with "a wink to the police" while making pretence of "shrugging shoulder." (p. 302)

Browning dramatizes his belief that much of Napoleon's so-called democratic processes were really a farce, by creating different voices which, when juxtaposed against the protagonist's voice, become touchstones by which to judge him. The following lines are a typical example:

The power to speak, hear, print and read is ours?
Aye, we learn where and how, when clapped inside
A convict-transport bound for cool Cayenne.
The universal vote we have; its urn
We also have where votes drop, fingered-o'er
By the universal Prefect. (p. 303)

The third section of the poem changes from autobiography to biography. The Prince says: "Hear what I never was but might have been," (p. 307) and then goes on to paint an idealized figure who, ironically, is a figment of his own imagination. The ironic gap between imagination and reality is particularly evident here. Browning accurately records the events of December 2, 1851, "Sudden the clock told it was judgement time," (p. 309) when the Prince President issued two proclamations, which, to use the words of Irvine and Honan, "addressed to the people, explained the failure of the existing constitution, dissolved the Assembly and promised a plebiscite on a new constitution, of which the chief feature was to be a strong and responsible executive."[24] But Browning also exposes the trickery of this political move and suggests the moral unsoundness of the Prince through the words which end the speech:

Grant them, and I shall forthwith operate –
Ponder it well! – to the extremest stretch
O'the power you trust me: if with unsuccess,
God wills it, and there's nobody to blame. (p. 310)

This section is full of satire at political manipulation and knavery, at those who

strut, prate and brag their best,
Squabble at odds on every point save one,

And there shake hands – agree to trifle time,
Obstruct advance with, each his cricket-cry. (p. 309)

and also:

craft and greed and impudence
Of night-hawk at first chance to prowl and prey
For glory and a little gain beside,
Passing for eagle in the dusk of the age, – (p. 310)

This is Browning's presentation of the reality of politics as opposed to the "pattern of romance" imposed upon it by Elizabeth.[25]

At this stage the casuistry of the Prince takes a different turn. He attempts to disarm criticism by showing how an imaginary Prince who is true to his ideals has also to face criticism. This section is a mixture of truth and make-believe. The Prince identifies himself with the Head Servant and claims to have always acted virtuously in spite of temptations to the contrary put forward by Sagacity. Sagacity plays the role of the worldly, practical, cynically clever worshipper of power that the idealized Head Servant could have become but did not. But Browning reveals the sophistry of the speaker by choosing three incidents from Napoleon's reign and contrasting the imagined, ideal course of action with the sordid facts of reality. For a true view of Browning's ironic stand-point, we need to be aware of the historical facts; but even without this knowledge, we have a clue as to the manner in which we are to view Hohenstiel-Schwangau's creation of an idealized self, for the Prince himself is aware that it is an "unwritten chapter" in his history, i.e. has not materialized in fact.

On the matter of Italian liberation, Sagacity advices the Head Servant to leave things as they are, but the Head acts with vigour for the cause of liberty, championing war for the sake of truth alone. In actuality, however, the Prince acted not from altruistic motives but from the motives of a self-seeking politician. Irvine and Honan point out a time when "a French garrison was blocking the Italian unity which he himself had set in motion."[26] And though, in the poem, the Head Servant indignantly refuses compensation for his role in the unification of Italy, it is a fact of history that Napoleon annexed Nice and Savoy as his "snug honorarium-fee." (p. 316) Further, though the Head Servant ignores Sagacity's advice to secure the throne for his heirs, Napoleon attempted to do just this.[27]

This section, with its profuse words and phrases suggestive of swift, resolute action--"Heavily did he let his fist fail plumb." (p. 310) "too swift/And thorough his procedure" (p. 310). "Hands energetic to the utmost" (p. 316) becomes deeply ironical in the light of Hohenstiel-

Schwangau's own assertion that this is the kind of ruler he might have been, but never was. The contrast between the fact and the fiction is all the more incisive.

Veering between the opposite poles of sympathy and condemnation, Browning's judgement of the Prince is coloured by indignation for the man's unsteady vision. Nevertheless, a sensitive awareness of human fallibility is, in these later poems, shared both by Browning and his monologuists. In the very last section of the poem, the Prince repudiates his own arguments, accepts the truth about his situation, and verbalizes what we have felt to be his true character all along. He is brought face to face with reality: "Alack, one lies one's self/Even in the stating that one's end was truth," (p. 319) Intentions and actions remain poles apart. The "I" of the ghostly dialogue is far removed from the "I" who realizes that "nothing is done and over yet." (p. 319)

Prince Hohenstiel-Schwangau now accepts the fact that truth is deflected by considerations of expediency and that admirable motives tend to become ineffective in practice. He admits that all his arguments defending his ends and means have been casuistical:

> Somehow the motives, that did well enough
> I'the darkness, when you bring them into light
> Are found, like those famed cave-fish, to lack eye
> And organ for the upper magnitudes. (p. 319)

And again:

> Yes, forced to speak, one stoops to say – one's aim
> Was – what it peradventure should have been: (p. 319)

Browning reinforces the irony of this last section through Hohenstiel-Schwangau's last, characteristically indecisive words: "Double or quits! The letter goes! Or stays?" This giveaway exposes the real truth about the Prince's character, throwing into relief the hollowness, in actual, concrete terms, of the Prince's claims to disinterestedness and patriotism. The image created of a vacillating ruler, gambling with the fortunes of his country also provides an effective contrast to the image of the resolute ruler ("No trepidation, much less treachery," (p. 316) that had been previously painted by the Prince. His apology encompasses an idea spoken by Ogniben in *A Soul's Tragedy*: "There is truth in falsehood, falsehood in truth. No man ever told one great truth that I know, without the help of a good dozen lies at least, generally unconscious ones." (p. 464, Modern Library Edition) Nevertheless, as with the other casuistical monologues of the later period, the portrait of the Prince is redeemed by the acute self-awareness that he reveals.

In *Fifine at the Fair* Browning further explores the question of attaining to the truth in a world where truth is easily deflected, through establishing the disparity between potentiality and actual achievement, between aspiration and action, the conflict between the two opposing thrusts in man – the sensual and the spiritual – and relating all these issues to the central issue of love as the one constant truth in a world of change.

Irvine and Honan remark that very nearly, the motivating principle of Browning's life in the 1870's was "his urge to restore the lost sense of union" with his wife.[28] They follow Professor W.O. Raymond[29] in isolating Browning's proposal of marriage to Lady Ashburton and her refusal as being the source of his feelings of guilt and remorse. In choosing the themes of material infidelity in *Fifine at the Fair*, Browning embarked, as it were, on a personal course of expiation, and Irvine and Honan remark that "it did much to restore Browning to himself."[30] It is clear, therefore, that the implications of the poem range much farther than that of mere casuistry, though casuistry becomes an important means for the total development of the theme.

Fifine at the Fair is divided into three parts,-the prologue, entitled "Amphibian," the main monologue, and the epilogue, entitled "The Householder." The prologue is preceded by an excerpt from Moliere's *Don Juan*, the last lines of which are Donna Elvire's mocking interpretation of the words Don Juan would use to allay her fears about his constancy: "nor aught in nature can avail/To separate us two, save what, in stopping breath/May peradventure stop devotion likewise – death!" The two main ideas of the poem are thus contained in this epigraph, constancy (devotion) in love, and, as Donna Elvire doubts, but the Epilogue will prove, the possibility of an unbroken bond even after death.

The lyrical prologue is a contrast to the argumentative main monologue stylistically, but the ideas explored in the main body of the poem are initially postulated here. In spite of the limpid beauty of the lines, there is an undercurrent of distress, "Fancy which turned a fear" (I) at the thought of the yawning gulf that separates the living from the "spirit-sort." (XV) This gulf cannot be bridged except through man's imaginative vision, a vision provided mainly by poetic inspiration initially:

> Emancipate through passion
> And thought, with sea for sky,
> We substitute, in a fashion,
> For heaven – poetry. (XIV)

The eternal can be linked to the finite in a completer way through the power of love, the devoted love that provides stability amidst flux and remains unchanged even after death. For the speaker, however, this certainty has not yet been achieved. The dominant background imagery of *Fifine* is the sea, and appropriately, the speaker in the prologue is a swimmer who, through the buoyant power of the imagination feels himself in harmony with the world of the spirit, symbolized by the butterfly hovering above him and which is to him "Like soul." (IV) Roma A. King points out that "soul" here means "both the realization of the fullest, deepest, level of one's being and also, the recognition of affinities with and participation in something outside and beyond man himself – Eternilty, God."[31] The speaker wonders "If a certain soul/Which early slipped its sheath" (IX) looks down with pity and wonder at the grossness of a creature who welcomes the material world "Land the solid and safe," (XVIII) and has no desire to gain the "finer element" (XV) except imaginatively. The prologue juxtaposes land and sea, heaven and earth to provide a parallel to man's amphibian nature itself. Man may desire the refinements of the spiritual existence, but his nature binds him to the temporal and the material.

The main monologue explores the psychology of an amphibian, a man who realizes the value of the bond of love, and yet surrenders to the base impulses of his amphibian nature and yearns for freedom and change. It is based on a question common to all the casuistical monologues – how is a man impelled to justify a course of action which he himself realizes is not entirely admirable? The speaker is deliberately left nameless, implying that such a man can at best be only a cipher. But the assumption is that he is the legendary voluptuary and sensualist, Don Juan. The choice of such a protagonist at once gives an ironic cast to his self-justifications. At the same time, it helps Browning to view objectively ideas and lines of thought that must have had points of similarity with his own following the Ashburton affair. The paradoxial issue as Browning presents it is this: every man has in him some facets of a Don Juan. It partakes of the element of change and impermanence in nature itself. To deny it leads to hypocrisy. To attempt to rationalize it leads to sophistry. But to surrender to the impulse leaves him to confront negation and despair.

Browning's speaker is not the Don Juan of tradition. He is not, at least till the end, concerned with seduction. As has been pointed out, "he evades the depth, nature and extent of his sexuality by explaining how he is true." He also evades being thought a philanderer rather than boasting of it.[32] But it must also be mentioned that this is how Don Juan sees himself, and not always as the reader sees him. Nevertheless, his arguments are to a large extent related to the more serious scheme of illuminating human nature: "From a given point evolve the infinite!" (CXXIX)

The opening lines postulate the theme of marital fidelity: "Link arm with me!/Like husband and like wife,"(I) and its role in helping man to face the illusiveness of life, where nothing appears to be permanent. Yet, the speaker is "Frenetic to be free."(VI) Like the pennon fluttering in the wind, his "heart makes just the same/Passionate stretch, fires up for lawlessness." (VI) The fair is representative of the illusion that gilds the reality of life; and Don Juan makes a first exposure of his casuistry when he argues that the illusion of the fair is in itself a kind of truth because sincerely presented. He wonders what it is that makes a man fall a willing captive to what he knows is at the opposite pole reject the "chaste, temperate, serene" Elvire in favour of "what splutters green and blue, this fizgig called Fifine!" (XXXIII) Even as he surrenders, he sets about analyzing the reasons for the "acknowledged victory of whom I call my queen,/Sexless and bloodless sprite." (XVI) The flower imagery that follows is replete with sexual connotations, as Barbara Melchiori has shown,[33] and serves as a give away to Don Juan's allegedly intellectual stance; the adjectives used: "flavorous venomed bell," "gorgeous poison-plague" (XVIII) reveal the insidious attraction posed by the sensuous Fifine, in spite of Don Juan's avowed preference for the "daisy-meek.i (XVIII) This at once throws doubt on the validity of Don Juan's claim that

> . . . because the flesh that claimed
> Unduly my regard, she thought, the taste, she blamed
> In me, for things externe, was all mistake, she finds—
> Or will find, when I prove that bodies show me minds. (XXVIII)

Don Juan sketches portraits of the archetypal woman as represented by Helen, Cleopatra, Saint-Fifine, and playfully adds Elvire, the "phantom-wife," (XXVIII) with the fanciful illusion that the real Elvire has "cast this clog/Of flesh away." (XXIII) The masque is Don Juan's way of asserting that Elvire is not only equal to these beauties, but has predominance over them. Yet, it is clear that Fifine interests him the most, for to Don Juan, she is, as Roma A. King notes "at once an attractive body and a symbol of spiritual freedom, an incentive to self-realization. She appeals to the speaker's elemental desire to be himself, untrammelled by conventions."[34] But the morality that Fifine represents is merely "self-sustainment" and Don Juan's quest for the infinite debases itself through this attraction.

Proceeding on the assumption that the urge to lawlessness is a purely intellectual experience which in no way affects his essentially inviolable regard for his wife, Don Juan compares her value to that of a priceless painting by Raphael that he might possess. He might momentarily turn aside to "relish leaf by leaf, Dore's last picture-book," (XXXV) but in a crisis would risk everything to safeguard his "perfect piece." (XXXVI)

The lines which follow seem to merge fantasy and reality in an illusory haze with Elvire beneath a pall, "As if the vesture's snow were moulding sleep not death." (XXXVIII) These shifting perspectives in time and space leads Ryals to call the technique of *Fifine* as cinematic.[35] But they also point to Don Juan's inability to achieve stability; for him Fifine is always more real than Elvire. The Elvire created by Don Juan's imagination represents the untainted spiritual being: "How ravishingly pure you stand in pale constraint!/My new-created shape, without or touch or taint,/Inviolate of life and worldliness and sin" (XXXVIII) but it is significant that he associates her with death. Reverting to reality, he eloquently describes her brown hair: "So part rich rillets dyed/Deep by the woodland leaf, when down they pour, each side/O'er the rock-top, pushed by Spring!" (XXXIX) His sensuous nature is deeply emphasized.

Carrying his justification forward, Don Juan expands on the proposition: "In the seeing soul, all worth lies." (LV) He finds the artistic consciousness instinctively able to invest with beauty the commonplace, to strip away all the external superfluities to reach the essence of truth. The artist who tries to bring out the hidden possibilities of his medium and the lover who looks beyond the externals to the inner soul, are both trying, as Don Juan says he himself is with regard to Fifine, to find abiding value in a world of illusion and shifting appearances.

At this point we have an affirmation of the nature and purpose of art that reproduce Browning's own views:

And this corroborates the sage,
That Art, —which I may style the love of loving, rage
Of knowing, seeing, feeling, the absolute truth of things
For truth's sake, whole and sole, not any good, truth brings
The knower, seer, feeler, beside,—instinctive Art
Must fumble for the whole, once fixing on a part
However poor, surpass the fragment, and aspire
To reconstruct thereby, the ultimate entire. (XLIV)

This view of art as a means of expressing the infinite is expanded to encompass the role of art as a means of giving life to what is inert and dead. Don Juan finds in creativity "a foil/For a new birth of life, the challenged soul's response/To ugliness and death,— creation for the nonce." (LV) But

Don Juan's artistry, concerned as it is with demonstrating the value of Fifine, does not lift him out of himself and so becomes self-defeating.

Don Juan goes on to express a belief that is found very often in Browning's poetry – it is only in rare, visionary moments that the mind can pierce through the superfluities of existence to its essence. The contrast between "the varicolour" and the "achromatic white," (LIX) is the contrast between finite experience in all its variegated colours and the white light of "spiritual verities in their absolute essence,"[36] as W.O. Raymond describes it with reference to "Numpholeptos" (*Pacchiarotto and How He Worked in Distemper: With Other Poems).* A man can only strive to attain this ideal and await the moment of fulfilment:

> . . . what joy, when each may supplement
> The other, changing each, as changed, till, wholly, blent,
> Our old things shall be new, and, what we both ignite,
> Fuse, lose the varicolor in achromatic white! (LIX)

Don Juan, however, twists this idea to suit his own purpose. To reach the depths of a soul like Fifine's, for example, he argues ingeniously, "some flesh may be to pass." (LX) That the argument is sophistical is made clear by the bee-image which is used to illustrate Don Juan's contention. The bee's flight from flower to flower making "Matter-of-course snatched snack" is necessary, for "unless he taste, how try?" (LX) Similarly, says Juan, if his "soul tastes and tries/And trifles time" with Fifine, it is only to "bring honey home to hive." (LX) Ryals is of the opinion that there is very little sophistry in Don Juan's arguments, since they do not proceed from a "desire to deceive" his audience.[37] One ventures to suggest that Don Juan is a casuist because he is doing a much more dangerous thing – he is trying to deceive himself.

The mood becomes serenely grave with the return to one of the key themes of the poem – the fear of approaching death. The setting sun and the tombstones where the birds twitter are symbolic of the end that awaits all in nature. But death here, as in all Browning's poetry, is an awakening into a new life, a "rise into the true out of the false." (LXIV) Don Juan's casuistical mind at once seizes on this point in order to bolster his defence. Using the analogy of the swimmer who is upborne by the water around him, but which would overwhelm him should he attempt to "slip the sea and hold the heaven," (LXV) Don Juan comes to the convenient conclusion that since man is perforce bound by his nature, he must use every facet of it to his advantage:

> We must endure the false, no particle of which
> Do we acquaint us with, but up we mount a pitch
> Above it, find our heads reach the truth, while hands explore
> The false below: (LXV)

W.O. Raymond points out that "the imagery of swimming in the sea is used as an illustration of man's dealings with the false and shifting appearance of life, through which he learns to value the truth and permanence that reside in the heaven above."[38] Don Juan further argues that this working from the false to the true, from Fifine to Elvire, convinces him of the one essential truth, the reality of his own being amidst endless flux and change: "That I am, anyhow, a truth, though all else seem/And be not." (LXXX) In a clearly discernible exercise in casuistry, Don Juan asserts that life is an endless search for truth, where the unusual and the risky venture draws more merit than the commonplace and the solidly safe. The imagery is no longer that of swimming but of navigation. The "cockleshell" (LXXXI) that is Fifine tempts his seamanship more rigorously than the "superior ship" (LXXXIII) Elvire. And though he asserts: "I would the steady voyage, and not the fitful trip, – / Elvire and not Fifine, – might test our seamanship," (LXXXII) his impulses run counter to his words. Even as he speaks, he gives expression to the powerful temptations Fifine's quicksilver attractiveness poses for him. It is not always her mind that he sees:

> Though art so bad, and yet so delicate a brown!
> Wouldst tell no end of lies: I talk to smile or frown!
> Wouldst rob me: do men blame a squirrel, lithe and sly,
> For pilfering the nut she adds to hoard? Nor I. (LXXXII)

In the face of this surrender to the forces of the temporal, Don Juan loses the tenuous certainty of the truth of his being that he had won so hardily. As Claudette Kemper Columbus notes: "In Fifine's 'wash o' the world' all matter liquefies. The 'solid and safe' though the speaker time and again argues that firmness is possible, nevertheless never takes hold."[39] In lines reminiscent of Arnold's "Dover Beach," he laments:

> All false, all fleeting too! And nowhere things abide,
> And everywhere we strain that things should stay, – the one
> Truth, that ourselves are true! (LXXXIV)

But the way to truth is not through rationalizations of the fleshly path to the spirit. Don Juan is unable to overcome his casuistry. His argument comes to a full circle with Don Juan once again insisting on the essential "truth" amidst falsity that the fair represents. He has learnt nothing from his explorations and shows how misguided he still is by again equating falsity with truth. Don Juan admires both the fair folk and Fifine for frankly admitting their falsity. But as a casuist, he seeks to depend solely on reason and so finds that knowledge dissolves into "surmise and doubt and disbelief." (XC)

The second circle of arguments begins again with a bathe in the sea and Don Juan's return home to smoke and think about the fair. He plays Schumann's "Carnival," is filled with the idea that in Art as in Nature change is inevitable, falls asleep and has a long and vaguely ominous dream. The music lifts him out of ordinary experience into a dream-world, thronged with silent and grotesquely masked figures which arouse disgust, but become less repulsive and almost pitiful when viewed from close quarters. The dream carnival becomes representative of life itself with its mixture of good and bad, hate and love, glory and shame. But just as Don Juan had previously used Browning's pet theory of the necessity of change in every sphere of life as a forerunner of progress to justify his need for change in love, so he now gives another favourite Browning theory a sophistical twist when he insists that, since life is a matter of varied experiences, every experience, moral or otherwise, has value in his attempts at gaining self-knowledge. Thus, Don Juan would satisfy his "hunger both to be and know the thing I am,/By contrast with the thing I am not." (CIII) The contrast between these lines and the almost doggerel rhythm of those that follow, "Experience, I am glad to master soon or late,/Here, there and everywhere i' the world without debate!" (CIV) which brings to mind the specific situation to which Don Juan's arguments are being directed (his petty intrigues) creates a juxtaposition that is sharply ironical.

The dream represents the sum total of Don Juan's questionings on the nature of perception and subjective judgements. His awareness of the shifting changeable, even illusory nature of all tradition – in Art, Science, Philosophy, History, morality, even religion – again brings him to the problem, can man ever know anything truly? The ambiguity that surrounds him everywhere merely leads him back to the primary impulse in his own heart – his innate conviction that if there is change there is also a permanent truth that exists unchanged. But, when "the multiform subsides, becomes the definite" it is not in this strife-ridden world, but "i' the blank/ Severity of peace in death." (CXIX) So much Don Juan gathers when he finds the multiform shapes of his dream world transfigured into the solidity of the Druid monument, which, in recounting his dream to Elvire, he reaches in actuality at this point. But Don Juan's casuistical mind cannot grasp fully the significance of the monument; he still believes that since change (death and the passing of time, symbolized by the Druid stones) is everywhere in nature, he will succeed in rationalizing change in love as a necessity.

But the monument symbolizes not only the reality of death but also the forces of regeneration. Browning stresses the latter aspect and Sutherland Orr comments: "It symbolizes life in its most active and perennial form. It means the force which aspires to heaven, and the strength which is rooted in the earth. It means the impulses of all being towards something outside itself which is constant amidst all variety."[40] Thus, change need not necessarily be mere falsehood, as Don Juan mistakingly supposes. That change is reality is undeniable. But this reality can have two aspects. The one that is creative is impelled upwards, the other, the mechanistic process, is a falling-away process, an inverse movement involving material objects and mechanistic laws, a process that becomes casuistic. The latter is Don juan's course.

Once again, Don Juan asserts the necessity of falsehood:[41]

> . . . truth is forced
> To manifest itself through falsehood; whence divorced
> By the excepted eye, at the rare season, for
> The happy moment, truth instructs us to abhor
> The false, and prize the true, obtainable thereby,
> Then do we understand the value of a lie; (CXXIV)

He argues that the impulse towards the unchangeable truth meets obstacles in the world of the temporal. The veils of illusion have to be transcended, but they are an everpresent feature of life. Truth perforce hides behind the false and each encounter with the latter is one more step towards the former. This is the education that the soul must pass through to achieve truth and permanence. Don Juan uses these doctrines to justify his false practices, even to glory in them, and so reinforces his image as a casuist. This is especially evident in his unashamed claim that the unmasked "Ultimate" is but the "sea-Fifine." (CXXV) Thus the inherent contradictions in Don Juan's claims to aim at truth and spirituality are ironically revealed. And he himself realizes that his "poetry" has turned to "prose." (CXXVI)

The prologue had raised the problem of the role of the imagination in approximating the true spiritual vision. Man's amphibian nature, his penchant for the earthly, always keeps his fancies and visions partial and incomplete. Thus Don Juan finds that for all his aspirations for the infinite, he is too bound to the finite to be wholly able to transcend it. His poetry has turned to prose. His dream of rationalizing inconstancy in love and of making it appear a means of attaining a higher spirituality has proved to be a failure. His attraction for Fifine is too sensual to lift him out of the body and into the spirit. It impels him towards death (negation) rather than life. For inconstancy to the truth of love is, according to the poet's personal views, to deny oneself anchorage in life. It is the denial of the essential instinct of the soul for the One amidst the Many. Don Juan realizes that "The wanderer brings home no profit from the quest/ Beyond the sad surmise that keeping house were best." (CXXIX) The thought that he has contemplated just this futile quest racks Don Juan and one can hear Browning's anguished voice in his words: "Will the saint vanish from the sinner that repents?/Suppose you are a ghost! A memory, a hope,/A fear a conscience!" (CXXX) Ultimately, he decides to let fate bolt the door of his "honest, civic house" "never to wander more." (CXXXI) In a neat link-up with the beginning of the poem, and thus completing the second circle of arguments, Don Juan points out that "The unlucky bath's to blame." (CXXXI) The image of the tower as representative of the life of self-indulgence which Don Juan now eschews, looks forward to a similar image and situation in *Red Cotton Night-Cap Country*, though in the latter poem the tower symbol has different connotations. In both these poems, however, the attractions of the sensual life are strong, though fraught with dangers:

> . . . because, though half-way down,
> Its mullions wink o'erwebbed with bloomy greenness, yet
> Who mounts to staircase top may tempt the parapet,
> And sudden there's the sea! (CXXXI)

Though Don Juan now resolutely wonders why the "foamflutter" of the sea should "mend or mar/ The calm contemplative householders that we are?" (CXXXI) the images used in this passage "landlocked," "die," "Door," reveal, as Roma A. King points out, "a tension, a spiritual restlessness that can never abide the restrictions that he affects to accept."[42]

Don Juan has not reckoned with the duality of his own finite nature; for with all his incursions into the philosophic world of the infinite, he remains, a wanderer, condemned to an eternity of wandering. The shift from the transcendental to the descendental (to use Ryals's terms) in the last verse is emphasized by the subtle change of rhythm with its suggestions of a debonair philanderer suavely making off for a tryst. Don Juan has found a note slipped into his palm by Fifine, and making this an excuse, leaves for a further meeting with her. This contrast between his philosophizing and his actual actions is almost pathetic. Clyde de L. Ryals finds the last lines ambiguous and is of the opinion that the "restoration of tension in the end underscores the metaphysical complexity of the poem."[43] But the ambiguity fades when we remember that Don Juan has, imaginatively, in the course of his argument defending infidelity, made Elvire "slip from flesh and blood, and play the ghost." (CXXXII) and it is her fate to become a ghostly presence with a husband like him. Irvine and Honan aptly remark: "Don Juan's ordeal dramatizes the logical and moral inconstancy of the romantic axiom that free love implies freedom of the spirit, since he revolves into eternity in sexual chains."[44] Philip Drew is of the opinion that the final reversal "presents dramatically the central theme of the poem—that to abandon wilfully constancy in love is to leave oneself no certainty but death."[45]

The main poem treated as a major theme the fear of approaching death. In the Epilogue, death is accepted, even welcomed.[46] "The Householder" is concerned with the polarities of life and death, and the one sure link between the two, undying, unchanging love. It presents the affirmation that had evaded the casuistry of Don Juan, in which he had been "endeavouring to joint/ Together, and so make infinite, point and point:/ Fix into one Elvire a Fair-ful of Fifines!" (CXXIX) all the while forgetful of the "given point" which should have been the base from which to "evolve the infinite" (CXXIX)—the fact of love.

There seems to be some disagreement among critics as to the identity of the speaker. DeVane says: "The Epilogue, called 'The Householder,' is a dialogue, jocular, yet tender, between the householder and his dead wife who comes back to visit him; that is between Browning and his wife. . . . For Browning it is a scene of reconciliation between himself and his wife after the affair with Lady Ashburton has been put definitely behind him."[47] Ryals on the other hand, following Orr, is of the opinion that "the speaker here is not the poet, but the speaker in the Prologue and the main monologue, the speaker I have been calling Don Juan. He is even linked through imagery with the speaker of the main body of the poem, wherein householding is frequently used to suggest permanence."[48] Reconciling these two points of view, Philip Drew comments: "The householder, partly Juan and partly Browning himself, has just been reunited by death with his wife."[49] And this seems the most logical view. The last lines of the main monologue had hinted that in spite of his assertions to the contrary, Don Juan will not keep his promise of returning from his meeting with Fifine in five minutes, and that when he does, he will find Elvire gone. In the Epilogue, the householder feels he has denied himself the privileges of continuing love because of his shameful experience in the world. Reassurance comes in the shape of the spirit of his dead wife, who assures him that the finite and the infinite are not as far apart as he had supposed. The prologue had asked whether there was any possibility of continuity in love even in the after world. The epilogue answers in the affirmative, not even death can stop devotion. The wholly unexpectedness and poignancy of the meeting is heightened in the poem by the use of short, precise words and phrases. The contrast between the sincerity of these hurried, broken rhythms and the controlled sentence structure of the monologue is very marked.

The "fancy that turned a fear" in "Amphibian" was the fear, to quote J.L. Kendall, that "divine love may be imaginably purer than human love."[50] It is this fear that leads Don Juan to rationalize his baser impulses. The epilogue shows that this fear is unfounded. Even the bliss of the after-life is incomplete ("And was I so better off up there?" [l.24]) until the union of two lovers is complete. For true love is the love that accepts the innate nature of the partner and loves it notwithstanding. But this can operate only under the condition of constancy. Poetic fancies cannot approximate this ideal truth, only intuition can, and Don Juan's casuistry is the result of his dependence on his reasoning faculties alone.

Thus, the point is not so much that "man's devotion can never become single and all-satisfying until he is transplanted from time into eternity," as Roma A. King opines[51] but this devotion is an enduring link between time and eternity. To deny it would lead to hypocrisy and spiritual negation, as Don Juan's monologue proves. To be defeated by the temptations that beset the course of true love in this world and so to come to doubt its validity and consequently to exalt the perfection of the next world, is again frustrating. For love bridges the gap between the here and the after. "Death is naught" (1.32) in the sense that death makes no essential difference to the quality of love that exists between two individuals. Thus, the question posed in the epigraph is answered; death does not "stop devotion."

The difficulty of assessing *Fifine at the Fair* as a poem lies in the fact of the frequent closeness of Juan's position with Browning's own, which resists any arbitrary labelling of Don Juan's arguments as wholly unsound.[52] Irvine and Honan note that "Juan's yearning for personal liberty, his sensuous intensity, and impressionism, and scorn for institutions: all partake of a side of Browning's personality richly expressed from *Dramatic Lyrics* to *The Ring and the Book*."[53] DeVane observes: "Most of the consternation of Browning's readers in the years following 1872 was caused by the fact that the villain had most of the tastes, opinions and feelings upon these matters [contemporary matters] which were generally accorded to Robert Browning. The effect was that of Satan quoting Scripture."[54] Thus Don Juan's arguments about human life as a state of probation, of evil being necessary for the apprehension of truth, of evil and falsehood being a part of the divine plan for the universe, of life as illusion as opposed to the permanence of eternity – all these ideas abound in Browning's poetry. But as Philip Drew observes, "whenever Don Juan applies his arguments to his own relationship to Fifine he is speaking disingenuously or with the intent to deceive Elvire, but elsewhere he offers as powerful arguments as Browning is able to devise."[55] Of Don Juan, as of Bishop Blougram, it may be said that "He said true things, but called them by wrong names."

Aristophanes' Apology is Browning's study of a poet who is forced into casuistry in order to justify his artistic methods. Aristophanes' defence of his comic art falls into two divisions: in the one, he justifies his own poetic theory and practice, and in the other, he attacks Euripides for what he feels is an essentially unrealistic conception of poetry. His argument uses a contention common to all Browning's casuists – the necessity of adapting one's resources to the limitations of the finite world.

Aristophanes assumes the role of the preserver of the traditional order of things, as opposed to the destructive forces of "restless change/ Deterioration" (p. 836) unleashed by the sophists, who would make "all we seemed to know prove ignorance." (p. 836) He attacks the "poison-drama" (p. 824) of Euripides, in which the tragic poet would "Boast innovations, cramp phrase, uncouth song,/Hard matter and harsh manner, gods, men/And women jumbled to a laughing stock." (p. 838) He is sceptical of the value of the challenge that Euripides has extended to the traditional sanctity granted to gods, heroes, priests, legislators, poets, and feels that "There's left no longer one plain, positive/Enunciation incontestable/Of what is good, right, decent here on earth." (p. 838) He scornfully rejects Euripides' advice to "Discard the beast, and rising from all fours,/Fain would paint, manlike, actual human life,/Make veritable men, think, say and do." (p. 827) He satirically presents Euripides' theory of poetry:

> Encircled with poetic atmosphere,
> As lark emballed by its own crystal song,
> Or rose enmisted by that scent it makes!
> No, this were unreality! the real
> He wants, not falsehood, – truth alone he seeks,
> Truth, for all beauty! Beauty, in all truth –
> That's certain somehow! Must the eagle lilt
> Lark-like, needs fir-tree blossom rose-like? No!
> Strength and utility charm more than grace,
> And what's most ugly proves most beautiful.
> So much assistance from Euripides! (p. 838)

He justifies his rejection on the grounds that the "now impossible cloud-cuckooburg" (p. 839) that Euripides envisioned got him nowhere in the world of men; and consoles himself with the thought that the tragedian rarely won a prize, while his own comedies won "applause, perhaps/ True veneration." (p. 840)

But Aristophanes exposes himself as a casuist when he begins his justification by admitting that his art is a "club" as opposed to the "polished steel" (p. 822) that it ideally should be. Arguing on the premise that the deeprooted layers of ignorance and folly cannot be rectified in one life-time's work, Aristophanes justifies his crude methods on the grounds that they created a deeper impression on the "vulgar" mob than refined argument. He reveals himself as an opportunist who ensures success by catering to his audience. His art has won him the adulation of the mob, and "What made them laugh but the enormous lie?" (p. 832) In a burst of casuistry, he claims that his lies have done the work of truth since "Truth's in thing not word,/ Meaning not manner." (p. 841) He reinforces his appeal as to the necessity of compromise by claiming that his audience restricts him—"In no case, venture boy-experiments!/ Old wine's the wine: new poetry drinks raw." (p. 823) But the validity of his argument is undermined by his admission that his prime concern is with success. Browning intends us to judge Aristophanes through the concept of the poet as a leader of society and a creator of value for mankind. Viewed against this lofty standpoint Aristophanes is found wanting. His comedy does not guide public opinion, but echoes it; it sets up no exalted ideal or high standards. It caters to the man in the market place and merely responds to his thoughts.

Aristophanes' attempts to sustain the old order has been a negative process. He has lost touch with the creativity of art and is content to patch and "vary vintage-mode." (p. 824) Throughout his justification there is evidence of Aristophanes' awareness of inadequacy, made the more obvious by his attempts to shift blame from himself to society. Concerned as he is with championing "truth," he yet is uncomfortably cognizant of the fact that his way of "flagellating foe" with "gibe and jeer" which "leers condonation too" (p. 832) differs markedly from the passionate sincerity of Euripides, whose "balled fist broke brow like thunder-bolt,/ Battered till brain flew." (p. 832)

In a more direct way, Aristophanes' casuistry is exposed by Balaustion who takes up his arguments one by one and shows their hollowness. She points out that the Comedy practised by Aristophanes has emphasized man's baser nature without making it "the nobler spirit's vehicle" (p. 852) and has used the doubtful method of telling exaggerated lies in order to point by contrast to the truth. This method has not been successful – though Aristophanes satirized warmongering, war continues; the statues at which he flung mud, still stand. She quotes various passages from Euripides to show how the latter had attained nobler ends than his opponent by far more civilized means. Essentially, therefore, the question around which the argument develops is one of ends and means. Euripides strives to see good in evil, beauty in ugliness. Aristophanes would banish evil through hate. There is evidence in plenty of Aristophanes' disdainful attitude to the people he caters to – "who think men are, were, ever will be fools." (p. 831) Thus his failure on the ethical side lies in his inability to establish a bond of sympathy with his fellowmen or to have compassion for human frailty. His failure on the artistic side lies in his compromising attitude to his art. Aristophanes' approach is very similar to Prince Hohenstiel-Schwangau's who finds man's brief life-span inadequate for the realization of ideals, and so opts for immediate gain in the form of "sustainment," thus compromising the very ideals he is aware of. It is not enough in the Browning canon to have lofty ideals. Man must aspire vigorously to attain, scorning worldly consequences, even if achievement falls short of the summit.

Euripides had believed in the continuity of the poetic tradition: and had dared to experiment with new forms and concepts, "Dared bring the grandeur of the Tragic Two/Down to the level of our common life,/Close to the beating of our common heart." (p. 879) The realism of Euripides aims at structuring a more relevant and hopeful world for man: ("Because Euripides shrank not to teach,/ If gods be strong and wicked, man, though weak,/ May prove their match by willing to be good." [p. 817]) Aristophanes, on the other hand, stands for the common coarse-as-clay/ Existence," (p. 844) but his realism is negative, because he has taken his stand on grounds lower than truth. The climax is reached with Balaustion's words: "Friend, sophist-hating! I know worst sophistry/Is when man's own soul plays to its own self false,/Reasons a vice into a virtue," (p. 852)

In 1881, Browning wrote to Swinburne: "Indeed I am no enemy of that Aristophanes – all on fire with invention – and such music!"[56] and a close reading of the poem makes clear the fact that Browning is not without sympathy for Aristophanes' point of view. As in the other casuistical poems, the feeling emerges, to quote W.O. Raymond, that "no creature, however mean, is without a case or a cause that has not latent in it a germ of truth, even though encrusted with error.[57] Aristophanes' ideals are not dissimilar to those of Euripides:

> I, loving, hating, wishful from my soul
> That truth should triumph, falsehood have defeat,

> –Why, all my soul's supremacy of power
> Did I pour in volley, just on him
> Who, all his whole life long, championed every cause
> I called my heart's cause, loving as I loved,
> Hating my hates, spurned falsehood, championed truth,– (p. 832)

Even Balaustion is forced to admit that Euripides had not entirely been successful. Though he had admitted the possibility of seeing truth from a number of planes, he had held on to a single plane, the High and Right. Though Balaustion does not admit it directly, she is fleetingly aware that Euripides' dictum, "raise soul, sink sense" (p. 829) may have been a denial of man's dual nature. Thus, Browning gives us another perspective to help us in our judgements. In fact, he shows Aristophanes himself as having a finer perception of this duality: he can envisage a higher stage of poetic development than either he or Euripides attained, one which incorporated "august head and enthroned intellect,/ With homelier symbol, of asserted sense,–/ Nature's primal impulse, earthly appetite!" (p. 289)

The tension created within Aristophanes by idealism on the one hand and cynicism on the other, gives his apologetics a forcefulness of such convincing intensity that Browning often hastens to prove a very obvious exposure of his casuistry. Hoxie N. Fairchild has called this device the "giveaway."[58] In *Aristophanes' Apology*, the translation of the "Herakles" acts as the initial giveaway, but significantly, of both the protagonists. The monologues of Balaustion and Aristophanes have been coloured by their own predilections and idiosyncrasies. Balaustion has no sympathy for Aristophanes' point of view, for she sees no need, as Browning himself put it in the letter previously quoted, for magnanimity towards Euripides' opponent, while Aristophanes' self-justification ("in which, as DeVane observes, he is chiefly concerned with satisfying his own conscience about his conduct towards the tragic poet")[59] becomes all the more vehement because he smarts under the supreme insult of Euripides' indifference to his jibes:

> No sign of wincing at my Comic lash,
> No protest against infamous abuse,
> Malignant censure – naught to prove I scourged
> With tougher thong than leek and onion plait. (p. 824)

So that, in the structural framework of the poem, the "Herakles" is, as Ryals points out, "the objectification and resolution of different points of view."[60] In a mad frenzy, Herakles has butchered his wife and children, but whereas

Oedipus blinded himself and sought exile, the wise Athenian Theseus consoles Herakles with the commonsense truth that no man can be stained with guilt by deeds done in ignorance and welcomes him to Athens. Thus, Balaustion's idealistic conception of Euripides is shown to be a distortion, for Euripides here shows the destructive, animalistic forces within man at its most terrifying; while Aristophanes' charge that Euripides "left no longer one plain positive/Enunciation incontestable/Of what is good, right, decent here on earth" (p. 838) is shown to be an exaggeration, for in the "Herakles," Euripides has shown the healing value of the simple virtues – pity, friendship, fortitude.

The final giveaway, which is more conclusive, comes at the end, where we are told how Euthukles flung the "choric flower" (p. 879) of the *Electra* and so saved Athens from destruction, while the Peirian bulwarks were demolished to the strains of comic dance and song. Sutherland Orr is thus partially correct when she opines that *Aristophanes' Apology* is "more conclusive than the other casuistical poems, and the only one in which the question raised is not in some degree left open."[61] At the same time, one must be careful in not arbitrarily linking the opinion at the speaker with the poet's opinions. To a certain extent, it is true that Aristophanes stands condemned when he asserts in the end that the poet must "remain the man nor ape the Muse!" (p. 574) when it is contrasted with Browning's assertions in other poems about the necessity of aspiration. On the other hand, characteristic of the later poetry in general, is the awareness of the subjective nature of judgement: and in the conception of an "imaginary Third" (p. 875) who would "take in every side at once,/And not successively, – may reconcile/The High and Low in tragicomic verse," (p. 873) Browning gives us the material for a more tentative judgement of both poets.

Thus, it may be seen that even as he makes a case for a position that is suspect, Browning shows a more sensitive awareness of human fallibility than is discernible in the earlier casuistical monologues, and of the difficulties of attaining to the truth. These later monologuists are not only impelled to justify their positions, they show a remarkable acceptance of the fact that their positions are not, in fact, admirable, thus lending greater complexity to their arguments. Each one, in the end, is forced to accept his nature, not in the complacent fashion of Blougram or in the unashamed manner of Sludge, but, one feels, guiltily, for the very process of their justification has confronted them with a selfhood which they recognize is ideal, but which they cannot sustain.

NOTES

1. DeVane, *Handbook*, p. 362.
2. DeVane, "The Harlot and the Thoughtful Young Man: A Study of the Relation between Rossetti's Jenny and Browning's *Fifine at the Fair*," *Studies in Philology*, XXIX (1932), pp. 463-84.
3. Douglas Bush, *Mythology and the Romantic Tradition in English Poetry* (Cambridge: Harvard University Press, 1937; Reissued with new preface, 1969), p. 374.
4. DeVane, *Handbook*, p. 360.
5. William Irvine and Park Honan, *The Book, the Ring, and the Poet: A Biography of Robert Browning* (London: The Bodley Head, 1974), p. 290.
6. *Loc. cit.*
7. *Dearest Isa*, ed. McAleer, p. 343.
8. *Ibid.*, p. 344.
8. *Ibid.*, p. 344.
9. *Ibid*, p. 347 and p.348.
10. *Ibid.*, p. 356.
11. *Ibid.*, p. 357.
12. *Ibid.*, p. 371.
13. *Browning to His American Friends: Letters between the Brownings, the Storys, and James Russell Lowell*, ed. Gertrude Reese Hudson (London: Bowes and Bowes, 1965), p. 167.
14. Leo A. Hetzler, "The Case of *Prince Hohenstiel-Schwangau*: Browning and Napoleon III," *Victorian Poetry*, 15, July-December 1977, pp. 335-50. I follow throughout Hetzler's stimulating suggestions regarding the structure of the poem.
15. Quoted in Robert Scholes and Robert Kellogg, *The Nature of Narrative* (London: Oxford University Press, 1966), p. 203.
16. *The Focusing Artifice*. p. 170.
17. *The Book, the Ring, and the Poet*. p. 291.
18. *Ibid.*, p. 461.
19. Park Honan, *Browning's Characters: A Study in Poetic Technique* (New Haven: Yale University Press, 1961), p. 131.
20. *Ibid*, p. 138.
21. Cf. "Bishop Blougram's Apology": "My business is not to remake myself,/But make the absolute best of what God made." (ll.354-55)
22. *The Infinite Moment*, pp. 137-38.
24. *The Book, the Ring, and the Poet*, p. 288.
25. Browning wrote to Isa Blagden on July 19, 1870, "...put not your trust in princes neither in the sons of men, Emperors, Popes, Garibaldis or Mazzinis, the plating wears through, and out comes the copperhead of human nature and weakness and falseness too!" *Dearest Isa*, p. 341.
26. Irvine and Honan, p. 373.

27. For Browning's view on this matter, see his letter to Isabella Blagden, dated July 19, 1870: "I never, when liking Napoleon most, sympathized a bit with his dynastic ambition for his son." *Dearest Isa*, ed. McAleer, p. 340.
28. *The Book, the Ring, and the Poet,* p. 454.
29. See "Browning's Dark Mood: A Study of *Fifine at the Fair*" in *The Infinite Moment*, pp. 105-20.
30. Irvin and Honan, p. 463.
31. *The Focusing Artifice*, p. 173.
32. Claudette Kemper Columbus, "*Fifine at the Fair:* A Masque of Sexuality and Death Seeking Figures of Expression," in *Studies in Browning and His Circle*, 2 (Spring 1974), p. 23.
33. Barbara Melchiori, *Browning's Poetry of Reticence* (London: Oliver and Boyd, 1968), p. 165.
34. *The Focusing Artifice*, p. 176.
35. *Browning's Later Poetry,* p. 60.
36. *The Infinite Moment*, p. 209.
37. Ryals, p. 67.
38. W.O. Raymond, p. 118.
39. "*Fifine at the Fair*: A Masque of Sexuality and Death Seeking Figures of Expression," p. 36.
40. Orr, *A Handbook to the Works of Robert Browning*, p. 159.
41. His contention reminds us of Mr. Sludge's argument that "every lie/Is quick with the germ of truth." (ll.1323-24) Both these casuists place a great deal of emphasis on the role of delusion in life.
42. *The Focusing Artifice*, p. 186.
43. *Browning's Later Poetry*, p. 80.
44. *The Book, the Ring, and the Poet*, p. 464.
45. *The Poetry of Browning*, p. 317.
46. cf. Browning's letter to Furnivall, March 2, 1889: "Absolute success being only attainable for the body in full manhood for the soul, in its full apprehension of Truth--which will be, not here, at all events." (*Letters*, ed. Hood, p. 301)
47. DeVane, *Handbook*, p. 369.
48. Orr, p. 80.
49. Philip Drew, p. 317.
50. J.L. Kendall, "Browning's *Fifine at the Fair*: Meaning and Method," *Victorian Newsletter*, No. 22 (Fall, 1962), p. 18.
51. Roma A. King, p. 188.
52. This is a feature common to all casuistical monologues. Mr. Sludge, for example, uses Browning's favourite doctrine of the immanence of God in creation, to defend his dishonest practices. If God is everywhere, he argues, could it not be that he, Sludge, is being used by God for purposes of his own? For an excellent discussion of this point, see Isobel Armstrong's "Browning's 'Mr. Sludge, The Medium'" in *Robert Browning: A Collection of Critical Essays*, ed. Philip Drew, pp. 212-22.

53. Irvin and Honan, p. 468.
54. DeVane, *Handbook*, p. 368.
55. *The Poetry of Browning*, p. 318.
56. *Letters*, ed. Hood, p. 193.
57. *The Infinite Moment*, p. 142.
58. Hoxie Neale Fairchild, "Browning, the Simple-Hearted Casuist," in *University of Toronto Quarterly*, April 1949, p. 234.
59. DeVane, *Handbook*, p. 378.
60. *Browning's Later Poetry*, p. 104.
61. Orr, *Handbook*, p. 144.

THE SATIRIC MODE

The casuistical monologues show how casuistry emerges from the gap between the ideal and the actual, and though Browning does not exculpate his casuists, he at least views them with sympathy. In many poems of the later period, however, the awareness of this gap leads Browning to a more forthright form of exposure, and one in which the balance is weighted more in favour of judgement, i.e. satire. This satire is all the more effective because it is supported in most cases by a narrative interest, and more trenchant (if somewhat less subtle) because it is direct, unlike the oblique satire of the earlier dramatic monologues.

Browning's political scepticism, earlier evinced in *Sordello* and the *Plays*, finds expression in the later phase in *Prince Hohenstiel-Schwangau*, with its ironic view of political processes and of politicians who style themselves as saviours of society. Browning himself called the poem "a sort of political satire,"[1] exposing the workings of the mind of a politician when called upon to defend his course of action. In *Aristophanes' Apology*, the comic poet speaks of the demagogue whose folly he satirizes:

(Noisome air-bubble, buoyed up, borne along
By kindred breath of knave and fool below,
Whose hearts swell proudly as each puffing face
Grows big, reflected in that glassy ball,
Vacuity, just bellied out to break
And righteously bespatter friends first,)
I loathing, . . .
The fawning, cozenage and calumny
Wherewith such favourite feeds the populace
That fan and set him flying for reward: (p. 832)

A more extended attack on political demagoguery is made "Parleying with George Bubb Dodington" (*Parleyings with Certain People of Importance in Their Day*, 1887). This is the only parleying in which Browning extensively uses the satirical method to show up the shortcomings of a particular point of view. His intention is to expose and condemn the time-serving behaviour of politicians. Browning sets about ruthlessly tearing off the disguise from time-honoured malpractices in politics and revealing them in all their ugliness.

James Sutherland says: "The satirist is most devastating when he appears most disengaged."[2] Browning achieves this disengagement by a device unique in the parleyings. He speaks, not in his own voice, but in the cynical, man-of-the world voice of one who recognizes charlatanry as an accepted principle in politics, and is unconcerned about the end, but cares only for the means used, the question being what sort of means achieve the desired end of success. This device is reminiscent of Swift, for Swift also spoke often through a persona that he assumed for the occasion. By using an unreliable narrator to reveal the aberrations of a point of view, Browning's dialectical method becomes an instrument of satire. And his exposure is all the more hard-hitting because it is spoken by a narrator who accepts this state of things as a matter of course. By identifying with a morally unacceptable point of view, Browning's narrator unwittingly exposes to the reader its internal contradictions. The speaker's responses introduce ironies at the expenses of the subject, which would not emerge had Browning chosen to speak directly in his own voice as in the other parleyings. As Roma A. King says: "By accepting Dodington's naturalistic premises and arguing the failure of his means rather than the evil of his ends, the speaker doubly exposes the inhumanity of a contemporary perspective against which Browning protested."[3] The poem is complex, simultaneously presenting four different perspectives – the views on political action of Dodington, Disraeli, the speaker, and, by implication, Browning himself.

"Parleying with Dodington" opens on an easy, neutral, conversational note that sets the tone of the piece: it is cynically matter-of-fact. Once again, we are reminded of Swift, who uses a similar non-committal tone to make the most outrageous statements. The speaker's unquestioning acceptance of underhand practices in politics leads to an ironic gap between his viewpoint and the author's, which is never stated, but the reader is aware of the disparity. In "Clive" (*Dramatic Idylls*, Second Series), the obtuseness of the narrator was a foil to the sensitive character of the protagonist. Here, the narrator's obtuseness in sympathizing with and finding excuses for evil and wrong-doing serves to emphasize the enormity of the crimes he is condoning. His argument, that it is natural for a statesman to pretend that he is working for the common good even while he is concerned only for his "private welfare" (I) is doubly ironical in the light of his pious affirmation "Intends/Scripture aught else." (I) He further reinforces his contention with an example from the world of nature – the bird who builds a nest with a rough outside, but "contrived himself/A snug interior, warm and soft and sleek."(I)

The ironies inherent in the situation are obvious. The speaker's advocacy of hypocritical attitudes, his eagerness to assert his sympathies with Dodington when the latter says: "What fool conjectures that profession means/Performance?" (II)[4] and again: "All outside show, in short, is sham," (II) merely discredits these attitudes. The speaker here reveals the kind of intellectual aberration that we see in the speaker in "Tertium Quid" in *The Ring and the Book* to whom men are little more than animals. In both, the use of animal imagery with reference to man reveals the extent of their dehumanization. To the speaker in the parleying, men are

> . . . a herd, whereof
> No unit needs be taught, his neighbours trough
> Scarce hold for who but grunts and whines the husks
> Due to a wrinkled snout that shows sharp tusks. (IV)

Political manipulation comes in for satirical treatment and the satire is all the more deadly for being put into the mouth of a cynic: "Disinterested slaves, nay--please the Fates – /Saviours, and nothing less:" and again:

> O happy consummation! – brought about
> By managing with skill the rabble rout
> For which we labour (never mind the name –
> People or populace, for praise or blame) (II)

The speaker, as well as Dodington and Disraeli, stand condemned because they have blurred the distinction between black and white, committed the worst kind of sophistry which, as Balaustion puts it in*Aristophanes' Apology* "Is when soul plays its own self false/Reasons a vice into a virtue." (p. 852)

Although these politicians recognize the sorry state of man, "Sloth-stifled genius, energy disgraced/ By ignorance high aims with sorry skill,/ Will without means and means in want of will," (IV) it is, for them, a spectacle to be exploited not redeemed. In their playing up of man's baser nature, they have done an injustice to his soul. The sympathy which redeemed Browning's judgement of Napoleon is wholly lacking here. For Prince Hohenstiel-Schwangau's ideals were real and laudable, even if they were not translated into action. Dodington and others like him lack any kind of ideals whatsoever, being the basest kind of human being, one who thinks of no one but himself. When Prince Hohenstiel Schwangau uses the words "save society," he is sincere if misguided. When the speaker in the "Parleying" uses the word "Saviour," he does so in a patently cynical fashion. His conclusion is that Dodington's methods have been a failure. Mere strength and intelligence are not enough. Man must now manipulate the supernatural in order to create any impression of superiority. He unashamedly admits that it is this sort of quackery that "men quail/Before." (VI)

Set off against the poet of the preceding parleying, Christopher Smart and the painter of the succeeding one, Francis Furini, the politicians are exposed for the knaves that they are. In contrast to Smart, whose vision of the supernatural was "one blaze of truth/ Undeadened by a lie" ("Parleying with Christopher Smart," (VI) and who uses his power to show men "by what degrees/Of strength and beauty to its end Design/Ever thus operates," (VII) these charlatans would use the supernatural for the sake of gratifying selfishness and greed. They stand condemned for their lack of reverence for the men whom they profess to serve: "No use/ In men but to make sport for you, induce/ The puppets now to dance, now to stand stock-still." (VII) How vivid is the contrast between these politicians and the artist Furini with his reverential attitude to man as a symbol of the Prime Mind.

Browning's attitude becomes more explicit if think of earlier poems with political themes. In *The Return of the Druses*. Djabal exploits the supernatural and proclaims himself a divinely sent Hakeem only in order to redeem his people. The interest in the welfare of the common people which Browning lauded in Valence in *Colombe's Birthday* and earlier in *Sordello* is totally lacking in Dodington and Disraeli. Browning is satirical about the men who would exploit man's baser nature, his ignorance and gullibility instead of contending with it. And what he invites us to ridicule is the whole process of specious rhetoric and false reasoning. The bland and persuasive arguments of the narrator may give rise to confusion in the mind of the reader were it not for the fact that Browning establishes him as an unreliable narrator at the very outset. His moral norms are shallow. What he (the speaker) admires is the deviousness of "exquisite disguise/ Disguise abjuring, truth that looks like lies." (VII)

In Dodington and Disraeli, Browning presents the insidious distortions of excessive intellectualization that kills the common goodness in a man's heart. Placed between two men who value the imaginative and the intuitive, Dodington represents Browning's condemnation of the ratiocinative. In their absolute dependence on materialistic reason, the politicians have cut themselves off from the sources of truth. Instead of dealing with truth, these men deal with delusion and falsehood. Their opportunism is more reprehensible than that of either Chiappino or Prince Hohenstiel-Schwangau. The former is misguided, the latter is weak. Browning's delineation of the Prince shows his shortcomings, but is coloured by his feeling—"I think he struggles against these."[5] In *Dodington*, there is no struggle at all, the leaders are depicted as wallowing in their knavery. DeVane says of *The Soul's Tragedy*: "Chiappino is a lost leader, in truth, and Browning's faith in liberalism – at least in the virtue of its leaders – shows itself disillusioned almost to the point of cynicism. The taste one gets of politics and politicians in *Luria*, published with *A Soul's Tragedy*, is likewise unsavoury."[6] This unsavouriness reaches its climax in Dodington, where the characters are entirely opposed to Browning's conception of heroes as "men and women who act in the light of ideal principles and honest convictions, scorning worldly consequences."[7]

Institutionalism of all kinds, political, legal and above all religious, is Browning's particular target for satire. A major theme in *Red Cotton Night-Cap Country* is the satirical exposure of the "none-excluding, all collecting Church!" (p. 383). Browning's sympathy for the hero Miranda, whose emotional confusions have been aggravated not allayed by religion, leads to a bitter indictment of the Church for its failure to guide souls in need. One remembers a similar indictment in *The Ring and the Book*. There also the churchmen hold rigidly to the letter of their religion while neglecting its true spirit. In *Red Cotton Night-Cap Country*, the parish priest and the nun who hasten to counsel Miranda return with "each palm well crossed with coin/ And nothing like smutch perceptible." (p. 410) Their rationalization of their covetous greed is highlighted: "Monsieur Leonce Miranda might compound/ For sin? – no surely! but by gifts – prepare/ His soul the better for contrition, say!" (p. 410). At the end of the poem the narrator offers his own assessments of the chief characters and his harshest estimate is reserved for the religious authorities:

> . . . the couple yonder, Father Priest
> And Mother Nun, who came and went and came,
> Beset this Clairvaux, trundled money-muck
> To midden and main heap oft enough,
> But never bade unshut from sheath the gauze,
> Nor showed that, who would fly, must let fall filth,
> And warn "Your jewel, brother, is a blotch:
> Sister, your lace trails ordure! Leave your sins,
> And so best gift with Crown and grace with Robe!" (p. 423)

"Cenciaja" (*Pacchiarotto* volume) is another instance of Browning's satire against the corrupt practices of the church prelates, who would make even innocence appear guilty if it suited their purposes. In *The Ring and the Book* we are shown how the Church has become a centre of wealth and power, attracting to its service men who are anything but religious in their attitudes and behaviour. The Pope is aware that clerical privilege is being used to protect crime. An incident of this nature is the theme of the present poem. Browning probes for the true motives behind the murder of Castanza Santa Croce by her son Paolo and the conviction of the elder son Onofrio, for alleged complicity in the crime. The Cardinal's zeal in hunting out the criminal, his lofty pronouncement, "Who sins must die," (l.229) is seen in an ironical light, for his motives are of the basest kind. He promises the judge the "Hat and Purple" if he would secure the conviction of the innocent Onofrio, because he desired a woman who favoured Onofrio. Much of the satirical import of the poem resides in the asides uttered by the narrator, as when he begins with "When Cardinal Aldobrandini (great/ His efficacy – nephew to the Pope!)" (ll.119-20)

Following this poem which satirizes aberrations in religious feeling is one on religious intolerance. In "Filippo Baldinucci on the Privilege of Burial" Browning uses the technique of the unreliable narrator, one whose point of view is clearly flawed, in order to heighten the effects of satire against a man narrow-minded enough to praise the "honest zeal to stop the voice/ Of unbelief with stone-throw." (stanza III) As we see in the "Parleying with Francis Furini," Browning despised Baldinucci, calling him a blockhead, and "scruple-splitting, sickly-sensitive/Mild-moral-monger." (II) Browning's conviction, that religion is a matter of love in a man's heart rather than blind interpretations of traditional dogma, is embodied here in the ironical treatment meted out to Baldinucci's tale. Through the dramatization of a distorted point of view, the reader is made to perceive ironies of which the character himself is unaware. The poem's satiric intention emerges from what Hintner calls "the grotesque of fragmentation"[8] and distortion, which is mainly a matter of language which mirrors perverted religious feeling. The poem satirically portrays a man who has denied humane brotherliness in his concern for the superficial trappings of religion. This is reminiscent of Browning's satirical treatment of the monk in "Soliloquy of the Spanish Cloister" whose holy concepts have hardened into formalisms. The picture we get is of a man who has equated superstition with religion. The frequent use of animal imagery-- "giving hogs a hoist," (IV) "just where sought these hounds to hide/Their carrion," (VIII) "Grey as a badger, with a goat's/Not only beard but bleat," (XII) "these dogs" (XXII) emphasizes the nature of the speaker himself as one devoid of humanity, for he equates men with brutes. Baldinucci's neglect of the essence of religion – tolerance and love – is exposed in the last lines:

In Christ's crown, one more thorn we rue!
In Mary's bosom, one more sword!
No, boy, you must not pelt a Jew!
O Lord, how long? How long, O Lord? (LVIII)

Satire against Roman Catholicism is the motive force of two narrative poems in the *Asolando* volume, "The Cardinal and the Dog" and "The Pope and the Net." The former satirizes the superstitious atmosphere that surrounded the prelates. DeVane explains that "Cardinal Crescenzio was obnoxious to the Protestants because he would make no concessions,"[9] so that the story of how the cardinal sickened and died after he had a vision of a huge dog springing on him, may also concern the judgement visiting those who practise religious intolerance. In fact, this point of view is reinforced by the contrasted tolerance of the narrator towards the end of the poem: "Heaven keep us Protestants from harm: the rest . . . no ill betide." (l.15) The latter poem exposes the duplicity of another churchman, whose humility becomes a means to an end, and is then discarded once the end has been attained. The dramatic impact of the last line – "Why, Father, is the net removed?" "Son, it hath caught the fish" (l.24) – intensifies the satire.

Browning's satire against the legal profession in *The Ring and the Book* is too well-known to need elaboration. To the poet, lawyers represented that class of people who "subordinated truth for personal gain."[10] In "Ponte Dell Angelo, Venice," (*Asolando*) Browning combines the themes of religious superstition and legal corruption in the story of an extortionate lawyer who maintained an outward semblance of virtue, and who sought to foil Satan, who had been sent to convey him to "punishment's place," by erecting a statue of an angel over his house.

Literary satire is also to be found in Browning's later poetry. *Fifine at the Fair*, as O.P. Govil has shown in his essay "Satire in Browning's *Fifine at the Fair*,"[11] may be viewed as an extended satire against the Pre-Raphaelite conceptions of art, the satiric burden being borne mainly by the innumerable half-concealed allusions. Satire against literary quacks is the intention of *The Two Poets of Croisic*, in which Browning records the meteoric rise and tame downfall of two long-forgotten poets. The dominant tone is one of bland good-humour at the follies of petty rhymesters. Browning's gift for comic, satiric verse is very much in evidence here. His method of saying the most outrageously funny things in a tone of mock-solemnity is reminiscent of Dryden in "Macfleknoe" "A poet born and bred, his very sire/A poet also, author of a piece/Printed and published, 'ladies – their attire'." (XXIX) The satire here is good-natured; it is the good humour of a man who can afford to be generous to a fool. The eight-line stanza reminds us of Byron and echoes the same, off-hand contemptuous manner. In the story of the success of the second poet, Paul Desforges Maillard, a success which is based on deception, Browning satirizes the evaluators of literary works, whose judgements are motivated not by the intrinsic worth of the produced work but by extraneous, often irrelevant, considerations.

Satire against literary critics is a major theme in the poems of the *Pacchiarotto* volume, in which Browning attacks by means of ridicule not only a personal enemy (Alfred Austin), but the whole tribe of critics that Austin represents.

The personal fury that motivated the title poem of the volume "Of Pacchiarotto and How He worked in Distemper" may be gauged from a letter that Browning wrote to Edmund Gosse on August 19, 1876:

> One particular piece of blackguardism headed 'Men of Letters: R.B.' – could only save its author from a kicking by the charitable hope that he was too small for that treatment. I never was unlucky enough to set eyes on the man: if he is physically as well as morally and intellectually a dwarf – you may be sure I should have considered him a pygmy had his stature been that of Goliath. But I really meant nothing except to enliven my visionary dance of chimney-sweeps by a grotesque monkey-image which had been thrusting itself upon my notice this long while: and it seems that one fillip more than avenges fifty flea-bites. The 'Examiner' may be sure, moreover, that Mr. Alfred Austin will take his own part in every rag of newspaper to which he has free access. What man of the ordinary size ever yet ducked down so low, – hooted from his hiding at what he presumed to call his 'fellows', – and then tried to stand on tiptoe by their side, as a 'poet' just as if nothing had happened?[12]

In *Aristophanes' Apology* (1875), he had satirized Austin as the critic whom Euripides finds too insignificant even to acknowledge:

> He reasoned, I'll engage, – "Acquaint the world
> Certain minuteness butted at my knee?
> Dogface Eruxis, the small satirist,
> What better would the mannikin desire
> Than to strut forth on tiptoe, notable
> As who so far up fouled me in the flank?"
> So dealt he with the dwarfs:. . . (p. 832)

In "Of Pacchiarotto and How He Worked in Distemper," Browning treats in a lighter vein the sad fate that met the reforming zeal of Giacomo Pacchiarotto, a mediocre artist and petty dabbler in politics in fifteenth century Siena, and indirectly warns his critics, and especially Austin, who is intended to be a parallel to Pacchiarotto, of the consequences of their attempts at reforming him as a poet. Browning's object here is essentially the satirist's object of directing the reader away from sympathetic identification and moving him instead to amusement and contempt. His method is that of straight-forward diminution that tears away the masks from pettiness and absurdity. Pacchiarotto's obtuse egotism is highlighted by the ironical grandeur of his ambitions:

> Man, devil as now he found him,
> Would presently soar up angel
> At the summons of such evangel,
> And owe – wht would Man not owe
> To the painter Pacchiarotto?
> Ay, look to thy laurels, Giotto! (Section 111)

This is almost like the mock-heroic method of linking the trivial with the grand in order to emphasize the insignificance of the former. The reader is invited to ridicule the absurdity of his apparent rhetoric and specious reasoning. The sheer comedy of Pacchiarotto's oration to his painted frescoes, with all its accompaniment of grotesque flourishes is nevertheless laced with the satirical exposure of his "hop, skip, jump" technique of changing sides. Browning's method is to descend abruptly from the insignificant to the ludicrous, thus underscoring the fact that a pigmy was posturing as a Goliath:

> He, one by one, with asperity
> Stripped bare all the cant-clothed abuses,
> Disposed of sophistic excuses,
> Forced folly to abandon,
> And left vice with no leg to stand on.
> So crushing the force he exerted,
> That man at his foot lay converted!
> True – man bred of paint-pot and mortar! (X-XI)

The amused detachment masks Browning's sense of superiority to a very foolish opponent; and behind the rollicking good humour lies the concentrated force of Browning's contempt. In retaliation to what Austin had called, with reference to Browning, "the most astounding and ludicrous pretension,"[13] Browning creates a parallel character who really assumes ludicrous pretensions and comes to an extremely sorry end. Pacchiarotto receives his warning:

> Lest haply thyself prove besotted
> When stript, for thy pains, of that costume
> Of sage, which has bred the imposthume
> I prick to relieve thee--of, – Vanity! (XXII)

The latter half of the poem lays a great deal of emphasis on the poet's own good-natured acceptance of criticism and his straightforward manner of dealing with his critics in contrast to the peevish and mischievous destructiveness of the troop of critics themselves. At one point alone does Browning's equanimity desert him, and significantly it is connected with the critic's demand for "clearness of words which convey thought." (XXVIII) The obscurity of which Browning was regularly accused was a sore point with him even as early as his love letters to Elizabeth.[14] And in the present poem, this indignation expresses itself through the crushing intensity of invective:

> Ay, if words never needed enswathe aught
> But ignorance, impudence, envy
> And malice – what word-swathe would then vie
> With yours for a clearness crystalline?
> But had you to put in one small line
> Some thought big and bouncing – as noddle
> Of goose, born to cackle and waddle
> And bite at man's heel as goose-wont is,
> Never felt plague its puny os frontis –
> You'd know, as you hissed, spat and sputtered,
> Clear cackle is easily uttered!

Reformers of all kinds, moral as well as literary, with their holier-than-thou attitudes are sharply satirized by Browning. In the "Parleying with Francis Furini" Browning launches a virulent attack against the prudishness of John Calcott Horseley who had spoken out against the nude in art:

> Paints he? One bids the poor pretender take
> His sorry self, a trouble and disgrace,
> From out the sacred presence, void the place
> Artists claim only. What – not merely awake
> Our pity that suppressed concupiscence –
> A satyr masked as a matron--makes pretence

To the coarse blue-fly's instinct – can perceive
No better reason why she should exist –
– God's lily-limbed and blushrose-bosomed Eve –
Than as a hot-bed for the sensualist
To fly-blow with his fancies, make pure stuff
Breed him back filth – this were not crime enough? (III)

Such heights of fury and scorn are reached nowhere else in Browning's satiric verse.

When Browning satirizes aberrations from a moral norm he is almost always able to maintain a sense of proportion in distinguishing the serious faults from the trivial; but when that norm is a very personally held belief, or when, as in the case of his satire against his critics, his sense of fair-play is touched to the quick, his scorn sometimes descends to invective. Though his understanding of man's mortal nature leads him to view with a certain sympathy his shortcomings, his desire for the truth impells him to expose folly when he sees it. Though sympathy is less evident in the later satire, Browning's irony is never destructive. In exposing the reality behind the mask, he really seems to be lamenting the failure of human nature to fulfil its ideals.

Browning's grudge against his critics is rooted in what he felt was their misrepresentation of his works and so he is often led, directly or indirectly, to present the aesthetic ideas that shaped his poetry. The following chapter examines this aspect of the later poetry.

NOTES

1. *Browning to His American Friends*, ed. Hudson, p. 166.
2. James Sutherland, *English Satire* (Cambridge: The University Press, 1956), p. 72.
3. *The Focusing Artifice*, p. 256.
4. Maisie Ward mentions an incident between Browning and Disraeli: "In his speech he [Disraeli] had praised 'the imagination of the British School of art,' but when Browning later asked for his opinion, he said, 'What strikes me is the utter and hopeless want of imagination.' This led Browning to remark to Allingham: 'What a humbug he is! Won't I give it to him one of these days.' in *Robert Browning and His World: Two Robert Browrings*?, p. 138.
5. Letter of January 1, 1872, to Edith Story, See *Browning to His American Friends*, p. 167.
6. DeVane, *Handbook*, p. 192.
7. W.O. Raymond, *The Infinite Moment*, p. 150.
8. John Meigs Hintner, "Browning's Grotesque Period," in *Victorian Poetry*, 4(1966), p. 8.

9. DeVane, *Handbook*, p. 536.

10. See Browning's letter to Furnivall, February 12, 1889: "I have always had a supreme contempt for the profession." *Letters*, p. 237.

11. See *Nineteenth Century Studies*: Essays presented to Dr. A. Bose (Calcutta: The World Press, 1973), pp. 143-61.

12. *Letters*, pp. 175-76.

13. Quoted in DeVane, *Handbook*, p. 397.

14. cf. letter of February 6, 1846, in which Browning defends himself against Miss Mitford's charge of his "raying out darkness": "Of course an artist's whole problem must be, as Carlyle wrote to me, 'the expressing with articulate clearness the thought in him' I am almost inclined to say that clear expression should be his only work and care for he is born, ordained, such as he is and not born learned in putting what was born in him into words what ever can be clearly spoken, ought to be: but 'bricks and mortar' is very easily said and some of the thoughts in *Sordello* not so readily even if Miss Mitford were to try her hand on them." *Letters of RB and EBB*, I, p. 439.

AESTHETIC THEORY IN THE LATER POETRY

Browning's later poetry presents the surprising spectacle of an ostensibly "dramatic" poet frequently setting aside the dramatic mask in order to speak out explicitly in his own voice. This element is not entirely new. In *Sordello*, Browning diverges occasionally from the narrative in order to speak out on the role of the poet and on the nature of poetry. Its re-emergence in the later poetry is not merely the result of his growing need to tell the truth (in a much more unambiguous fashion than dramatic indirection would allow) of his feelings on the perennial problems of life, art and faith, but as a response to contemporary pressures. The chief of these was the necessity of defending his art against the hostility of its detractors.

Though Browning explicitly disavowed personal self-revelation in poetry, he was not averse to dealing with the problems of his art therein. In poems like *Balaustion's Adventure, Aristophanes' Apology* and *Fifine at the Fair* Browning presents his views on art through the mouths of his characters, using the theories to illuminate and develop the particular situations in these poems. In *Balaustion's Adventure* poetry is a "power that makes," (p. 782) and which "brings forth now good, new beauty from the old." (p. 808) The creative aspect of poetry is emphasized in order to justify a reinterpretation of the original tragedy by Euripides. In *Aristophanes' Apology* Donald Smalley points out that Browning's "exposition of the poetic principles of Euripides represented in large part a justification of his own principles as a poet."[1] Smalley further says: "it is clear that Browning believed with his Euripides that realism is justifiable only when it searches for a spiritual 'truth' beneath all coarseness and bestiality."[2] In *Fifine at the Fair* art becomes a means by which the artist reconstructs the whole and primal truths out of the fragment so afforded by life. (XLIV) Don Juan asserts: "Art is my evidence/That something was, is, might be; but no more thing itself,/ Than flame is fuel." (XLI) The transfiguring, resuscitating power of the artistic imagination becomes a key theme in Don Juan's argument. In *Red Cotton Night-Cap Country* Browning as narrator comments on the necessity for poetry to look beyond the bare facts to the psychological truth:

Along with every act – and speech is act –
There go, a multitude impalpable

To the ordinary human faculty,
The thoughts which gave the act significance.
Who is a poet needs must apprehend
Alike both speech and thoughts which prompt to speak
Part these, and thought withdraws to poetry:
Speech is reported in the newspaper. (p. 412)

Pacchiarotto and How He Worked in Distemper: With Other Poems (1876) is the first collection of shorter poems since *Dramatis Personae* (1864), and DeVane remarks that the volume "must remain a book of great importance to the critic and biographer of Browning, for here the poet speaks more directly than anywhere else in his poetry concerning his own art and his feelings towards it."[3]

The title poem repudiates the idea of the artist as reformer:

"Let tongue rest and quiet thy quill be!
Earth is earth and not heaven, and ne'er will be."
Man's work is to labour and leaven
As best he may – earth here with heaven,
'Tis work for work's sake that he's needing:
Let him work on and on as if speeding
Work's end, but not dream of succeeding! (Stanza XXI)

The latter half of the poem castigates the critics who complain of the poet's "harsh analytics," bad grammar, broken rules, of "ear, so tough-gristled – /He thought that he sung while he whistled," and above all, of his obscurity.[4] Browning asserts his right to continue "whistling and singing" as he chose:

Mine's freehold, by the grace of the grand Lord
Who lets out ground here, – my landlord,
To him I pay quit-rent – devotion,
Nor hence shall I budge. . . . (XXVII)

This establishment of a personal link between the poet and God is reminiscent of the poet's relationship with "our Lord the King" in "How it Strikes a Contemporary." As regards obscurity, Browning's stand remains unchanged – complex thoughts demand complex utterance.[5]

In "At the Mermaid," "House," "Shop" and the "Epilogue" Browning asserts that the business of the poet is not with personal expression but with his craft, and that the critical emphasis should be not upon the poet but upon the poetry.

The speaker of "At the Mermaid" is ostensibly Shakespeare, but the identification between the speaker's views and Browning's own is so complete that it is almost as if Browning himself is the speaker. He asserts that he claims recognition on the basis of his works: "Mine remains the unproffered soul." (1.28) The poem is also an affirmation of Browning's hopeful view of life, and a re-iteration of the life-after-death theme that recurs so often in the later poetry: "My sun sets to rise again." (1.80) Linked with his hopes and beliefs is Browning's resentment against his critics that forms the motive force of this volume. Browning must have remembered the critic in *Fraser's Magazine*, who in his review of *Men and Women*, wrote of the "selfish temper and carelessness for the gratification of others which lie at the root of all Mr. Browning's faults."[6] In "At the Mermaid," he states his refusal to compromise with his art for the sake of fame:[7]

> . . . not to buy your laurel
> As last king did, nothing loth
> Tale adorned and pointed moral
> Gained him praise and pity both (ll.57-60)

Unlike the posturings of certain poets who "sell you cheap their souls for fame," (1.32) he has been true to his own self, "never once have wished/Death before the day appointed:/ Lived and liked, not poohed and pished!" (ll.126-28) The reference is to poets like Byron who made a parade of their personal emotions.[8] For, as Preyer points out, "he knew that Romantic disillusionment, romantic contempt for normal living, could easily turn into something contemptible, an evasion of moral choices and a striking of attitudes."[9] In this poem, Browning expresses an opinion similar to T.S. Eliot's who says in "Tradition and the Individual Talent": "Poetry is not a turning loose of emotion. . . it is not the expression of personality but an escape from personality."[10] This does not mean that a poet should not have something to say, but that what the poet has to say should be objectified, and that it is with the shape and character of this object that the critic should properly be concerned.

In "House" Browning asserts: "Outside should suffice for evidence." (1.33) The poem is not only a plea for personal privacy, it maintains that the highest art is impersonal. Though DeVane is of the opinion that Browning's view as expressed in "House" "agrees so little with his practice, especially in his apprentice years and again in his decline."[11] It must be noted that what Browning set himself against is the uninhibited exposure of personal feelings, and not objectified (however perfunctorily) affirmation of beliefs that would have some value for mankind in general. Browning's contempt is reserved, not for those who revealed themselves through their poetry, but for those who made of poetry a confessional rather than a dramatic art. To Browning this meant all the difference between a concern for the self and its own point of view, and the higher concern of fitting the infinite into the finite.

In "Shop" we have the flesh-spirit dichotomy that forms the base of much of the poetry of the later period. It is Browning's imaginative reconstruction of the theme, "Man lives not by bread alone":

> Because a man has shop to mind
> In time and place, since flesh must live,
> Needs spirit lack all life behind,
> All stray thoughts, fancies fugitive,
> All loves except what trade can give? (ll.100-5)

The poet stresses the need for man's imaginative vision in order to give life to his everyday world. He also criticizes the poet whose "shop" is all his "house"—who exposes his personal affairs to the public view for cheap popularity. The poem is an attack on those who treat their vocation as a "trade" merely, and neglect its essential function as a nourisher of the spirit. Thus Andrea's art becomes a commodity to be traded in, because he has perverted the values of the spirit.

In the "Epilogue," Browning uses an extended simile of poetry (and, by implication, truth) as wine, and contrasts its opposing qualities "stark strength" and "sheer sweet." The analogy had previously been used in "Popularity," where the true poet praises God: "Others give best at first, but Thou/Forever set'st our table praising/ Keep'st the good wine till now." (ll.18-20) In *Fifine at the Fair*, when Don Juan comes to accept the permanence of truth, in spite of its changing forms, the realization to him is "No fresh and frothy draught, but liquor on the lees,/ Strong, savage and sincere." (CXIII) Later, in the prologue to the *Parleyings*, wine is again linked to the poetic imagination. In this poem, Browning brings together the two central themes of this volume by affirming that in poetry "Mighty and mellow are never mixed" (l.106) and also arraigning his critics who, while ostensibly lauding Shakespeare and Milton, have essentially a very superficial acquaintance with their works. Browning angrily contends that the critics will not see diamonds even if they are there in plenty. His poetry is made from "man's thoughts, and loves and hates!" (l.153) and he refuses to sweeten it with "cowslips" to please his audience. In fact, he says, the ingratitude of these critics will not allow them to appreciate him even if he made "wine of the memories/ Which leave as bare as a churchyard tomb/

My meadow, late all bloom?" (ll.198-200)[12] In the poems of the *Pacchiarotto* volume Browning refuses to pander to the current demand for conventional poetry celebrating conventional notions of beauty, great ideas or significant actions. All these views are crystallized in the poetry of his later period.

In *The Two Poets of Croisic* (1878) the attempt at factual narration is replaced towards the end by the poet's own thoughts about matters suggested by the main body of the poem. Browning's desire to explore the nature of poetic creation and poetic fame underlies the satiric intention of the poem. The tale of Rene Gentilhomme, the shoddy rhymester, whose heavensent moment of inspiration changed the course of his career, leads Browning to a consideration of the nature of poetic inspiration. The moment of inspiration, fleeting though precious, is the ultimate truth. Its transforming power leaves the common poetaster a changed man for the moment, "luminous, erect,/ Triumphant, an emancipated slave." (XLI) The moment is described in terms of light and fire, "burning moment," "bright escape of soul." Browning's purpose becomes more explicit in Stanza LIX and in the following stanzas, in which he speculates on the kind of attitude to life a man would have after such a visitation:

> Well, I care – intimately care to have
> Experience how a human creature felt
> In after-life, who bore the burden grave
> Of certainly believing God had dealt
> For once directly with him: (LIX)

His conclusion is that "we must play the pageant out, observe/ The tourney regulations." (LXIII) This idea will receive greater attention in the "Parleying with Christopher Smart."

In *The Ring and the Book* the poetic imagination, often divinely inspired, was the fancy that made "dead" fact come alive. In *The Two Poets of Croisic*, however, Browning hastens to insist that truth (the fact) is the "gold," and that:

> . . . All fume and fret
> Of artistry beyond this point pursued
> Brings out another sort of burnish: yet
> Always the ingot has its very own
> Value, a sparkle struck from truth alone. (CLII)

Art, now, becomes a means of highlighting the inherent significance of facts. The poet does not invest facts with truth; his task is rather to give new eyes to people by which they might pierce beneath the surface impressions to the truth within.[13]

The question of poetic fame was one that concerned Browning intensely.[14] In *The Ring and the Book* we have his rueful summary of his relationship to his reading public. (I, 1378-86) In *La Saisiaz* the issue of fame becomes more urgent, with Browning wishing for the fame of a Byron or a Rousseau, so as to set off their pessimism with his own "brand flamboyant" his message of hope. But fame, though desirable, is not to be acquired at the expense of ideals. The career of the second poet of Croisic is satirized because its success is based on cunning. Sordello's fault had been that he loved song's results, not song. In *Fifine at the Fair* Browning speaks through Don Juan of art as "the love of loving, rage/ Of knowing, seeing, feeling the absolute truth of things/ For truth's sake." (XLIV) The creation of poetry is its own reward in so far as the process repeats the divine act of creation.

Browning further affirms that the poet who lives with joy ("led a happy life") is to be regarded as the best poet, for pessimism is an acknowledgement of defeat.[15] The joyful poet is not necessarily one who feels, sees or suffers less. His joy, rather, gives him the strength to gain mastery over sorrow. This is Browning's view of his optimism. Further on, he awards the palm to the poet who dares, who chooses the "vivid horse/ Whose neck God clothed with thunder" (CLIX) in preference to "the steer/ Sluggish and safe." (CLIX) Stanza CLVIII of *The Two Poets of Croisic* is among the more important assertions about the nature of Browning's own poetry and is particularly relevant to the later poetry in general:

> Who knows most, doubts most; entertaining hope,
> Means recognizing fear: the keener sense
> Of all comprised within our actual scope
> Recoils from aught beyond earth's dim and dense.
> Who, grown familiar with the sky, will grope
> Henceforward among the groundlings? That's offence
> Just as indubitably; stars abound
> O'erhead, but then – what flowers make glad the ground!

This passage is Browning's answer to those who accused him of being unaware of disharmonies in existence. It also firmly bases poetry on earthly experience. Even the divinely inspired poet cannot spurn the finite.

The "Epilogue" to *Dramatic Idylls, Second Series*, "Touch Him Ne'er So Lightly" is, in DeVane's opinion, "one of the most important of his later utterances upon the function of the poet and of poetry."[16] The poem repudiates the notion of an overflow of lyrical emotions as most expressive of a "poet-soul". He describes, rather, the rigours of the poet's task, and the ruggedness of his nature. If he produces no flowers, the forbidding rocks of his poetry nurture the pine-seeds of truth. Browning thus champions the cause of the prophet-poet rather than the lyric poet and indirectly justifies his poetry as he had done earlier in the "Epilogue" to the *Pacchiarotto* volume.

The problem of encompassing the infinite within the finite is Browning's major preoccupation as a poet and as a theorist of poetry. In his later poetry Browning evolves a theory of imagination that both aesthetically and morally resolves this problem.

The Prologue and the Epilogue to the *Parleyings* create overtly dramatic situations, but the main speaker in each is used quite directly as a spokesman for the poet's own views. There is no ironic distancing of the speaker's point of view as in the dramatic monologue, so that through Apollo and Fust, the poet appears to speak in his own voice on the role of imagination in life.

The contention of the Fates, in the Prologue, that happiness in life is an illusion is a major idea that Browning would refute in the "Parleying with Mandeville." Evil is without doubt a reality. And yet, as Apollo argues, there is the possibility that there is in man "Some power in himself, some compensative law." (p. 686) This power, as the Prologue goes on to show, is the power of the imagination symbolized by the wine that Apollo offers to the three sisters. The Fates mockingly hold that though "Life mimics the sun," (p. 686) the reality proves to be nothing more than "an ice-ball disguised as a fire-orb." (p. 686) In "Mandeville" Browning would show that it was just this mimicry that helped man to "infer immensity," (p. 695) and though good and evil were blent in life, there was always the hope, made possible, once again, by the imaginative faculty, that good would eventually triumph. For even the Fates are forced to admit that good and evil are not fixed entities—"Worst, best/Change hues of a sudden." (p. 690) It is the imagination that compounds "Fancy with fact" so that the "lost secret is found." (p. 689) The worth and beauty of human life is no illusion because of the infinite possibilities of the human spirit. Not "what is," but "What may be" is man's essential. (p. 689) Defeat in this life means triumph in the next, and death is not extinction but something that "completes living, shows life in its truth." (p. 690)

Since Browning views the poet as a leader and a teacher of men, the importance of the kind of creative imagination that the Prologue describes for the poet is axiomatic.

In the "Parleying with Christopher Smart" Browning focuses his attention once again on a poet in order to clarify his ideas on poetry and the poetic imagination. As Roma A. King writes: "Smart's one triumph illustrates the means of apprehension (intuitive, imaginative) and of communication (symbolic, artistic) by which man grapples with reality."[17]

The parleying once again discusses the problem of the relationship between the infinite and the finite. Since it is only rarely that the whole truth can be comprehended in a single flash of vision, the ambitious attempt to understand the infinite while impatiently rejecting the particular, can only lead to futility.[18]

Browning's insistent highlighting of the uniqueness, almost miraculous nature of Smart's experience becomes a necessary device for the elaboration of his argument. Significantly, Smart's visionary moment is defined in terms of fire and flame–"A fire-ball wrapping flesh and spirit both/ In conflagration." (V) It was during this transfiguring moment that the poet

> . . . pierced the screen
> 'Twixt thing and word, lit language straight from soul–
> Left no fine film-flake on the naked coal
> Live from the censer–shapely or uncouth,
> Fire suffused through and through, one blaze of truth
> Undeadened by a lie . . . (VI)

But this is patently a rare visitation. More often than not, man has to come to terms with the limitations of his human perspective. Nevertheless, Smart's experience can set an example for other poets wishing to embody the truth:

> . . . and who saw for once could tell
> Us others of her majesty and might
> In large, her lovelinesses infinite
> In little, (VII)[19]

Acknowledging the strengths and beauties of the natural world are a step towards the apprehension of the infinite being. Yet even here, the complexities inherent in the case are embodied in a poet like Aprile, of whom W.O. Raymond says: "He yearns to reveal and transfigure the beauty of the natural world by reclothing it in the glorious forms of art. Thus his works would remain in the sight of all as pledges of the love which exists between himself and the beautiful. But desiring to grasp the whole sum and absolute essence of beauty, he cannot rest with any finite manifestation of it. Dazzled by his vision of the infinite, the poet is in danger of dissipating truths in dreams and abstractions."[20] The solution lies in what Browning in *Sordello* had termed the concept of the Maker-See, i.e. the poet's progress from the stage of merely seeing and telling what he sees to the highest stage in which he can "Impart the gift of seeing to the rest." (III, 868) Such poetry will be of the synthesist type – a representation not only of the inner psychological import of external objects but of its transcendental implications.

The idea is resuscitated in the present parleying. The true poet's task is to point out hitherto unsuspected beauties on earth and to trace a primal Design operating through all:

> For Man to know by, – Man who, now – the same
> As erst in Eden, needs that all he sees
> Be named him ere he note by what degrees
> Of strength and beauty to its end Design
> Ever thus operates – (VII)

It is significant that this assertion of the functions of the poet resembles Browning's description of the subjective poet in his *Essay on Shelley* as one who "lifts his fellows with their half-apprehensions, up to his own sphere, by intensifying the import of details and rounding the general meaning."[21]

Browning's conception of poetry with a purpose was not merely a feature of his later poetic development, as is revealed by a letter he wrote to Ruskin in 1855: "It [poetry] is all teaching, and the people hate to be taught. . . . A poet's affair is with God, to whom he is accountable and of whom is his reward."[22] To Carlyle's definition of the true poet as "ever a Seer, whose eye has been gifted to discern the godlike mystery of God's Universe",[23] Browning would add that the true poet's function is to convey his spiritual comprehension, to "rule" and not merely to "please." It is essentially a religious undertaking.

Moreover, the poet must convey his awareness of the infinite *through* the finite. Will, Power and Love, the three attributes of God, can be discerned not just through soul-shaking visions, but through their finite manifestations on earth itself. Scrutinizing the rose before embarking on an investigation of the meteor's birth is the correct method for the poet to adopt. Like Paracelsus, who ultimately finds in the smallest "chance-sown plant" the laws of the spiritual world, man must accept the finite as the defining human quality. As Browning puts it in the "Parleying with Bernard to Mandeville": "In little, light, warmth, life are blessed – /Which, in the large, who sees to bless?" (XI) Through the poet's imaginative, symbolic, finite representation of the infinite, man can gain his conception of the formless and the illimitable. Philip Drew sums up Browning's viewpoint aptly: "Browning is here repudiating two distinct types of poetry. The first is the kind that merely entertains, which does no more than particularize the wonders of the world. This is inadequate because it offers no guidance to mankind: it pleases simply, whereas the poet's 'function is to rule.' He rejects also the kind of poetry, at present even more popular, which offers 'the end ere the beginning,' that is, pretends to teach the inmost secrets of the universe without having studied things as they are. In between lies the recommended middle way, which is to proceed from a limited but adequate observation of the earth step by step to such general conclusions about universal laws as are possible in a man's lifetime."[24]

The "Parleying with Christopher Smart" is thus not only a resumé of Browning's characteristic conceptions of poetry, it is also a refutation of current notions of the Aesthetic School of poetry. That particular school was in revolt against the idea that art was linked with morals. To Swinburne, who, as DeVane has pointed out,[25] was the main target of Browning's attack, the pursuit of beauty and the pursuit of uninhibited experience was an end in itself. In fact Browning would have found totally alien Swinburne's idea (as described by Mario Praz in *The Romantic Agony*) that "God smites equally the just and the unjust, and perhaps the former rather more than the latter; also the other idea that pain and death are everywhere in Nature, that crime is Nature's law; and the conception of God as a Being of supreme wickedness ('the supreme evil, God') and the revolt of man against the divinity he disowns." The Aesthetic School urged the artist to experience sin and corruption; it exalted immediate, personal, sensory emotion, often borrowed poetic experience from the visual sense alone. All this must have seemed to Browning to be an abrogation of poetic responsibility. To Browning the mere "raw material" of poetry without the "spiritual comprehension" behind was unthinkable. In "Saul" he had shown David as "fashioner" informing Saul of the physical truth, and then, in the higher role of "seer," of spiritual truth.

The "Parleying with Smart" affirms Browning's belief in the importance of the poet's role as a link between the temporal and the spiritual.[27] It also asserts that spiritual reality is not very far away from our world of ordinary perceptions. God's immanence is evident in nature, and more directly, within man himself if he has but eyes to see.

The Epilogue to the *Parleyings* carries to a conclusion the informing idea of the Parleyings, that of the imagination as an aid to truth. "Truth is God" says Fust, so that the pursuit of truth by means of the imaginative faculty becomes man's means of salvation. This is the ultimate message of the *Parleyings*. Fust's imaginative creation (the printing press) has linked fancy with fact. The toil leaves him a transformed man: "Creation/ Revealed me no object, from insect to Man,/ But bore thy hand's impress: earth glowed with salvation." (p. 738) Thus Fust joins the ranks of the men who receive the highest commendation in the *Parleyings*, those who see imaginatively and acknowledge the hand of God in their creations, who humbly recognize that it is the Creator himself who "concedest a spark/Of thy spheric perfection to earth's transitory/ Existences!" (p. 740)

The Epilogue further embodies a recurrent theme in the *Parleyings* – the impossibility of gaining complete knowledge of the infinite. Yet, the enlargement of the consciousness brought about by the imagination leads the artist to strive for higher goals: "So approximates Man – Thee, who reachable not,/ Hast formed him to yearningly follow Thy whole/ Sole and single omniscience!" (p. 741) One gets an idea of the closeness of the relationship between Browning's moral and aesthetic theories.

The "Prologue" to *Asolando* records the change that has come with maturity in the poet's vision. It is Browning's answer to the sense of loss recorded in Wordsworth's "Immortality Ode" and an affirmation of his belief in the beneficent effects of change. For if man has lost one way of seeing life – the fanciful vision, "falsehood's fancy-haze," (l.20) that embued with "ruby, emerald, chrysopras,/ Each object," (ll.13-14) he has attained to another and truer vision:

> The very naked thing? – so clear
> That, when you had the chance to gaze,
> You found its inmost self appear
> Through outer seeming – truth ablaze. (ll.16-19)

The poem is a reiteration of Browning's favourite theme as expressed earlier in the "Parleying with Gerard de Lairesse" – facts are superior to fancies. The Biblical reference to the burning bush gives a religious dimension and resonance to a poem essentially concerned with poetic vision, and emphasizes the essential quality of Browning's poems – their awareness of a loving, powerful Divine Being in the universe. It also marks the culmination of Browning's poetic progress from the poetry of subjective experience through dramatic poetry to a poetry where the subjective and the objective are fused in the interests of spiritual truth. It is a progress recorded as early as *Sordello* where the ascent to the highest level of perception begins with beauty and delight for its own sake and ends when the various aspects of beauty are seen as a unity representing the sum of all beauty – God.

"Development" (*Asolando*) records Browning's reminiscence of his father, who could transform even the most formidable subject into a delightful concoction of comic rhymes and games, making it vividly alive and interesting. It records how the poet's father not only introduced him to the story of the *Iliad* by means of a game, but, in the words of Irvine and

Honan, "softened Homer's Greek by beginning with Pope's *Iliad*, encouraging Robert to get the *Iliad* by heart before mastering the original, as he did at the age of twelve."[28] It also marks the culminating stage in Browning's continued interest in the role of fact and fancy in poetry. The poem softens Browning's own contention Prologue to *Asolando* as to the superiority of facts over fancy. As in "A Death in the Desert" he asserts the necessity of myths and fancies at the undeveloped stages of man's perceptions, for it is by their means that man can attain to the awareness of truth that would otherwise be beyond his comprehension. But as in the image of the ring in *The Ring and the Book* where fancy is needed to temper the "gold" of fact till it is able to "take its own part as truth should,/ Sufficient, self-sustaining" (I, 373-74) so in this poem, fancy is but an aid to fact till truth is firmly perceived by the mind – "in my heart of hearts/ And soul of souls, fact's essence freed and fixed/ From accidental fancy's guardian sheath." (ll.78-80) Clyde de L. Ryals sums up thus: "During the course of his development, he comes to realize that 'facts' as well as myths are but provisional constructs never to be taken as truth itself alone since, as the Pope in *The Ring and the Book* pointed out, truth is always in advance of any formulation of it."[29]

It is interesting to trace the changing connotations of the concepts of "fact" and "fancy" through Browning's later poetic theory. In *The Ring and the Book* fact is the untempered gold that needs fancy, the poetic imagination, to transform it. Fancy here is creative: "I fuse my live soul and that inert stuff,/ Before attempting smithcraft." (I, 469-70)

In *La Saisiaz* fancy assumes the nature of conjecture and surmise as opposed to the facts provided by reason. But these concepts, initially seen as opposites become, as the poem progresses, to be twin adjuncts in the process of belief. Both fact and fancy are supplemented by a superior force – hope.

In *Fifine at the Fair* Don Juan opposes fancy and truth, the former being "Mere/Illusion." (XXVI) Yet, in the idea of the seeing soul he comes to giving fancy the same imaginative, creative force that Browning gives it in the ring analogy in *The Ring and the Book*: "And naught in the world, which, save for soul that sees, inert/ Was, is, and would be ever, – stuff for transmuting." (*Fifine at the Fair*, LV)

In *The Two Poets of Croisic* we see the beginning of the process by which Browning in his later poetry came more to insist on the superiority of fact over fancy:

> But truth, truth, that's the gold! and all the good
> I find in fancy is, it serves to set

Gold's inmost glint free, gold which comes up rude
And rayless from the mine.

In *Ferishtah's Fancies* fancy is once again equated with illusion:

When shall we rest upon the thing itself
Not on its semblance? – Soul – too weak, forsooth,
To cope with fact--wants fiction everywhere!
Mine tires of falsehood: truth at any cost!

("A Bean-Stripe," ll.292-95)

Ferishtah is of the opinion that the facts of our experience are sufficient to enable us to infer the absolute truth.

In the "Parleying with Mandeville" fancy once again becomes the scapegoat whose soaring visions, because unrealizable on earth, lead men to pessimism and despair. While earlier fancy had been a means of man's communion with the infinite, it is now explicitly rejected: "Abjure each fond attempt to represent/ The formless, the illimitable!" (VI) Browning now advocates the truth that can be apprehended through finite manifestations of fact. Nevertheless, in place of fancy Browning brings in something very like it, the myth or the symbol as the earthly representation of the divine. As in the Prologue to the *Parleyings* poetic imagination is the link between fancy and fact.

In the "Parleying with Gerard De Lairesse" the issue of fact and fancy is stated unequivocally. Referring to the decorative mythologizing of Greek art, Browning states his modern approach:

Oh, we can fancy too! but somehow fact
Has got to – say, not so much push aside
Fancy, as to declare its place supplied
By fact unseen but no less fact the same,
Which mind bids sense accept.

In the "Prologue" to *Asolando* fact and fancy are sharply separated, the one representing truth, the other falsehood; but in "Development," finally, the two come together again as indispensable aids for the apprehension of truth.

We may note in passing the striking similarity of Browning's views on the imagination with that of Coleridge, who wrote: "The primary Imagination I hold to be the living power and the prime agent of all human perception, and as a repetition in the finite mind of the eternal act of creation in the infinite I Am."[30] It is in Coleridge's "Dejection: An Ode" that we have the lines: "Ah! from the soul itself must issue forth/ A light, a glory, a fair luminous cloud/ Enveloping the Earth." (IV, 53-55) Much of the *Parleyings* deals with men from whom this light did issue forth, and in contrast, with their opponents, detractors or anti-types in whom this light has been deadened by hyper-intellectualization. In fact Coleridge's account of the aesthetic reconciliation wrought by the imagination – "Imagination . . . reveals itself in the balance or reconciliation of opposite or discordant qualities . . . the idea with the image; the individual with the representative; the sense of novelty and of freshness, with the old and familiar objects"[31] – forms the base of all the ideas presented in the *Parleyings*. Ultimately, the reconciliation of opposites includes another and more complex pair (and one which engaged Browning most intimately), the inner human spirit and the outer transcendental or supernatural entity.

In the "Parleying with Christopher Smart" Browning's description of the poet's functions had religious overtones. The poet's symbolic representation of the beauties of the earth turns men's eyes to the presence of a Design in the universe. But Browning saw all artists, whether poets or painters, attempting to join the infinite to the finite. In the "Parleying with Francis Furini" he chooses a painter to parley with, one who feels that "art is a natural accompaniment to his priestly calling, because in both he saw himself fulfilling religious functions."[32]

The poem is the same multi-layered composition as the other parleyings, encompassing a juxtaposition of two images of Furini's character, Browning's and Baldinucci's, leading to a defence of the nude in art and a tirade against the Darwinian Evolutionists. In the first part, Browning reiterates a theme presented earlier in "Fra Lippo Lippi" and again in the "Parleying with Smart" – the artist as communicator who gives eyes to people to look into the significance of reality.

The conflict presented in the poem is once again between a sterile, narrow-minded conception of art, and a dynamic one that deals with the actual in order to derive meaning and significance from it. Against the kind of people like the prior in Fra Lippo Lippi, who protests:

> . . . it's devil's game!
> Your business is not to catch men with show
> With homage to the perishable clay,
> But lift them over it, ignore it all,
> Make them forget there's such a thing as flesh.
> Your business is to paint the souls of men. (ll.178-83)

Browning sets a painter-priest who believes in the significance of the flesh. The idea is consistent with Browning's life-long belief in the physical and the finite as the pathway to the spiritual and the infinite, the former being no less important than the latter. In the present poem, the apex of "each rendered loveliness" lies in

> . . . Art's endeavour to express
> Heaven's most consummate of achievements, bless
> Earth by a semblance of the seal God set
> On woman his supremest work. (III)

By using the flesh to illuminate soul, the true artist sees meaning in what is beautiful in the world. This is valuable to other men, who are brought by art to see what there is inherent in the world of nature all along, but invisible to them. Art becomes the means whereby the essentials are separated from the outward shows:

> Where else the uninstructed ones too sure
> Would take all outside beauty – film that's furled
> About a star – for the star'self. . . . (V)

This idea had earlier been expressed in "Fra Lippo Lippi":

> . . . We're made so that we love
> First when we see them painted, things we have passed
> Perhaps a hundred times nor cared to see;
> And so they are better painted – better to us,
> Which is the same thing. Art was given for that –
> God uses us to help each other so,
> Lending our minds out. (ll.300-6)

The parleying places a more explicit emphasis on the truth that is the essential centre of all beauty. The true artists are those who "Have the grace to see Thy purpose, strength to mar/ Thy work by no admixture of their own,/ Limn truth not falsehood." (VII)

Browning's conception of the union of the body and the soul is symbolized in the poem through the figure of Andromeda. As Douglas Bush points out: "He is not now, as in *Pauline*. mainly content with romantic picture-making . . . and Andromeda is not simply a beautiful girl rescued by a heroic champion. Her body is the work of God which the artist can see and make others see."[33] Art becomes the means whereby man may render gratitude to God. It is also a repetition in finite terms of God's creative acts: "(Man, poor elf,/ Striving to match the finger-mark of Him/ The immeasurably matchless)." (II) In painting as in poetry, Browning champions realism transformed by the imagination that integrates the world of nature with the world of the spirit.

The "Parleying with Francis Furini" emphasizes the need for apprehending the particulars from one's personal experience as a means of gaining insight into the universal. Browning champions the cause of realism in painting on the assumption that if man was represented exactly as he was, the soul would, of necessity, shine through. In the "Parleying with Gerard de Lairesse" he moves a step further in this proposition by choosing a painter who began as a realist, who felt that the artist should recognize the worth of the "trivial commonplace," (II) who believed that

> . . . Beyond
> The ugly actual, lo, on every side
> Imagination's limitless domain
> Displayed a wealth of wondrous sounds and sights
> Ripe to be realized by poet's brain
> Acting on painter's brush!

Yet, with mistaken zeal, this artist became bent on banishing "All except beauty" and rejected the "daily and undignified" for "Fancy's rainbow-birth/ Conceived 'mid clouds in Greece." (IV)

In contrast Browning presents his own temperament, content with "hard, fast wide-awake/Having and holding nature for the sake/ Of nature only." (V) He describes himself as one "who, bee-like, sate sense with the simply true,/ Nor seek to heighten that sufficiency/ By help of feignings proper to the page." (V)

The parleying thus becomes an assessment of two modes of poetic practice and the functioning of two opposed forms of the poetic imagination – the imagination that seeks to heighten reality by decorating it with myth, and the imagination that seeks to express reality by looking deep into its psychological truth. In effect, it is the contrast between the Hellenic and the "modern" psychological approach to art.

Browning seeks to find an explanation for the need to heighten and add to reality. It is probably based, he says, on the fact that sense "Cannot content itself with outward things, /Mere beauty: soul must needs know whence there springs – / How and why – what sense but loves." (V) This particular desire Browning finds entirely legitimate. It is merely an indication of the chasm that exists between heaven and earth, the infinite and the finite. What he rejects is the "Fancy" which is the product of the "freakish brain." (VI) This kind of fanciful mythologizing merely distorts the truth with its trappings of "Joves and Junos, nymphs and satyres." (V) One remembers Browning's vindication of the poetry of Euripides in *Aristophanes' Apology*. Euripides refused to encircle himself "with poetic atmosphere" (p. 838) or to live apart from the unpleasant realities of the world. Aristophanes comments: "the real/he wants, not falsehood, – truth alone he seeks,/ Truth, for all beauty! Beauty, in all truth – ." (p. 838) Beauty is not something to be added to truth, but inherent in it.

In "Lairesse" too, Browning advocates a different kind of fancy, an imaginative realism which presents "fact unseen, but no less fact the same,/ Which mind bids sense accept."(VI) He upholds the psychological art that reveals the inner meaning without having recourse to mythological apparatus. Thus, as Langbaum puts it, "Browning defined his realism precisely through opposition to myths as overt subject-matter."[34] A higher reality can be made manifest if the artist faithfully reproduces the world of his perceptions and tries to illuminate its significance by using the double vision mentioned in the parleying, but not by linking the outward world to some imagined, outworn concepts of value.[35]

In his earlier poetry Browning had praised those artists who had achieved in their work a fusion of the flesh and the spirit, the real and the ideal. For what may technically be perfect may, nevertheless, like Andrea's paintings, lack soul. What really matters is the insight that transforms, that enables the artist to break through the boundaries of the here and now to participate in the limitlessness of eternity. This is what Browning means by its assertion: "If we no longer see as you of old,/'T is we see deeper . . . Progress for the bold,/ You saw the body, it is the soul we see." (VII). Progress implies continued development. In "Old Pictures in Florence" Browning expressed his preference for early Christian art as against Greek art not only on the basis of the realism of the former, but also because of its inherent possibilities for improved excellence:

> Today's brief passion limits their ranges;
> It seethes with the morrow for us and more
> They are perfect – how else? they shall never change,
> We are faulty – why not? we have time in store. (XVI)

Perfection in art is rejected as implying negation. Ultimately, Browning's concept of "soul" in relation to art is based on the worth of the artistic vision in revealing to man the truth that lies beyond the finite apprehension. Even the most powerful and gorgeous poetry is insignificant if it cannot do this.

The "Parleying with Gerard de Lairesse" closes on a note of renewal as represented by the pattern of death and rebirth in the vegetation cycle. In the "Parleying with Charles Avison" this idea is examined with reference to music and its changing patterns. The parleying is, in fact, the culmination of Browning's characteristic conceptions of music, its functions and its effects. As in *Pauline*, "A Toccata of Galuppi's," *Fifine at the Fair*, "the effect of music upon the poet," says DeVane," is to people melody with the figures of ancient men, now dead."[36] This linking of the past and the present leads Browning to a comparative assessment of the two.

In the "Parleying with de Lairesse," too, Browning had examined the past in the light of present needs and had found it to be deficient. Greek art, which had reached the very acme of perfection in the past, was now outworn as touchstones for modern man, chiefly because of its underlying pessimism which provided empty answers to man's hopeful, enquiring spirit. Both these parleying posit change as an essential feature of the human condition and of art in particular. In "Avison" Browning writes:

> . . . Ah, but such and such
> Beliefs of yore seemed inexpugnable
> When we attained them! E'en as they, so will
> This their successor have the due morn, noon,
> Evening and night. . .
> So will it be with truth that, for the nonce
> Styles itself truth perennial: (XII)

In the "Parleying with de Lairesse" Browning had asserted: "Nothing has been which shall not bettered be." (XIII) In the "Parleying with Avison" he propounds the even more vigorously hopeful belief that while it was given to the past to "Nourish truth merely" it was for the future to achieve "Novel creation." (XIII) If music was the myth of the inner life, this principle of symbolic transformation represents a fresh fountainhead, a generative force providing fresh motives. Thus the transitoriness of the arts as a repository of truth becomes for Browning not a pessimistic conception, but a hopeful one, for it repeats the pattern of life itself.

The paradoxical idea emerges that while truth remains essentially unchanged, it yet assumes new shapes: "Truth was at full within thee long ago,/ Alive as now it takes what latest shape/ May startle thee by its strangeness." (XIII) This idea had been treated at great length in *Fifine at the Fair*, surprisingly by means of the imagery of food. Don Juan plays Schumann's *Carnival* and sees

> . . . how food o' the soul, the stuff that's made
> To furnish many with thought and feeling, is purveyed
> Substantially the same from age to age, with change
> Of the outside only for successive feasters. (XCII)

He comes to realize the inevitability of change in art no less than in nature. Thus we see that in both the parleyings, "Lairesse" and "Avison," Browning opposes himself to the mythical attitude which, as Langbaum says, "idealizes the past in order to set it up as a permanent criterion of value."[37] Myths that had value previously may change and fade away; but nothing can change the "corolla" of truth that these myths safeguard, (XIII) and the essential hopefulness embodied in these truths.

What is needed is the double vision mentioned in "de Lairesse" (V) to apprehend the intrinsic as distinguished from the externals, to feel intuitively the deeper truth beyond the surface impressions. Thus music becomes for Browning the highest art in so far as it not only bridges the gulf between Mind and Soul, as the other arts do, a "star" (as he writes in "Abt Vogler," l.52) musical creation becomes the closest analogue to God's creative act. The other arts produce novelty, not creation:

> . . . Arts arrange
> Dissociate, re-distribute, interchange
> Part with part, lengthen, broaden, high or deep
> Construct their bravest, – still such pains produce
> Change, not creation: simply what lay loose
> At first lies firmly after, . . (VIII)

W.O. Raymond remarks: "Music to Browning was always a symbol of the infinite, the art in which, above every other, the soul may aspire towards the spiritual, eternal and divine."[38] In *Paracelsus* the poet Aprile "To perfect consummate all" (l.475) rises above poetry to the sphere of music. In "Abt Vogler" painting and poetry are triumphant arts, but art "in obedience to laws" (l.47); it is in music that one can see "the finger of God." (l.49)

Thus for Browning the best art is that which instinctively apprehends the soul beneath the surface flesh and acknowledges the hand of God in all artistic creation. In *La Saisiaz* the term "soul" had been used to denote man's knowing faculty. In the "Parleying with Avison," however, the "soul" becomes the feeling faculty or the non-rational, as Roma A. King calls it.[39] And art becomes the means that helps to

> . . . shoot
> Liquidity into a mould, – some way
> Arrest Soul's evanescent moods, and keep
> Unalterably still the forms that leap
> To life for once. (VIII)

But if music is the art which embodies the soul's feelings most exactly, it is also the most evanescent. This is what makes it all the more precious. In "Abt Vogler" the musician's failure to hold on to his transcendental moment is converted into an assertion of triumphant optimism: "And what is our failure here but a triumph's evidence/ For the full hope of the days?" (ll. 81-82) In the "Parleying with Avison" too, with the awareness of fleetingness comes the promise of renewal:

> . . . off they steal –
> How gently, dawn-doomed phantoms! back come they
> Full-blooded with now crimson of broad day –
> Passion palpable once more. (VIII)

Unlike the complex, structure of Master Hughes of Saxe-Gotha's music ("those spider-webs," l.95) which would obliterate "God's gold" (l.114) Browning finds in Avison's march-music a "Truth which endures re-setting." (XIV) The image of fire is again used to indicate the spiritual implications of this truth:

> . . . Still lives the spark enough
> For breath to quicken, run the smouldering ash
> Red right through. . . (IX)

The unchangeable truth lies in man's ceaseless march forward into the future. But the future does not invalidate the core of truth that resides in the art of the past. To illustrate his point, Browning goes back to recreate what had been created in the past in order to infuse it with fresh meaning and so reveal its essential truth. His imaginative shaping of Avison's *March* fills the "vacant sky with stars/ Hidden till now." (XV) and becomes a paean to the continuity of human aspirations. Once again, Browning emphasizes the importance of the imagination as a guide to the truth and as a link between the past and the present. The creativity of art – "new good, new beauty, from the old" – as Balaustion says in *Balaustion's Adventure* is also stressed.

To sum up: Browning in his later period sets himself against the convention by which the criticism of poetry tended to become the criticism of the character and way of life of the poet. He demands that his work be judged by its literary merits alone. He affirms that his poetic make-up is optimistic and joyful rather than pessimistic, not because he is insensitive to realities, but because as a poet he has attained to the larger consciousness; and he explicitly repudiates the romantic pose of disillusionment as unworthy of the high calling of the poet.

Realism in art receives considerable attention in Browning's later pronouncements on art. He rejects sentimentalizing and poeticizing in poetry and decorative mythologizing in painting and poetry. He affirms that the material for poetry could be found in the ugly as much as in the beautiful, that "Strength and utility charm more than grace" and that beyond the beauty that appeals to the sense is the truth that speaks to the soul.

As regards poetic style, Browning answers the charge of obscurity and harshness with the contention that complex thoughts cannot be couched in mellifluous language. He opposes the traditionally-held assumptions as to the appropriate subject-matter for poetry.

In the importance laid on the imagination as the shaping power in all artistic endeavour we can discern a movement towards a theory that defines the means by which the fusion of the poet's role as fashioner and seer, (as envisaged initially in the *Essay on Shelley*), takes place. Between the external phenomena that is the sphere of the objective poet and the ultimate view that the subjective poet aspires to, lies the synthesizing faculty of the imagination that controls the material so as to enhance the value of both. The poet's imagination helps him in his symbolic representations, for the symbol is the embodiment of the infinite within the finite. The symbol thus becomes the via media between the actual and the ideal, the representation in concrete of the most abstract conceptions. Through its uses, the objective poet, who reproduces "things external" and appeals to the "aggregate human mind" can give depth to his poetry by establishing the relationship between the world and God. On the other hand, the subjective poet who appeals to the "absolute Divine mind" is enabled to shape his experience, which are often inchoate, into intelligible form and to curb his impulse to reach the truth instantly by impatiently rejecting the particulars. For the poet is essentially a communicator, of the strengths and beauties of this earth as much as of the moral significance that is to be discerned through them. And the best kind of communication is achieved through the symbolic method which uses finite means towards illuminating the infinite.

Though Browning's aesthetic theory holds a high estimate of the importance of artistic creation, it does not support a vague loftiness. One thinks of such phrases occurring through Matthew Arnold's critical writings as high seriousness," the "noble and profound application of ideas to life" and the "grand style" that arises when "a noble nature, poetically gifted, treats with simplicity and severity a serious subject." The contrast that Browning presents is telling, a contrast particularly evident in Browning's treatment of Greek myths and legends, in which he translates his aesthetic theory into practice and examines the contemporary cult of Hellenism from his own particular point of view.

NOTES

1. Donald Smalley, "A Parleying with Aristophanes," *PMLA*, 55 (1940), p. 827.
2. *Ibid.*, p. 833.
3. DeVane, *Handbook*, p. 392.
4. As early as 1855, Browning was defending himself against this charge. In a letter to John Ruskin, he wrote: "I cannot begin writing poetry till my imaginary reader has conceded licenses to me which you demur at altogether. I *know* that I don't make out my conception by my language, all poetry being a putting the infinite within the finite. You would have me paint it all plain out, which can't be, but by various artifices, I try to make shift with touches and bits of outlines which succeed if they bear the conception from me to you. You ought, I think, to keep pace with the thought tripping from ledge to ledge of my 'glaciers' as you call them, not stand poking your alpenstock into the holes and demonstrating that no foot could have stood there, suppose it sprang over there?" in W.G. Collingwood, *Life and Works of John Ruskin* (London: Methuen, 1900), p. 163. And as late as 1882, he wrote to Edmund Yates of the "Fifty-years long charge of unintelligibility against my books." *Letters*, p. 212.
5. In *Sordello*, obscurity is seen as a matter of language "brothers speech," (V, 635) where nuances of suggestion and association are conveyed without explicit recourse to language. In the later period, obscurity is seen mainly as a matter of complexity of thought.
6. Quoted in *Browning: The Critical Heritage*, ed. Boyd Litzinger and Donald Smalley (London: Routledge and Kegan Paul, 1970), p. 169.
7. Browning wrote to Isa Blagden on August 19, 1865: "As I began, so I shall end, taking my own course, pleasing myself or aiming at doing so, and thereby, I hope, pleasing God." *Dearest Isa*, p. 220.
8. cf. Browning's letter to Miss Anne Egerton Smith, August 16, 1873: "I never said or wrote a word against or about Byron's poetry or power in my life; but I did say, that, if he were in earnest and preferred being with the sea to associating with mankind, he would do well to stay with the sea's population; thereby simply taking him at his word, had it been honest whereas it was altogether dishonest, seeing that nobody cared so much about the opinions of mankind and deferred to them, as he who was thus posturing and pretending to despise them." *Letters*, p. 159.
9. Robert Preyer, "Robert Browning: A Reading of the Early Narratives" in *Robert Browning: A Collection of Critical Essays*, ed. Philip Drew, p. 174.
10. T.S. Eliot, *Selected Prose*, ed. John Hayward (Penguin Books, 1963), p. 29.
11. DeVane, *Handbook*, p. 401.
12. The idea of the obtuseness of the critics had found expression in *Sordello*. Sordello learns "to live in weakness as in strength." Even when he gave the best of himself, wrote dramas and adopted the language of common speech for greater effect, Naddo, the busybody, the mouthpiece of the crowd, charged him with lack of originality on the ground that he gave them only what they could understand. (ll. 775-867)

13. In *Paracelsus*, the hero asserts that truth is an "imprisoned splendour" (I.735) which is within man; but while this becomes a source of egotism for Paracelsus Browning's stress is always on the altruistic motives of art.
14. In *Sordello* Browning dramatized the twin impulses within the poet his desire as a human being to secure fame by offering what the public want the obvious and the commonplace, and his aim as a poet to cling to the truth at all costs. "Pictor Ignotus" and "The Grammarian's Funeral" also treat the problem of fame.
15. See "Preface to *Lyrical Ballads*, 1800" in *Wordsworth's Literary Criticism*, ed. N.C. Smith (London, 1905), p. 15.
16. DeVane, *Handbook*, p. 458.
17. *The Focusing Artifice*, p. 242.
18. Browning had earlier explored the problem in *Paracelsus* where the hero "attains" only when he comes to realize that absolutes cannot be achieved by man in his imperfect, finite state of being, and that man must gracefully accept his limitations. cf. V, 889-98.
19. This is reminiscent of Paracelsus' final realization of a Being "in whom life is evermore/ Yet whom existence in its lowest form/ Includes." (V. 646-48)
20. *The Infinite Moment*, pp. 165-66.
21. *Essay on Shelley* in *Browning: Poetry and Prose*, selected by Simon Nowell-Smith (London: Rupert Hart-Davis, 1967), p. 675.
22. Quoted in DeVane, *Handbook*, p. 237.
23. Quoted in Philip Drew, *The Poetry of Browning*, p. 6.
24. Philip Drew, p. 55.
25. DeVane, *Handbook*, p. 508.
26. Quoted in Douglas Bush, *Mythology and the Romantic Tradition in English Poetry*, p. 341.
27. cf. Browning's description of the subjective poet: "...he digs where he stands preferring to seek them in his own soul, as the nearest reflex of that absolute, according to the intuitions of which he desires to perceive and speak." *Essay on Shelley*, p. 38.
28. Irvin and Honan, p. 6.
29. *Browning's Later Poetry*, p. 232.
30. Coleridge, *Biographia Literaria*, Chapter XIII. Quoted in William K. Wimsatt, Jr. and Cleanth Brooks, *Literary Criticism: A Short History*, 1957 (Second Indian Reprint, Oxford and IBH, 1964), p. 389.
31. *Ibid.*, p. 395.
32. *Browning's Later Poetry*, p. 217.
33. *Mythology and the Romantic Tradition in English Poetry*, p. 381.
34. Robert Langbaum, "Browning and the Question of Myth" in *The Modern Spirit*, p. 86.
35. Browning's idea that instead of employing fanciful tales or antiquated myths the poet should draw upon the actual material of the times which alone can furnish material for the presentation of valid truths, is, reminiscent of Carlyle's: "The ordinary poet, like the ordinary man, is forever seeking in external

circumstance the help which can be found only in himself. In what is familiar and near at hand, he discerns no form or comeliness: home is not poetical but prosaic, it is in some past, distant, conventional heroic world, that poetry resides. . . . Let them be sure that heroic ages and heroic climates can do little for them. . . . The poet, we imagine, can never have far to seek for a subject: the elements of his art are in him, and around him on every hand; for him the Ideal world is not remote from the Actual, but under it and within it: nay, he is a poet precisely because he can discern it there." *Essay on Burns in Critical and Miscellaneous Essays* (London: Chapman and Hall, 188, I,205)

36. DeVane, *Handbook*, p. 320.
37. "Browning and the Question of Myth," p. 80.
38. *The Infinite Moment*, p. 51.
39. *The Focusing Artifice*, p. 264.

GREEK MYTHS AND LEGENDS

Browning's approach to the question of subject matter taken from the Greek literary past in modern poetry is entirely dissimilar to that of Arnold and Swinburne, two other Victorians who dealt extensively with Greek themes in their poetry:

In the 1853 Preface to his *Poems* Arnold wrote:

> I fearlessly assert that Hermann and Dorothea, Childe Harold, Jocelyn, "The Excursion," leave the reader cold in comparison with the effect produced upon him by the latter books of the *Iliad*, by the *Oresteia,* or by the episode of Dido. And why is this? Simply because in the three last-named cases the action is greater, the personages nobler, the situations more intense: and this is the true basis of the interest in a poetical work and this alone.[1]

In the Advertisement to the edition of 1854, Arnold again asserted the suitability of great actions as subject matter for poetry. Swinburne's *Atlanta in Calydon* was his tribute to Aeschylus and Sophocles, whose poetry he loved; it was his attempt to reproduce the poetical spirit which he found in these Greek poets. Though the form was not strictly Greek, its subject and spirit were. Both these poets were consciously and deliberately endeavouring to revive old modes and moods. In the heroic actions of the past, they found a beauty and dignity which their own world could not provide. Their love of the past was in part an escape from the contemporary situation. In reproducing the form of Greek tragedy, Arnold sought the beauty and dignity of the Hellenic discipline and restraint. Swinburne, besides this, sought also the essential poetry, the indefinable essence which he found in the tragedies of ancient Greece.

But Browning's views on this matter had been influenced by Elizabeth Barrett. As early as the period of their courtship, she wrote to him:

> I am inclined to think we want new forms as well as thoughts. The old gods are dethroned. Why should we go back to the antique moulds, as they are so improperly called? . . . Let us all aspire rather to Life, and let the dead bury the dead. . . . For there is poetry everywhere,[2]

In his reply on May 17 to Elizabeth's letter dated May 16, 1846 (wherein she severely criticizes Mrs. Jameson's views that the present age is not heroic and undeserving of expression in art, and maintains that "genius in the arts is not a mere reflection of the times") Browning shows his perfect accord with her views:

> All you write about Art is most true. Carlyle has turned and forged, reforged on his anvil the fact "that no age ever appeared heroic to itself". . . and so, worthy of reproduction in Art itself. . . . The cant is, that an "age of transition" is a melancholy thing to contemplate and delineate – whereas the worst things of all to look back on are times of comparative standing still, rounded in their important completeness.[5]

This view that perfection in art means stagnation is one premise on which Browning based his opposition to the unquestioning adulation accorded to Greek art. For Browning art meant an unceasing progress towards newer goals. In "Old Pictures in Florence" Greek art is "perfect of lineament, perfect of stature," (l.117) but then "what's come to perfection perishes." (l.130) Early Christian art, though imperfect, is awarded the palm because of its tremendous possibilities for development:

> Today's brief passion limits their range,
> It seethes with the morrow for us and more.
> They are perfect – how else? they shall never change:
> We are faulty – why not? we have time in store.
> The Artificer's hand is not arrested
> With us; (XVI, 121-26)

The other premise is linked to Browning's view of the artist as attempting to join the finite to the infinite. Greek art, which portrayed the body so beautifully, did not go beyond it to the inner soul. This was the point in which the Christian painters scored over their alleged superiors: "To bring the invisible full into play!/ Let the visible go to the dogs – what matters?" ("Old Pictures in Florence," 151-52)

In his later period, Browning particularly develops this idea. For him, beyond the requirement of poetic beauty was that of poetic truth, and truth was that which entered into and modified experience. Browning's attempt in his Greek poems was not to literally reproduce the Greek experience, which he felt time had rendered inadequate, but to transcend the time barrier and reach an insight into the essential reality that underlay all human experience.

Contrary to Arnold's emphasis on a great subject as a repository of timeless values, Browning insists on the need for the shaping spirit of the poetic imagination to penetrate the past and shape it afresh. The forms of the earlier ages could not embody the contemporary consciousness, which needed psychological truth rather than external beauty or grandeur. Browning's treatment of Greek myth challenges the view that the subject-matter taken from the heroic past was inherently invested with "immortal strength." He is rather of the opinion that it is the kind of interpretation given to the myth that matters, the particular imaginative rendering of it that gives it abiding value. Browning believes in exercising the imagination to create life and not just to imitate it. In his later poetry, he uses mythology to interpret, rather than to escape his age, adding by his reconstructions to the sum of living experience.

After the publication of *The Ring and the Book*, Browning renewed his explorations into Greek literature. Earlier he had written "Artemis Prologizes," published as a dramatic lyric in *Bells and Pomegranates*, Number III, in 1842, which DeVane says, was intended to be a prologue to a tragedy in imitation of Euripides.[4] Browning's admiration for the Greek dramatist was further demonstrated in the Pope's monologue in *The Ring and the Book*. Euripides was one of the earliest voices of European liberalism and Browning was attracted by that. Moreover, Euripides' pathos and humanity had particularly appealed to Mrs. Browning, as indicated by the lines from her poem "Wine of Cyprus" which Browning used as an epigraph to *Balaustion's Adventure*. With her death, a study of her favourite classical poet became, for Browning, a homage to her memory.

Douglas Bush suggests that "Browning may have had a surfeit of his more or less modern and sordid realism."[5] Moreover DeVane points out that an unappreciative introduction to the tragedies of Euripides by T.A. Buckley, published in 1868, and further, Augustus Wilhelm Schlegel's opinion in his *Lectures on Dramatic Art and Literature* that "Euripides wrecked classical poetry" roused Browning's ire. (*Handbook*, p. 377) As Donald Smalley has shown, Browning identified closely with Euripides.[6] In Euripides he found a kindred soul – a realist, an ironist and psychologist and a champion of truth and justice, the man whose "strong style" showed men the true path through "the mire of cowardice and the slush of lies," as he wrote in the Pope's monologue. (X, 1786 and 1789) It is thus wholly appropriate that when Browning came to choose themes from the Greek for his poetry, his interest in Euripides shaped his choice.

Balaustion's Adventure, Including a Transcript from Euripides (1871) is a recasting of the Greek myth of Alcestis, the woman who chose death to save the life of her husband. "No Greek tragedy has been better translated"[7] wrote one of the early reviewers of the poem. More recently, *Balaustion's Adventure* has variously been described as "a vindication of Euripides,"[8] an "effort to deal in his art with the living problem of his marriage to Elizabeth"[9] and "the embodiment of Browning's ideas on Christian love and what it means to be a poet."[10]

For Browning a myth was not merely a recapturing of past glory and nobility but a base from which to embark on his characteristic exploration into man's heart and mind. "A myth may teach" (VIII) he would say in the "Parleying with Bernard de Mandeville" and the essence of his teaching was the revelation of the eternal pattern of the victory of good over evil that survives through time. Thus his method is to use the double vision, treating the myth both literally and symbolically. As Browning puts it in the "Parleying with Gerard de Lairesse":

> . . . for sense, my de Lairesse
> Cannot content itself with outward things,
> Mere beauty: soul must needs know whence there springs—
> How, when and why—what sense but loves, . . . (V)

This is what Langbaum terms the "psychological use of myth."[11] For while Browning delighted in the beauty of the Greek myths, his sensuous response to them as evident in *Pauline* underwent a progressive change as he formulated his ideas on the Incarnation; so that, seen in the light of Christianity and the divine love of Christ, the spiritual emptiness of the classical world became more pronounced. "Life's inadequate to joy," (l. 249) cries Cleon, yearning for a state of being "Unlimited in capability/ For joy, as this is in desire for joy," (ll. 326-127) and rejecting as insane the one path that promises him this blessedness. This is the third premise on which Browning bases his criticism of Hellenism. It was the Greek philosophy that ultimately led men to despair that Browning found anti-pathetic; and against it he set the Christian revelation of a God of Love which gave men hope of immortality.

Thus, Browning accepts neither the Hellenic forms nor its values, and *Balaustion's Adventure* translates his ideas into practice.

Structurally, *Balaustion's Adventure* is one of the most innovative of Browning's longer poems—a translation of a Greek play spoken by a narrator-commentator (Balaustion), who not only enlarges upon the significance of the various scenes, but gives her own interpretation of the action to suit her own predilections, the whole being set in the framework of a boldly sketched-in historical framework. Browning's characters are not mere symbols for metaphysical concepts (as are Shelley's for example, in *Prometheus Unbound*), rather their humanity is emphasized to make them psychologically adequate for present-day conditions. The use of the narrator-commentator gives Browning a dramatic mask from behind which he can bring to bear his keen insight and questioning modern spirit upon the ancient myth and derive from it a meaning of a fresher and more relevant kind.

The three major stages in the action of *Balaustion's Adventure* correspond to the three main themes of the poem – poetic power, perfect love and salvation, first through the vigorous action of a legendary hero and then, through the power of love itself. The poem thus deals with some of the recurrent themes in all Browning's poetry – poetry, love and religion, and embodies Browning's mature views on these subjects.

The "poetry is power" theme is stated at the very beginning, when Balaustion describes how her love and knowledge of Euripides' poetry saved her own life and that of her companions. The hostile Syracusans would have forced their ship back to be a prey of a pursuing pirate bark, had not Balaustion pleased them by reciting the *Alcestis* as she remembered seeing and hearing it at the theatre at Kameiros. "What's poetry except a power that makes?" she asks, a power that gives the auditors the capacity to "link each sense on to its sister-sense/Grace-like." (p. 732) This is the raison d'etre of her interpolations. Balaustion is not content to merely explicate the action, she must explore its psychological basis. The texture of the play thus becomes richer and more meaningful. Though her soaring imagination has been questioned by "A brisk little somebody,/ Critic and whippersnapper." (p. 781) Balaustion argues that the power of poetry.

> . . . so breeds
> I' the heart and soul o' the taker, so transmutes
> The man who only was a man before,
> That he grows god-like in his turn, can give –
> He also: share the poet's privilege,
> Bring forth new good, new beauty, from the old. (p. 808)

The immediate effect of her comments is to add imaginative fervour and lyrical splendour to the narrative. But it is clear that Browning is using Balaustion as a mouthpiece to voice a defence of his interpretative recreation of Greek legend against the literalists.

The *Alcestis* of Euripides was a semi-satyric play governed by Greek conventions and attitudes, but not wholly. For the ironist in Euripides, even while presenting an ideal king in Admetos, who appears to be quite justified in accepting his wife's sacrifice and who is delivered from his fate because he has put his duty as a host above his own personal sorrow, cannot quite accept or condone Admetos' selfishness. And so he created the intensely real, intensely moving Alcestis, who consents to sacrifice herself, but who dies with a despairing, contemptuous awareness of her husband's weakness. This realistic psychology is repeated by Browning. But even Euripides falls a prey to the Greek concept of arbitrary fate, and though he superficially tries to bridge the moral gap between Alcestis and Admetos, with him, the repentance of Admetos is little better than an increasing self-pity. Browning, with his subtler reasoning, and his demand for psychological verity, makes this the focal point of his treatment of the story; his stress of the development of "soul" in Admetos.

Approaching death has, for Alcestis, been a means of removing the veils of illusion. The commercial imagery used with reference to Admetos—"Saw him purse money up" (p. 786) emphasizes his foolish selfishness. "The man was like some merchant who, in storm/Throws the freight over to redeem the ship." (p. 789) The process of Admetos' repentance and his growth in moral stature constitutes the action of Balaustion's narrative. Throughout we have the voice of Balaustion herself, pinpointing moral ambiguities, suggesting norms for judgement, highlighting the inner complexities.

The bitter confrontation with Pheres, his father, reveals to Admetos the extent to which selfishness can descend, and he recoils in horror as he sees himself mirrored in the old man's "poor, pretentious talk." (p. 796) This is one step towards Admetos' regeneration. Balaustion remarks:

> You see the worst of the interruption was,
> It plucked back, with an overhasty hand,
> Admetos from descending to the truth. (p. 795)

Yet, Admetos is "Only half-selfish now, since sensitive," (p. 798) and he moves to the anguished realization that he has gained nothing by exchanging death for life. Balaustion marks the stages in Admetos' awareness of the truth of the situation, and, in a beautiful analogy, she comments:

> That was the truth. Vexed waters sank to smooth:
> 'Twas only when the last bubble broke,
> The latest circlet widened all away
> And left a placid level, that up swam
> To the surface the drowned truth, in dreadful change. (p. 803)

This dramatic development, according to DeVane, is "Browning's rather than Euripides', and is modern rather than Greek."[12] Balaustion seems to express Browning's impatience of the earlier poet's rather hesitant treatment of the myth when she says:

> I would the Chorus here had plucked up heart,
> Spoken out boldly, and explained the man,
> If not to men, to Gods. (p. 797)

The advent of Herakles, with its influx of "light and life/ And warmth and bounty and hope and joy," (p. 798) is delineated in terms that go beyond the pagan myth to Christianity. He is not only the Euripidean heroic adventurer, but, as Douglas Bush puts it, "the supreme example of the poet's favourite mythological type, the divine helper of mankind."[13] Ryals calls Herakles "a Greek hero made Christ-like."[14] He is the "Helper of our world." (p. 802) As Margaret Oliphant, reviewing the poem in the *Edinburgh Review* of January 1872, remarked:[15]

> He [Euripides] has left it as human problems have to be left so often, without explanation, a revelation of the dread gaps and breaks that come into life, without any suggestion of a cure or even any strong sense of its necessity. He goes off into an easier, arbitrary world of gods and miracles with a light heart, ignoring all the difficulties. But not so Browning.

Browning puts great emphasis on the restoration scene, where the element of dramatic suspense is not so important as the final testing of Admetos' regenerated self, carried to great lengths to prove him "Risen to the heights of her." (p. 807)

The filtering of the Greek myth with Christian connotations is one step in transposing the past for the purposes of meeting the demands of the present. In the original play, the resolution had been brought about by means of an external agency. But Browning not only reproduces the original version, he goes a step further. With Balaustion's assertion that "One thing may have so may sides," (p. 808) she proceeds to "mould a new/ Admetos, new Alcestis." (p. 808) Once again, her stand is modern rather than Greek. In this particular aspect of Browning's rendering we may discern a characteristic idea of his later poetry, and one that he used as the hub of his arguments in favour of the modern as against the ancient – his insistence on man as the creator of values and not on external structures as repositories of value.

In Balaustion's idealized version of the story, Love is the saviour, the noblest kind of love that is both creative and self-sacrificing. The regenerative powers of love are embodied in the image of the seed:

> Say, does the seed scorn earth and seek the sun?
> Surely it has no other end and aim
> Than to drop, once more die into the ground,
> Taste cold and darkness and oblivion there;
> And thence rise, tree-like grow through pain to joy,
> More joy and most joy, – do man good again. (p. 802)

In Browning's version destiny is not something external to man, it lies in his self-hood. Admetos now speaks the words that had earlier been conspicuous in their absence:

> Let the flesh perish, be perceived no more,
> So thou, the spirit that informed the flesh,
> Bend yet awhile, a very flame above . . . (p. 810)

His nobility matches the perfect goodness of Alcestis; for Balaustion's version makes Admetos a truly just and unselfish king under Apollo's influence. Alcestis convinces him the oneness of her soul with his, so that, in a sense, she cannot be said to have died. But Persephone sends her back from Hades – "Two souls in one were formidable odds." (p. 811) Thus the old myth is modernized to the point where there is no need for a Divine Saviour at all.

Yet even in the midst of this triumphant assertion of the infinite capacities of the individual soul, comes the recognition (as so often in Browning's later poetry) that all affirmation is partial, that the ideal is circumscribed by the actual. Balaustion's idealized version ends on a note of sadness and with a sensitive awareness of the contraries within human existences – its promises and its failures. Nevertheless, *Balaustion's Adventure* marks an important stage in Browning's progress towards affirmation of the importance of the creative self. It also presents vividly Browning's conception of myth as "developing articulations of a truth inherent in the nature of human life."[16]

Aristophanes' Apology is a poem dealing with special pleading and has already been discussed with the other casuistical poems of the later period. In the present context its importance lies in the manner in which Browning uses a debate on poetic theory and practice, not only, as Donald Smalley has shown,[17] to justify his own poetic principles, but to point to the differences between the traditional notions of poetry and the modern.

Aristophanes' rigidly conventional views on life and art represent the orthodoxy of Greek art, which is perfect within its narrow range; while the poetry of Euripides, which seeks to break the bounds of the conventional in the interests of a higher truth, becomes representative of the modern approach to poetry – its realism and psychological insight. For the debate in *Aristophanes' Apology* is not merely one between Comedy and Tragedy, but the wider one between art and morality, sense and soul, between humane realism and a pragmatic naturalism. In Euripides, Browning sees the sympathetic response to mankind's frailties and an upward-looking vision that is desirable even if impossible to realize in totality. Aristophanes' poetic practice is based on utilitarian grounds, and as such rejects the idealism that ennobles. So that, while Euripides is "modern" by virtue of his deeper insight, Aristophanes exemplifies the limitations of the Greek mind that sees the body but not the soul. This idea is further elaborated in the "Parleying with Gerard de Lairesse."

In the "Parleying with Gerard de Lairesse" Browning does not treat a Greek theme directly, but by choosing to parley with a painter who glorified Greek myths in his work, he presents his answer to the contemporary cult of Hellenism.

The poem is centred on the contrast between de Lairesse's art, which seeks to invest a subject with significance by adorning it with mythology, and Browning's own art, realistic, psychological and analytical. He distinctly repudiates the idea that a subject from the past has inherent significance. Browning's emphasis is on the particular treatment given to the subject. It is on this point that Browning crosses swords with the contemporary Hellenists. Idealizing the past, he feels, is no solution for modern ills. To those, like Matthew Arnold, who turned to antiquity to find symbols of values they found lacking in their own times, Browning would say that these symbols had become outdated and outworn. As Douglas Bush puts it: "He thought his vision of the infinite carried him as a modern beyond the finite rationalism of the Greeks. He cannot forgive the Greeks their lack of a satisfying belief in Christian immortality."[18]

It was on a similar count that Master Hughes of Saxe-Gotha's music had been rejected; its technical achievements, however superior, merely obscured and did not illuminate. It offered only empty answers to the problems of temporal existence:

> Is it your moral of Life?
> Such a web, simple and subtle,
> Weave we on earth here in impotent strife,

Backward and forward each throwing his shuttle,
Death ending all with a knife. (XXII, 106-10)

In *Balaustion's Adventure* Browning had asserted that "one thing may have many sides." Now he puts this principle into practice by revealing a totally unsuspected side of Greek mythology. Throughout the "Walk," in which Browning proposes to parallel de Lairesse's creations with his own, Browning employs the double vision. The two interpretations of the myth are not presented successively as in *Balaustion's Adventure*, but simultaneously. As Roma A. King says: "Like Lairesse, he sees and admires the external grandeur of these old figures; unlike Lairesse, however, he discovers beneath their grandeur a human insensitivity and a spiritual void that culminates in despair and ultimately in disintegration."[19]

The series of vignettes highlight the malice of Jove, the cruelty of Artemis ("Not one spark/ Of pity in that steel gray glance," [IX] cruel indifference of Lyda who turned from the satyr's "rustic homage in disdain,/ Saw but the poor uncouth outside of thee," (X) and so changed the satyr's love for her into lust and savagery. Darius and Alexander confronting each other "wrath-molten each,/ Solidified by hate" (XI) are no longer heroes to be admired, but feared for the chaos they bring.

The conclusion reached is that "The dead Greek lore lies buried in the urn/ Where who seeks fire finds ashes." (XIV) This is in consonance with Browning's theory of progress, which holds that "Nothing has been which shall not bettered be/ Hereafter." (XIII) Ultimately, Browning's rejection of Hellenism is based on the belief that a philosophy of life that offered no hope was dead. In "Cleon" Browning had shown that Greek culture had no answer to man's yearnings for something beyond this finite life. All man's progress towards perfection leads to nothing but terrible negation if he does not have this hopeful view of life to cling to. Cleon is tortured by the question: "the years and days, the summers and the springs,/ Follow each other with unwaning powers. . . . What, and the soul alone deteriorates?" (ll. 128-29) To him, a future state "Unlimited in capability/ For joy, as this is in desire for joy" (ll.326-27) seems a figment of his imagination: "Zeus has not yet revealed; and alas,/ He must have done so, were it possible!" (ll. 334-35)

In contrast, Browning presents his Christian view of immortality after death in the "Parleying":

. . . come what will,
What once lives, never dies – what here attains

To a beginning, has no end, still gains
And never loses aught: (IV)

The opposition between these two views is resolved in the lyric which closes the poem. It re-inforces the theme, "All's change, but permanence as well" (CXXIV) that had been presented in *Fifine at the Fair*. Change is no longer an occasion for pessimism, because it is linked with continuity. Langbaum comments of the lyric: "Christianity, Browning implies, makes such realism possible by confirming our deepest intuitions that the vegetation cycle is, indeed, symbolic of our fate after death."[20]

Three poems in *Dramatic Idylls* have themes taken from Greek legend or mythology – "Pheidippides" in the *First Series* (1879) and "Echetlos" and "Pan and Luna" in the *Second Series* (1890). The first two deal with the theme "The great deed ne'er grows small," but in keeping with his artistic theories, the great deeds that Browning celebrates concern the heroic action of unassuming men who do their duty without thought of reward. In each poem the simple nobility of the hero is contrasted with the selfish, time-serving attitude of those in power. Browning's choice of his protagonists is a telling repudiation of conventional notions of the hero. Both are in the tradition of Herakles in *Balaustion's Adventure* the helper of mankind. The great names of Miltiades and Themistokles have been ground to the dust, but the simple heroism of a Pheidippides or of an Echetios can "never decline, but, gloriously as he began/ So to end gloriously." ("Pheidippides," ll. 114-15)

In contrast to "Artemis Prologizes," where Browning presents the action through the mouth of Artemis herself without comment, in the idylls, the narrator stands outside the action, which helps to emphasize its moral significance. The emphasis is on the moral value of each character's response to a particularly testing moment. The subtle working of man's soul is Browning's theme in these later Greek poems, illustrating in practice his views regarding deeper insight in modern poets. The nameless "holder of the Ploughshare" has "a clown's limbs broad and bare," but once the battle is won, he does not stay to seek praise. In contrast to Miltiades, whose first words are about the reward Pheidippides might have received from Pan, the Greek runner praises Pan, rejoices in Athens' victory and has no thoughts of personal gain beyond going home to marry his girl. Douglas Bush points out that the changes Browning makes in the original Greek legend are "mostly in the way of dramatic compression, heightening and realistic verisimilitude."[21] Beyond this, however, Browning's characteristic interpretation of Greek legends makes them a means of asserting fundamental human values which are relevant for all times. In "Pheidippides" and "Echetlos" the idea emerges that when man can labour selflessly to help others for no other reason than the love in his heart, he becomes a prototype of divinity "...the noble, strong man/ Who could race like a god, bear the face of god, whom a god loves so well." ("Pheidippides," l. 112)

The two poems discussed above deal with heroic action and its implications in the mortal world. "Pan and Luna" has for its theme the unpredictability of motivation and action. The Greek myth, as related by Virgil in the third *Georgic*, tells how Luna, the chaste, "full-orbed" moon was enticed by Pan, disguised as a cloud in fluffy wool, and how she followed him to his domain in the woods. The psychological incongruity of the Virgilian interpretation must have struck Browning, so that his narrator qualifies the original, Virgilian version – " and so she followed" (l.99) – with his own line, "In her sleep/ Surely." (ll.99-100) In the context of the *Idylls* the poem emphasizes the difficulty of making absolute judgements about "what's under lock and key/ Man's soul." (Epilogue; *Second Series*) This is Browning's way of seeing deeper, of linking psychological veracity with the imaginative faculty. Mere sensuous beauty is not enough, neither is mere grandeur. Both must be psychologically true.

In "Ixion" (*Jocoseria*, 1883) Browning sets himself against the Greek idea of malign destiny. The Christian concept of the immortality of the soul and of a beneficent loving Being exerted too strong a hold on his imagination for Browning to accept the idea of eternal punishment. In *Aristophanes' Apology* he had expressed the idea that the arbitrariness of the gods nullifies their divinity. Herakles says of Hera – " What she has willed, that brings her will to pass/ . . . who would pray/ To such a goddess?" (p. 871) It is inconceivable that deeds done in ignorance should be punished, for if punishment exists, ignorance and illusion must be dispersed so that man can choose between right and wrong:

> What were the need but of pitying power to touch and disperse it,
> Film-work – eye's and ear's – all the distraction of sense?
> How should the soul not see, not hear, perceive and as plainly
> Render in thought, word, deed, back again the truth – not a lie?
>
> (ll.37-40)

Man can only worship a being that reciprocates fully his own love, faith and hope. So Ixion's imagination soars "past Zeus to the Potency over him." Thus Browning's protagonist turns away from the Greek concept of Gods who use man for "a purpose of hate," (l.4) who pay the price of man's endeavour by striking him down, to an assertion of the values of striving and aspiration until "despair's murk mist blends in a rainbow of hope." (l.116)

Once again, one can see Browning's modernizing influence at work in his treatment of an ancient Greek legend. For Browning's hero is not the treacherous murderer and ingrate that Ixion is in Virgil's *Georgics*. The Ixion in the *Dramatic Idylls* is rather the injured party, in that Zeus had first encouraged him to look upon himself as an equal and friend of the gods at Olympus, and then wreaked vengeance on him for presuming to love Hera. Therefore, says DeVane, "Browning voices the revolt of an outraged humanity in the manner of Shelley in *Prometheus Unbound*, against the heartless decree of the tyrant."[22] Browning's conception of godhood would rather emphasize its "grand benevolence," as in his delineation of Herakles and Pan. He makes Balaustion say:

> I think that this is the authentic sign and seal
> Of Godship, that it ever waxes glad,
> And more glad, until gladness blossoms, bursts
> Into a rage to suffer for mankind,
> And recommence at sorrow: (*Balaustion's Adventure*, p. 802)

The most convincing evidence of Browning's antagonism to the Hellenist position in his translation of the *Agamemnon of Aeschylus* in 1877. Sutherland Orr, in her biography of the poet, makes the following comment:

> Mr. Browning's deep feeling for the humanities of Greek literature, and his almost passionate love for the language, contrasted strongly with his refusal to regard even the first of the Greek writers as models of literary style. The pretensions raised for them on this ground were inconceivable to him; and his translation of the *Agamemnon* published in 1877, was partly made, I am convinced, for the pleasure of exposing these claims and of rebuking them. His preface to the transcript gives evidence of this. (p. 294)

It is clear that Browning translated the Agamemnon in a meticulously literal manner in order to expose the claims of Arnold and the other Hellenists of the day about the fitness of Greek themes of treatment in modern art. The following excerpt from the preface bears ample testimony to this fact:

> Fortunately, the poorest translation, provided only it be faithfull, though it reproduce all the artistic confusion of tenses, moods, and persons, with which the original teems, – will not only suffice to display what an eloquent friend maintains to be the all-in-all of poetry – "the action of the piece" – but may help to illustrate his assurance that "the Greeks are the highest models of expression, the

> unapproached masters of the grand style: their expression is so excellent because it is so admirably kept in its right degree of prominence, because it is so simple and so well subordinated, because it draws its force directly from the pregnancy of the matter which it conveys . . . not a word wasted, not a sentiment capriciously thrown in, stroke on stroke!" So may all happen!
>
> (Preface to the *Agamemnon of Aeschylus*, pp. 511-12)

Browning was evidently thinking of Arnold's position in the Preface to the *Poems* of 1852. His own preface can be seen as an ironical retort.

Thus, Browning finds neither Greek philosophy nor Greek art suitable for present-day conditions. In the "Parleying with de Lairesse" (as also in "Cleon" in the earlier phase) he gives his opinion of the former:

> What was the best Greece babbled of as truth?
> "A shade, a wretched nothing, – sad, thin, drear,
> Cold, dark, it holds on to the lost loves here,
> If hand have haply sprinkled o'er the dead
> Three charitable dust-heaps, made mouth red
> One moment by the sip of sacrifice;
> Just so much comfort thaws the stubborn ice
> Slow-thickening upward till it choke at length
> The last faint flutter craving – not for strength,
> Not beauty, not the riches and the rule
> O'er men that made life life indeed". Sad school
> Was Hades! (XIV)

His opinions of Greek art are embodied in "Old Pictures in Florence" and in the "Parleying with Lairesse." But what Browning rejects are not the Greek myths and legends in themselves, but those particular interpretations of them that have uncritically invested them with value. In "Development" (*Asolando*, 1889) Browning explains the importance of mythology as a "guardian sheath" for "fact's essence." In his own poems Browning successfully demonstrates the vitality that could be infused into Greek themes provided they were made psychologically relevant to the modern situation.

NOTES

1. *The Poetical Works of Matthew Arnold*, ed. Tinker and Lowry (London: Oxford University Press, 1950), p. xx.
2. *Letters of RB and EBB*, I, p. 43.

3. *Ibid.*, II, p. 710.
4. DeVane, *Handbook*, p. 117.
5. *Mythology and the Romantic Tradition in English Poetry*, p. 364.
6. "A Parleying with Aristophanes," *PMLA*, 55 (1940), pp. 823-38.
7. Quoted in *Browning: The Critical Heritage*, ed. Litzinger and Smalley, p. 359.
8. DeVane, *Handbook*, p. 352.
9. Joseph R. Friend, "Euripides Browningised," *Victorian Poetry*, 2 (1964), p. 186.
10. Clyde de L. Ryals, *Browning's Later Poetry*, p. 41.
11. Robert Langbaum, "Browning and the Question of Myth" in *The Modern Spirit*, p. 86.
12. DeVane, *Handbook*, p. 335. See also DeVane, "Browning and the Spirit of Greece" in *Nineteenth Century Studies*, ed. H. Davis, W.C. Devane, and R.C. Bald (Ithaca: Cornell University Press, 1940).
13. *Mythology and the Romantic Tradition in English Poetry*, p. 371.
14. *Browning's Later Poetry*, p. 35.
15. *Browning: The Critical Heritage*, pp. 365-66.
16. Robert Langbaum, *The Poetry of Experience: The Dramatic Monologue in Modern Literary Tradition*, 1957 (rpt. Penguin University Books, 1974), p. 6.
17. cf. "A Parleying with Aristophanes."
18. *Mythology and the Romantic Tradition in English Poetry*, p. 385.
19. *The Focusing Artifice*, p. 261.
20. *The Modern Spirit*, p. 98.
21. Douglas Bush, p. 376.
22. DeVane, *Handbook*, p. 470.

NARRATIVE ART – THE LONGER POEMS

In a significantly large portion of the later poetry, Browning dispenses with the dramatic monologue and uses the form of the narrative. This shift is important in view of the rise of the novel as the dominant literary form in the nineteenth century. A wide-ranging mind such as Browning's could not but respond to the new impetus. The development of the novel towards a more inward rendering of experience was matched by Browning's creation of complex effects within the dramatic monologue.

Scholes and Kellogg are of the opinion that the "tendency of modern novelists to shy away from full omniscience in one direction or another . . . is tied to certain changes in the entire cultural climate which have made some facets of this nineteenth century device untenable in the twentieth century."[1] A crucial change lay in what Langbaum terms "the modern habit of allowing the literary work to establish its own literary judgement."[2] This could only be achieved through a rigorously objective presentation. Browning's dramatic monologues are a step in this direction. The form is, in fact, the ideal solution to the modern novelist's problem of presenting the mind of a character without having recourse to the authorial voice.

But, as Wayne Booth has shown in his masterly book *The Rhetoric of Fiction*, complete objectivity is a myth. He points out that "the emotions and judgements of the implied author are . . . the very stuff out of which great fiction is made."[3] For Browning, too, art was a means of telling the truth "obliquely." As he put it in *The Ring and the Book* – the writer may "write a book shall mean, beyond the facts,/ Suffice the eye and save the soul beside." (XII, 866-67) Browning himself probably realized that though dramatic indirection afforded opportunities for discrimination and qualification, the dramatic monologue was, of necessity, a brief vignette, positing a narrow range of viewpoints, and so did not always allow a completely unequivocal exposure of the truth. In *The Ring and the Book* Browning had sought to present a completer truth through multiple viewpoints raised through the pattern created by nine speakers. But, as John Killham points out, "the method of juxtaposing his monologues within the framework of explicit moral condemnation destroys the irony which elsewhere so stimulates the reader into admiration of his art."[4]

Browning's problem in his later period was to find a way to express truths while at the same time abjuring narrative omniscience. In the longer narrative poems, he holds in tension differing sets of ideas and viewpoints, sometimes controlling them through the consciousness of a narrator so that he has the simultaneous advantage of dramatic presentation and a wider range of perceptions. Thus, dramatic projection combined with a multiplicity of interrelated perspectives is the method adopted by Browning to present the ambiguous multiplicity of reality as also to derive moral values from it. The importance of this method lies in its continued use by twentieth century novelists as a way of giving the reader the multi-faceted "feel" of an experience.

Red Cotton Night-Cap Country (1873) is not only an attempt by Browning to study another morbid case of the soul, it is also an exploration from a different angle of the major theme of *Fifine at the Fair*—the conflict between the flesh and the spirit and the deceptiveness of appearances. But while in *Fifine*, the action is "internalized" and the problem a more or less hypothetical one (at least till the end), in *Red Cotton Night-Cap Country* external scene and event provide the base for a well-developed narrative line which gives Browning's speculations an air of immediacy. His concern in the poem is much the same as in *The Ring and the Book*—to delve into a sordid tale devoid of conventional poetic beauty for meaningful values. It is a process of moral exploration that ultimately transforms inert "facts" into "a thing/of truth."

In *The Ring and the Book* the dramatic exposition of the same incident by a number of characters from their own particular point of view lends to a shift in the focus from the action of the story (which is narrated in Book I) to the character's comprehension of that action. The focus-character's view initially appears to illuminate the central issue, but really tends to illuminate the viewer himself. But in *Red Cotton Night-Cap Country* Browning adopts only minimally this dramatically expressive point of view technique of presenting character and event simultaneously. His method is rather to focus the action through a narrator, who in this case is not directly involved in the story, but whose interest in it serves as means of directing attention to and laying emphasis on significant aspects of the story. The narrator assumes almost the same significance as he does in the fiction of Henry James and Conrad, a means of limiting and controlling the area and even the nature of the reader's responses.

It is important to note that in *Red Cotton Night-Cap Country* the narrator is the author himself; so that Browning really has recourse to two narrative voices—the one, that of the omniscient recorder of factual matter, and the other, the tentative ambivalent voice of someone who is feeling his way through arid "fact" to the psychological "truth," apportioning to it value in terms of moral action. It is when he assumes the latter voice as will be shown during the analysis of the poem, that Browning comes very close to using a technique characteristic of modern fiction, whose object is what Conrad termed a "moral discovery" – not the illustration of a preconceived moral truth, but by the very fact of artistically ordering certain facets of life, making a discovery about the meaning of life itself.

The poem opens with a firmly sketched-in, minutely observed descriptive backcloth which provides that "air of reality (solidity of specification),"[5] that Henry James so admired and whose outward clarity serves to define the artist's essential concern with "soul," to show that a person

> . . . if he lack not soul, may learn to know,
> Earth's ugliest walled and ceiled imprisonment
> May suffer, through its single rent in roof,
> Admittance of a cataract of light . . . (p. 372)

Browning's expansiveness, as he proceeds from an exposition of different kinds of night-caps and, surprisingly, violins, to an "incident of Ninety-Two, has special advantages." It allows him a variety of effects not possible in a more restricted, tightly ordered field. There is the tongue-in-cheek irony that laughs good-naturedly at the priggishness of small-town mentality in his description of the little church, "Our brand-new stone cream coloured masterpiece." (p. 372) The urbane, conversational tone creates an impression of normality that will contrast effectively with the actual tale of self-mutilation and suicide, and also serves to familiarize the reader with an important motif in the poem – the Church of Ravissante. The under-current of satire in Browning's treatment of the theme of religious superstition will have echoes throughout the poem and will function importantly in the presentation of Miranda's case. Further, Browning's ironic technique of frequently presenting events in the actual voices of the participants varies his narrative tone. J. Hillis Miller calls this "the method of indirection" and describes the movement of the poem as spiral one: "The idea is to reach the depths by lingering on the surface, by just that 'prolonged hovering flight of the subjective over the outstretched ground of the case supposed' for which James praised Conrad."[6]

Browning first presents Miranda as he appeared to the society around him and describes Clairvaux (Miranda's country-home) and especially the tower that he has built in terms of normal supposition. But appearances can be deceptive; and in his role of perceptive narrator, Browning notes "a sense that something is amiss,/ Something out of sorts in the display." (p. 380) The narrative tension is upheld at this point by two conflicting points of view: the auditor's, that insists on the "whiteness" or normalcy of what is being retold, which contrasts with the "redness" that the narrator seeks to demonstrate. This dual argument slowly builds up to an enunciation of the primary motifs which form the poem's symbolic frame of reference – "Notion of outside mound and inside mash,/ Towers yet intact round turfy rottenness." (p. 385)

The twin contrasted symbols of tower and turf, the former standing for the self-indulgent life of the flesh and the latter, the life of the spirit, with its struggle for self-mastery, are employed as a means of formal control over the massed details and are expressive of the moral intent of the poem. For Miranda's case, as the narrator sees it and is concerned to make the readers see, is essentially a problem of faith and of mistaken choices. Both the emotional and intellectual background to Miranda's problem is rendered in detail. Moliere's Sganarelle plays the role of the artful schemer, helping to salve a guilty conscience, (a role played by Sagacity in Prince Hohenstiel-Schwangau), advocating – "Youth, strength and lustihood can sleep on turf/Yet pace the stony platform afterward." (p. 387)

In the succeeding sections, Browning uses the epistolary method (Miranda's "airy record to a confidant") to dramatize the narrative, while building up through repetition of the symbols the strife within Miranda and his inability to make a firm moral base that would make it valid. "Trust me, I know the world, and know myself,/ And know where duty takes me – in good time!" (p. 389) Browning's ironical treatment of Miranda's dilettantish attitude reveals itself obliquely through his style. The technique of commentary from Miranda's viewpoint provides a more cogent picture of Miranda's character than direct comment: "At all points thus against illusion armed" – the very diction demands that the statement be read ironically.

The description of the meeting between Miranda and Clara, given in a tempo that has been speeded up to correspond to Miranda's flurried and fervent actions, is followed by slow-paced comment: "Truth I say, truth I mean, this love was true." (p. 390) But even so, moral definiteness is absent, for the narrator is aware of contradictions inherent in the situation:

> . . . there exists
> A falsish false, for truth's inside the same,
> And truth that's only half true, falsish truth. (p. 390)

The objective account of Clara's past history varied by recourse to a dramatic mode of third person commentary representing society gossip and direct presentation of Miranda's reactions: "Renounce the world for them – some day I will:/ Meantime, to me let her become the world." (p.

394) The ambiguity from Miranda's situation is highlighted. On the one hand, the narrator builds up an idea of the weakness in his character through direct comment: "Monsieur Leonce Miranda, meant to lean/By nature" (p. 394); and again:

> Monsieur Leonce Miranda probably
> Had else been loath to cast the mask aside,
> So politic, so self-preservative,
> Therefore so pardonable – though so wrong! (p. 395)

On the one hand, the narrator provides a foil by using particular incidents to portray Miranda's confused impulsiveness: his attempt to reproduce Parisian tastes at Clairvaux, his destruction of the old Norman priory. The incidents are so shaped as to inform our sense of character. Miranda's indecisiveness is not wholly of his own making; his mother further compounds it by ordering "Keep both halves, yet do no detriment/ To either!" (p. 399)

The heralding of the New Year, described by Browning in vivid poetic imagery, introduces another phase in Miranda's life. The crucial scene of Miranda's summons to his mother's death-bed has all the compelling vividness of Browning's best dramatic manner, while its significance is integrated into the symbolic framework:

> The tawdry tent, pictorial, musical,
> Poetical, besprent with hearts and darts;
> Its cobwebwork, betinselled stitchery,
> Lay dust about our sleeper on the turf,
> And showed the outer towers distinct and dread. (p. 402)

Beyond this Browning as narrator declines to either comment or analyze. The conflict within Miranda is not particularized except now and then, through telling phrases. The emphasis here is on the ironical portrayal of the money-grubbing Cousinry, through dialogue and visual particulars. The Cousinry help to enhance the complexity of the points of reference by which Miranda is to be ultimately judged. And because the narrative has told us what to make of the main character, not directly, but through the manipulation of the symbols of the tower, turf and intermediary tent, and also shown the character objectively, we can move to the next important episode with our expectations clear and intense.

The climactic scene of the burning of Miranda's hands is delineated by means of four different voices and is open to four different interpretations: that of the protagonist himself, to whom the burning of his hands becomes a sacrificial rite to achieve purity; the doctor, who pronounces his patient to be mad; the narrator, who finds in the concept of the distinction between the body and the soul, an explanation for Miranda's being "insensible to pain," and the Cousinry, who see in this an incentive to hasten their "purpose of reform." What follows is concentrated narrative that carries forward the action swiftly towards the next major event. The insistent use of the symbolic tower and turf to denote the twin impulses of Miranda's being is one means of imposing unity over the narrative structure. More interesting to the reader is Browning's concern, later developed so finely by Henry James, of illuminating his character's concern with the meaning of what is happening; so that the narrative can be said to encompass the development of the character's consciousness about life. Browning's aim here is the direct apprehension of the "truth," not just a partial point of view. And since truth's source is the human mind, an evaluation of truth necessarily becomes an evaluation of character.

But this evaluation differs from the process in a dramatic monologue. As Langbaum observes, "the dramatic monologue must at some point be abandoned where logical completeness is desired."[7] In *Red Cotton Night-Cap Country* we have a balance between the inside and the outside points of view that is reminiscent of a novel by Conrad: a filtering of the action through the consciousness of the main character, what it meant to him, what difference it made to him, and what difference it made in him, and also a general perspective, created mainly by the narrator's expository comments, which prevents the reader from uncritically identifying himself with the character's thoughts. But even here, the narrator is not omniscient, but rather concerned to throw as much light as possible on the action in order to aid judgement.

The digression on Milsand, who, according to the narrator, was better equipped to help Miranda "on the path/ Of rectitude" (p. 408) than conventional channels, prefaces another on the bases of faith and belief. Economy here is sacrificed in the interests of detailed exposition of what the narrator believes to be the proper area for analysis – the actions emerging from a man's beliefs and not the beliefs themselves. This theme adds an extra dimension to Browning's examination of the well-springs of human motive and action. As in *The Ring and the Book*, the institutions of revealed religion are inadequate guides. Browning sets Miranda's case against a religious background to emphasize the disparity between a cold-blooded, superficial dogma, devoid of intrinsic moral quality and an anguished quest for faith, however misguided. Miranda's doublings and twistings under the grip of circumstance are viewed sympathetically by the narrator – "According to his lights, I praise the man." (p. 411)

The actual scene of Miranda's jump from the tower, at once an emotional and moral crisis, is presented dramatically, an actual rendering of the event as it appeared to the character at the moment of its occurrence, the result of which is to make vivid and concrete what takes place deep within Miranda's soul. The narrator remains impersonal, the reader is invited to form his own judgements about the validity of Miranda's action. Browning's concern is with exposing a very compelling human situation to our view, and his narrative method awakens the perception of the reader.

Miranda seeks not to evade issues but to come to terms with them. It is what Conrad describes in *Lord Jim* as "the struggles of an individual trying to save from the fire his idea of what his moral identity should be."[8] The intensity derives from the juxtaposition of concepts – strength and weakness, despot and enchantress, acorns and life-apples, Queen and the "unrobed One." Miranda's conflict thus becomes one between opposing systems of thought and ways of life. Up till now, the narrator had made no direct comment (except obliquely, through the symbols of turf and tower) on the upheaval within Miranda that had led to various events like his renouncing Clara and then going back to her, his attempted suicide and the burning of his hands. Now he provides the rationale for these acts by dramatizing Miranda's inner conflicts. Miranda's speech is one-sided argument, yet the implied dramatic interplay between different perspectives gives added depth. The method of rhetorical questions gives his heart-searching a poignancy reminiscent of Lord Jim's. Like Jim, Miranda seems to be involved in "a dispute with an invisible personality, an antagonistic and inseparable partner of his existence – another possessor of his soul."[9] Like Jim, Miranda complicates rather than resolves issues by being so sensitive yet so naive. For him, the problem is just "managing to live on terms with both/ Opposing potentates, the Power and you," (p. 415) and its solution, an expression of indomitable faith in the miracle-working Virgin of Ravissante, and, as a means of pleasing her by this show of faith, leaping down from the high tower.

It is remarkable how Browning conditions our responses to Miranda through the diction even while remaining withdrawn in his narrator's stance. The first part of Miranda's speech reveals a tendency in him to think of his situation in terms of a bargain to be struck with the Ravissante. The frequent use of words like gain, loss, plain-dealing, instalment, purchase, tribute-money, is typical of this attitude. It is this reduction of a complex problem to such simplistic terms that leads to Miranda's self-delusion. In a manner similar to Conrad's exposure of Lord Jim, Miranda's emotional stresses are revealed from the inside by Browning, without any explicit judgement; but on the whole, the narrator's attitude to his confusions and somewhat immature reactions is one of sympathy and understanding. "I see no slightest sign/ Of folly," (p. 412) he says. We remember Marlow saying in Conrad's story: "It was tragic enough and funny enough in all conscience to call aloud for compassion, and in what was I better than the rest of us to refuse him my pity?"[10]

Miranda's fervent, exalted faith, even if self-centred, contrasts favourably with the cynicism of the clergy, who opine: "What folly does the madman expect?/ No faith obtains – in this late age, at least – / Such cure as that! We ease rheumatics, though!" (p. 414) Thus, Browning provides the material for a correct assessment without intrusive commentary. At the climax of his peroration, Miranda enlarges his own problem of faith for the world at large, but his position is not maintained, once more underlining his essential weakness. Miranda's leap is, in his own eyes, the resolution of his "Spiritual effort to compound for fault/ By payment of devotion." (p. 411) The gardener, who witnesses the catastrophe, emphasizes the irony inherent in the situation by his remark – "Angels would take him! Mad!" (p. 417) Just as Jim's action is assessed not by Marlow alone but by others like Chester who says: "What's all the to-do about? A bit of ass's skin . . . . You must see things exactly as they are . . ." (p. 125); and the French lieutenant: "And what life may be worth when ... the honour is gone – *ah ca! par exemple* – I can offer no opinion," (p. 115) so Miranda's action admits of different interpretations.

Browning's pointed intervention, using his authorial voice at this juncture, serves to minimize the tension, detaching the reader from the experience presented and preparing him for an assessment of the meaning. But before this can be done, the loose ends have to be tidied up in the interests of narrative coherence. Clara's speeches serve not only to round out the action but also to reveal character; her second confrontation with the cousinry shows her unexpected strength and reinforce the theme of the deceptiveness of appearances. In his more overt judgement of Clara's character, Browning uses a fully developed imagery that produces as much a sense of reality as "inside" representation would. As regards the judgements themselves, Browning as narrator deliberately keeps them fluid, for the complexity of interpreting motives precludes simple formulas of right and wrong. The reader's own evaluation, his perception of the significance of events are sought to be played off against a scheme of values, a general perspective which encompasses such favourite Browning theories as "Success is nought, endeavour's all" (p. 422) and "Love bids touch truth, endure truth, and embrace/ Truth, though, embracing truth, love crush itself." (p. 423) If the narrator had earlier praised Miranda – "According to his lights I praise the man," (p. 411) he is now critical – "Miranda hardly did his best with life." (p. 422) Clara is the "happier specimen" and yet we have the implicit irony of his description of the "finished little piece" (p. 422) who, "caterpillar-like" fed on "unlimited Miranda-leaf." (p. 423) Yet along with moral condemnation, there is pity and compassion. To aid our total apprehension of the characters, Browning sketches in, with biting sarcasm, the clergy who should have shown Miranda the true path, but rather chose to exploit his spiritual confusion for material gain-"trundled money-muck/ To midden and the main heap oft enough." (p. 423)

It was Turgenev who insisted – "Realism by itself is fatal – truth, however powerful, is not art."[11] It is interesting to note that Browning met the Russian author in 1871, during grouse-shooting in the Highlands.[12] In Turgenev's art, Browning may have found a corroboration of his intention of looking at real life, not as mere facts in themselves, but only through the human soul and in their effects upon personality. So that, in *Red Cotton Night-Cap Country* Browning "is not a journalist reporting the bold external facts of Miranda's case."[13] Through the use of a narrative persona, he assumes the role of the narrator as enquirer. His aim is "Truth, and nothing else" (p. 425); the imagery of light which Browning uses in this connection – flash, blaze, effulgence, reveals the illuminating nature of this experience of interpretation and evaluation. As in Conrad's fiction, the superiority of imaginative truth over empirical truth is affirmed.

Apart from its interest as a further attempt by Browning to find meaningful values in sordid matters, *The Inn Album* (1875) is noteworthy because of its special methods as regards structure and narrative technique. Most commentators have noted its affinities with the drama and the novel. Roma A. King writes: "*The Inn Album* does give evidence of having been conceived as drama."[14] Felgar comments: "Browning is trying to beat the novelists at their own game by having the best of both worlds, the concentration and intensity of poetry, in addition to the realism and melodrama of Dickens and Thackeray".[15] Philip Drew is of the opinion that "it gives the feeling of Victorian life that we find and value in the great novelists."[16] The present reading holds that through this unique combination of drama and novel, Browning comes very close to the point-of-view method of dramatized consciousness that is characteristic of the artistic achievement of a "modern" novelist like Henry James.

Browning rarely ever told a story for its own sake, and in *The Inn Album*, too, his aim is not merely to tell a sensational story where the plot is the sole concern and the action has little to do with the personal qualities of the characters. It is the personal reaction to circumstance that remains Browning's central concern, as it is the concern of novelists like James and Conrad. The apparatus of melodrama is used, but because this subserves his artistic vision, there is no sense of contrivance. Browning's intention in this poem is more serious and more imaginative than mere manipulation of curiosity and suspense.

In *Red Cotton Night-Cap Country* the truth of the situation was conceived by Browning in a sudden flash of illumination, but he conveyed it to the reader as meaning in the process of being shaped, exploring the moral implications in a slow, digressive fashion by means of a narrative persona. In *The Inn Album*, however, he achieves concentration and immediacy by adopting a dramatic structure within a narrative framework. The descriptive method is abandoned in favour of dialogue as a medium for advancing action and portraying character. Third-person narrative is pared down to a minimum. *The Inn Album* shows Browning superbly in control of his material, linking the intensity that drama provides with the fullness and completeness of a well-narrated story with all its elements of surprise, climax and excitement.

The story, a sensational one of intrigue, seduction, suicide and murder, is not very remarkable or promising from the aesthetic point of view. But for Browning it provides a base for a reading into human character and motivation. Stevenson remarked: "With each new subject . . . the true artist will vary his method and change the point of attack."[17] Browning does this by so constructing his narrative as to make the conduct of the main characters the subject of debate among themselves. We remember James' remark in this context: "I could think so little of any situation that didn't depend for its interest on the nature of the persons situated and thereby on their way of taking it."[18] The emphasis is on the tactics of presentation through the consciousness of characters rather than through an objective presentation of the author's viewpoint. This is the Jamesian technique of making the presented occasion tell all its story itself. Aesthetic distance is maintained, so that the moral significance emerges as a direct result of our perception of these characters, not as opinions imposed upon us by the author himself.

Browning's narrative in *The Inn Album* takes a single event that has occurred in the past and examines its repercussions on the present lives of all concerned (either directly or indirectly) with it. Both the Elder Man and the Younger Man have loved and lost the same lady, though they realize this only later. The youth has been rescued from a life of stagnation by the "much-experienced man," has been introduced to the pleasures of society life and then been advised to marry the Cousin, who in her turn seeks the advice of her friend, the Lady. The dual perspective of time past and time present at once enriches the narrative, for the past, recaptured in retrospect, at once acquires fresh meaning. The exposition, subtly carried out step by step along with the story, is done through dialogue, the narrator limiting himself to a brief description of the setting and the external features of the characters, which corresponds almost to the stage directions in a play.

The limitation of what we know and think about these characters to what they themselves know and think about each other at this point ensures objectivity. Browning cleverly ensures the reader's interest by maintaining the swift pace of the dialogue, releasing new information in a phased manner and abjuring psychological subtleties at least till we are familiar with the characters. The rich texture of the dialogue is evident from the Younger Man's first speech, which provides an elucidation of the present action: the two men have been playing cards and he, surprisingly, has won; an explication of the relationship between the two men: the Younger Man looks upon himself as a disciple; and a sketch of the social background against which the story is to unfold:

> I'm off for Paris, there's the Opera – there's
> The Salon, there's a china-sale, – beside
> Chantilly; and, for good companionship,
> There's such-and-such and so-and-so. (p. 428)

This last aspect, i.e. the social setting, is an important means of giving physical presence and credible existence to the characters themselves.

The conversations in Section I and II establish the potentialities and motive forces of the two principal characters, which are afterwards made evident by actual events, and also provide an indirect view of the third, the Lady. In true Jamesian manner, the protagonists are like players in a game. With each new revelation of fact in the present and succeeding sections, the situation takes a more meaningful turn. Browning shows a novelist's skill in selecting and accumulating significant detail to highlight the thematic opposition of concepts like innocence and experience, ignorance and knowledge, reason and intuition, vice and virtue and to lay unobtrusively the moral norms against which the characters are to be judged. This method is, as Henry James describes it in the Preface to *The Portrait of a Lady*, the method of a novelist who saw characters as "subject to the chances, the complications of existence, and saw them vividly, but then had to find for them the right relations, those that would most bring them out; to imagine, to invent and select and piece together the situations most useful and favourable to the sense of the creatures themselves, the complications they would be most likely to produce and feel."[19]

The Younger Man's innocence is established by the tone of his conversation with the Elder Man. Initially dazzled by the polished exterior that the Elder Man presents, he yet has gained enough perception from experience to see their relationship in a more realistic light. Nevertheless, commitment has destroyed the initial innocence and even his freedom to act. Experience has also shown him his folly in meekly and humbly accepting his lot, instead of making vigorous efforts to transform the situation. In the case of the Elder Man, experience has brought disillusionment, cynicism and hatred. He is a self-confessed failure: "so hate alike/ Failure and who caused failure." (p. 434) His cold materialism is evinced by the epithets he uses to describe himself – polisher, collector. Yet, even as he recognizes his deeds as "The devils doing," (p. 435) there is in him the saving grace of remorse:

> . . . yet I seem to think
> Now when all's done, – think with 'a head reposed'
> In French phrase – hope I think I meant to do
> All requisite for such a rarity . . . (p. 435)

He has "proved the fool" in misjudging the quality of the woman he has made a proposition to. Experience has brought him a kind of insight, which, in turn, increases his frustration. Each man acknowledges the saving, redeeming power of the woman's love, had it been given. In a crucial passage with tragic overtones the Elder Man speaks:

> But I see. Slowly, surely, creeps
> Day by day over me the conviction – here
> Was life's prize grasped at, gained, and then let go!
> That with her – may be, for her, – I had felt
> Ice in me melt, grow steam, drive to effect
> Any or all the fancies sluggish here
> In the head that needs the hand she would not take
> And I shall never lift now. (p. 437)

A little later comes our first intimation that the fault may not be wholly one-sided:

> Therefore I hate myself – but how much worse
> Do not I hate who would not understand,
> Let me repair things – no, but sent a-slide
> My folly falteringly, stumblingly
> Down, down and deeper down . . . (p. 437)

But lest we tend to sympathize too closely with this man, Browning would have us judge the quality of his reactions by juxtaposing them with the simplicity of the Younger Man's "I can't hate." (p. 434) It is this multiplication of view-points that highlights the significance of a character's perception of the particular situation, and at the same time gives us a sense of his character, even while it reinforces Browning's view of the essentially paradoxical nature of human behaviour and of the tentativeness of all judgements about it.

Having deliberately given up the digressive privileges of the traditional narrative form, Browning uses a well-integrated pattern of imagery and symbol to enrich and deepen the significance of the narrative, and to impose aesthetic order upon his material. The album at the inn is not only symbolic of the main themes of the story – friendship and love, it becomes a means of revealing character, as each person refers to it in his or her own particular manner. For the Elder Man, the Album is a convenient place to scribble accounts in, pointing to his role as a despoiler of innocence. But later, it becomes representative of his inmost thoughts:

> Love once and you love always. Why, it's down
> Here in the Album: every lover knows
> Love may use hate but – turn to hate, itself –
> Turn even to indifference – No, indeed! (p. 451)

The Younger Man reveals his intrinsic honesty when he finds that "To spout like Mister Mild Acclivity/ In album-language" (p. 429) goes against the grain. To the Younger Woman, the album is an inspiration to look at life poetically, but in the concluding section, it aids her task of facing reality with equanimity. The Lady's last reference to the album as she dies confirms our perception of her as a creature of extremes, who sees life solely in terms of black and white. Ryals comments that the Album "becomes symbolic of how truth and seeming are so often at variance."[20] The Eden imagery (with its recurrent references to the fruit of knowledge and the arch-enemy, Satan associated with the serpent) links the poem to the mythic pattern of the fall and redemption, and also emphasizes its character as a morality probing human codes and values. In a similar way, James attempts to increase the evocativeness of his narrative by the images of the dove and the serpent in *The Wings of the Dove* and a symbolic use of the flawed bowl in *The Golden Bowl*.

The probing of the inner life demands that the author delve deep into the subconscious. But much more takes place in the minds of the characters than they would speak out in everyday life. In order to communicate that "more" without stepping in himself as the omniscient author, Browning throws his characters into situations that call for evaluation of past conduct and of present positions. Thus, in Conrad's *Lord Jim,* Marlow's sympathetic interest leads Jim to unburden his inner confusions in a manner in which the unspoken is more revealing than the explicit. In *The Inn Album* the conflict between the Younger Woman's romantically naive view of love and marriage and the Lady's view which proceeds from "sad apprenticeship," in Section III, creates a similar situation. The girl looks upon her friend's married life as "trellised bliss/ Of blush-rose bower" and "One fairy tent with pitcher leaves that held/ Wine and a flowery wealth of suns and moons,/ And magic fruits whereon angels feed." (p. 442) In contrast, the Lady terms her married life as "Inferno." (p. 444) The allusiveness of Browning's art can be seen in the manner in which he packs dialogue with meaning: when the Younger Woman laughingly composes poetry, she refers to love, but the Lady thinks of death and oblivion. This is the indirect and oblique view of the characters that provides the "psychological reason,"[21] as James puts it.

The girl's terror ("face struck sudden white") is the outcome of her view of the murky depths of experience and of her sudden realization that her innocence is "easy ignorance." (p. 443) Further contrast between the girl's spontaneity and the elder woman's reticence ("You were/ Are, ever will be the locked lady," [p. 444]) is important in the light of subsequent developments, when her love for her friend is eclipsed by her love for the Younger Man, and when, in her innocence, she adopts a more positive attitude than has been possible for the more experienced woman.

Another situation of the same kind is created by the unexpected meeting of the Elder Man and the Lady at the inn parlour. It is a confrontation that leads each to accusation, explanation and justification. The process is more revealing of character and motivation than either intends or is aware of. Each is brought face to face with the ugly realities of existence devoid of love.

The conflict in Section IV is between acceptance of mistake, acknowledged with humble sincerity and a rigid pride of self-righteousness. Langbaum's remark with regard to the dramatic monologue is apt in this situation – "extraordinary motives in Browning come not from disordered subconscious urges, but, as in Henry James, from the highest moral and intellectual refinement."[22] And Browning's moral discrimination is as keen as James'. In the case of the lady, her moral sensitivity, laudable in itself, has encouraged self-deception; the refined sensibility has hardened into a conventional morality that becomes an end in itself, unresponsive to the actual issues of living. Her idealism is suspect. We have in her the kind of moral and emotional inadequacy involved in George Eliot's vision of the latter-day St. Theresas. Her martyred effacement of personality is not the redemptive action that she believes it to be. In chasing the chimera of the ideal, divorced from the real, she has deliberately rejected life in favour of a kind of spiritual death. Instead of using the Elder Man's confession as a means of purifying and deepening their relationship, she retreats behind a facade of martyred indignation and misguided idealism. She ignores the Elder Man's plea that her "angelic potency/ Lift me from out perdition's deep of deeps/ To light and life and love!" (p. 453) and instead retaliates in what the narrator calls "the hard, grey, grimly comic speech." (p. 454) In her "crowned contempt" she calls the Elder Man the "Arch-Cheat" and "the Adversary." But the ironical possibility emerges that her attitude has made him so. She has misused her potentialities for good. Hers is not the liberal and awakened sensibility that cuts across the surface of evil to the essential core of goodness. We remember in this context Browning's words in *Fifine at the Fair*:

> But touched aright, prompt yield each particle its tongue
> Of elemental flame, – no matter whence flame sprung
> From gums and spice, or else from straw and rottenness,
> So long as soul has power to make them burn. (LV)

Section V increases the complexity of the situation with the arrival of the Younger Man. But now that the facts are known, the emphasis is on the thoughts of each character about the situation at hand. Browning dramatizes the consciousness of each, as each is allowed the interpretations, inferences and explanations of which he or she alone is capable. Browning's narrative art at this point encompasses not so much the kind of psychological analysis presented in a dramatic monologue, but, as in Henry James, "the dramatic presentation of mental states as the characters themselves are conscious of them."[23] Simultaneously, however, an outside view of the characters is also provided thorough the subtle balancing of the dialogue, so that the presentation and evaluation proceed hand-in-hand. It is in this creation of multiple viewpoints, which in their inter-relationship define the conditions of the story and highlight its significance, that Browning shows his affinities with the technique of the modern novel.

The three-pronged situation of emotional conflict further reveals character at the same time that it advances the action. Browning shows his technical maturity in overcoming his reluctance (a reluctance which had proved a major drawback during his early experiments with drama) to give his characters only those qualities that are strictly necessary for the action. The Youth has advanced in his knowledge of the ways of the world, and though he says miserably "There's no unknowing what one knows" there is no trace in him of cynicism or of negation. His love for the Lady is intensely loyal:

> . . . Half an hour ago,
> I held your master for my best of friends;
> And now I hate him! Four years since, you seemed
> My hearts one love: well, and you so remain! (p. 455-56)

The Lady's stance as teacher and moral superior is ironical. Her words reveal the extent of her self-delusion and pride – "in my verdict lies your fate" (p. 456) and "That reptile capture you? I conquered him." (p. 457)

The most telling evidence against the Lady comes in glimpse of her duplicity; happiness in love, as she conceives it, is based on ignorance. She advises the Younger Man: "Never let her know/ How near came taint of your companionship!" (p. 457) She reveals an essential confusion of mind as to values – ignorance she calls a sin, yet she would have her husband remain ignorant of her past because that would abolish his faith in her as "pure and true." The idea emerges that for her, external impression counts a great deal. In the light of the narrator's indication of the change wrought in the Elder Man:

> "Ah" – draws a long breath with a new strange look
> The man she interpellates – soul a-stir
> Under its covert, as, beneath the dust,
> A coppery sparkle all at once denotes
> The hid snake has conceived a purpose (p. 457)

The lady's contention, "I yearn to save/ And not to destroy," (p. 457) shows itself as false. Experience and knowledge for her have not been nurturing, fostering influences. Her unbending attitude has destroyed the last vestiges of faith and truth in the Elder Man, and leads to his final descent to dastardly behaviour. In the succeeding section, (VI) he becomes Satan, tempting the Youth to "strip the tree/ Of fruit desirable to make one wise." (p. 462)

In Section VII, the tension between the protagonists is resolved in the clarity of discovery. The crisis has forced on each a sharper insight. The Lady now sees herself as blameworthy:

> I do believe I should have straight assumed
> My proper function, and sustained a soul,
> – Nor aimed at being sustained myself
> By some man's soul – the weaker woman's want! (p. 463)

The Young Man sees very clearly his duty – to rescue, redeem, avenge and protect. He has put his new experience and knowledge to fruitful action. His humility – "redeem myself/ The stupidest of sinners" (p. 464) highlights by ironic contrast the selfish obtuseness of the Lady:

> . . . Blame I take
> Nowise upon me as I ask myself
> – You – how can you, whose soul I seemed to read
> The limpid eyes through, have declined so deep
> Even with him for consort? (p. 462)

Unlike the narrator in *Red Cotton Night-Cap Country* the narrator in *The Inn Album* studiously avoids giving any explicit opinion about the Lady. Yet, we are subtly made aware of the inadequacies in her character, chiefly through the overtones in her speeches. The Elder Man, with his sordid proposal, arouses in her an almost physical revulsion ("Takes it as you tough carrion.") Roma A. King interprets this as an instance of "her maturity, her simultaneous devotion to the ideal and her clearheaded awareness of the ways of the world."[24] On the other hand, viewed in the light of the violent imagery that she uses – serpent, poison-seed, leprosy, plague-spot – we might see the extreme nature of her reactions as a symptom of her exaggerated refinement. The contrast with the simple, sincerely unpretentious nature of the Young Man's words is pointed.

The climax, when the Young Man springs upon the Elder Man and kills him and the Lady chooses her own "refining fire" by committing suicide, is handled with reticence and economy. There is a minimum of emotional display, but Browning maintains the dramatic tension by focusing attention on character as it emerges from the incident.

For the problem of incident has been resolved; what remains to be resolved is the matter of interpretation. Browning directs our attention to the point of intense interest – the ambiguity of the lady's character as an off-shoot of the paradoxical nature of all moral ideals and the tentativeness of all judgements. If the Lady's suicide is an affirmation of her devotion to the ideal, it is also seen as an escapist's way of coping with reality. We remember as an instance in contrast, Isabel Archer's proud assertion in *The Portrait of a Lady* "One must accept one's deeds" and her return to a future of moral challenge. A further contrast is presented by Pompilia's compassionate magnanimity in her dying moments: "I am saved through him/ So as by fire; to him – thanks and farewell." (*The Ring and the Book*, VII, 1738-39) In *The Inn Album* the Lady's reaction to the murder – "And that was good but useless," (p. 468) and her last references to the dead man as

"Villain," and "fool" – emphasize her hard, unforgiving nature. Unlike the positive idealism of the Youth, her idealism has led to negation. Her last words are characteristically full of the rhetoric that has throughout been the giveaway of her misguided line of action. It is significant that the narrator never makes the kind of explicitly approving remark with regard to the lady as he does with regard to the Youth and the Younger Woman, who are called the "good, strong fellow" and the "good, gay girl" respectively.

Thus, while one can agree with Philip Drew that the characters in *The Inn Album* "perform what is almost a masque of Vice and Virtue, enacting a basic conflict,"[25] our agreement has to be qualified with the observation that in keeping with Browning's trend of thought in his later years, these concepts are not viewed as absolutes. One remembers the lines in *The Ring and the Book*:

> Man, like a glass ball with a spark a-top,
> Out of the magic fire that lurks inside,
> Shows one tint at a time to take the eye:
> Which, let a finger touch the silent sleep,
> Shifted a hair's breadth shoots you dark for bright,
> Suffuses bright with dark, and baffles so
> Your sentence absolute for shine or shade. (Bk. I, 1367-73)

These were the years when Browning was becoming increasingly conscious of the subjective nature of judgement; and as Drew himself points out, "He is accordingly more ready to present a speaker without implying a single judgment of him, leaving the reader with the materials for a more tentative judgement."[26] Ultimately, however, Browning's narrative technique is not only concerned with directing judgements, but with carrying the reader thorough the process of the experience itself.

It has been said that "the ambition of the modern novelist is to apprehend the whole of human nature, including its shifting contradictions."[27] Viewed in this light, Browning seems very much the modern novelist, with the "voracious appetite for the salient" that Henry James attributes to Balzac.[28] Browning himself, in his letters, expressed a strong liking for the French novelist[29] and it is not fanciful to suppose that he transposed elements into his poetry that were derived from Balzac's novels. Balzac wrote: "The introduction of the dramatic element, of the image, the picture, of description, of dialogue, seems to me to be indispensable in modern literature. Let us confess frankly that *Gil Blas* is wearisome as form: in the piling up of events and ideas there is something sterile. The idea personified in a character, shows a finer intelligence."[30]

Gilbert Phelps notes that "at first his [Balzac's] version of the search for 'the true,' with its disregard for conventional morality, and of the limits traditionally regarded as proper to literature, inspired almost universal revulsion and the verdict of the *Quarterly Review* of April, 1836 – 'a baser, meaner, filthier rascal never polluted society' – was typical. But, Phelps further writes, "by 1889 Arthur Symons was hailing him as 'One of those divine spies, for whom the world has no secrets'."[31]

The points of affinity between the French novelist and the Victorian poet are evident. In his narrative poetry, Browning sought to create life in all its actuality, the immediate, the unpoetic and the material observed with intimate particularity, but, as Henry James says of Balzac, "with the inner vision all the while wide-awake, the vision for which ideas are as living as facts and assume an equal intensity."[32]

But it is not only as regards the matter that Browning has points of contact with the modern novel, his manner, too, breaks away with the traditional methods of presentation. Henry James wrote in the Introduction to *The Golden Bowl* about his point-of-view techniques:

> I have already betrayed, as an accepted habit, and even to extravagance commented on, my preference for dealing with my subject-matter, for 'seeing my story,' through the opportunity and sensibility of some more or less detached, some not strictly involved, though thoroughly interested and intelligent witness or reporter, some person who contributes to the case mainly a certain amount of criticism and interpretation of it. Again and again, on review, the shorter things in especial that I have gathered into this Series have ranged themselves not as my own impersonal account of the affair in hand, but as my account of somebody's impression of it – the terms of this person's access to it and estimate of it contributing thus by some fine little law to intensification of interest. The somebody is often, among my shorter tales I recognize, but an unnamed, unintroduced and (save by right of intrinsic wit) unwarranted participant, the impersonal author's concrete deputy or delegate, a convenient substitute or apologist. . . . My instinct appears repeatedly to have been that to arrive at the facts retailed and the figures introduced by the given help of some other conscious and confessed agent is essentially to find the whole business – that is, as I say, its effective interest – enriched *by the way*. I have in other words constantly inclined to the idea of the particular attaching case plus some near individual view of it; that

> nearness quite having thus to become an imagined observer's, a projected, charmed painter's or poet's – however avowed the 'minor' quality in the latter – close and sensitive contact with it. Anything, in short, I now reflect must have seemed to me better – better for the process and the effect of representation, my irrepressible ideal – than the mere muffled majesty of irresponsible 'authorship'. . . .

A little further on in the same Preface, James points out a changed narrative technique in *The Golden Bowl* itself:

> There is no other participant, of course, than each of the real, the deeply involved and immersed and more or less bleeding participants; but . . . the whole thing remains subject to the register, ever so closely kept, of the consciousness of but two of the characters. The Prince, in the first half of the book, virtually sees and knows and makes out, virtually represents to himself everything that concerns us . . . and yet after all never a whit to the prejudice of his being just as consistently a foredoomed, entangled, embarrassed agent in the general imbroglio, actor in the offered play. . . .

As we have seen in the preceding analysis of Browning's later narrative art, he too, like James, shows a marked preference for enriching the significance of the action presented by filtering it through the consciousness of either a narrator or a perceptive actor in the story itself. Browning is at his best when he is most dramatic in his narrative, but with him, the drama is almost as much a matter of a clash of ideas as a clash of character. This is best revealed in the *Parleyings*.

Any study of the narrative techniques of Browning's later poems would remain incomplete without a discussion of the techniques used in the *Parleyings*. In *The Ring and the Book* various points of view are presented in succession, this method being an attempt to permit an inclusive perception of the centre of truth round which many points of view organize themselves. Nevertheless, as has already been mentioned, this truth emerges not so much from the monologues themselves, as from their juxtaposition with the master perspective that establishes the right judgements in the first and last Books of the poem. And at these points, Browning abandons the dramatic monologue form in order to speak out in his own voice. In the longer monologues of the later period, we have an interplay of perspectives that create multiple levels of meaning, but they are often not wholly integrated into the framework of the poem, as in the debate between the Head Servant and Sagacity in *Prince Hohenstiel-Schwangau*. So the next step in Browning's experiments with form encompassed a closer fusion of the subjective and the objective, one which permitted multi-level perspectives to be presented, not disparately but simultaneously. In the *Parleyings*, he is both objective, in the sense of projecting characters external to himself with their own lines of thought, and subjective, in the sense of superimposing on their views his own particular interpretation of truth, and integrating both in a seamless web.

The form of the poem is complex. Roma A. King notes: "Browning achieves here a subtlety that evaded him even in *The Ring and the Book*. There are the various figures from the past, their modern equivalents and Browning himself, a complex, ambivalent, often ironic 'I'."[33]

Consequently, the parleyings, in spite of their overt structure as conversations between the poet and certain people of importance in their day, really becomes a clash of conflicting forces present in the mind of one man, Browning himself.

Browning speaks in his own voice, but he also manages to retain dramatic qualities in his poem.

Chiefly, this is brought about by the dialectical exchange of arguments conducted through various subsidiary voices and the resultant frequency in the shifts in the point of view. It is the movement of the poet's mind that constitutes the dramatic action, the conflict residing in the opposition of varied mental forces. When Browning treats an idea, not in the abstract, but as a personally held view-point, then the drama implicit in the idea becomes explicit.

The *Parleyings*, far from being "mere grey argument" are an interesting experiment in what may be termed as the drama of ideas. The dramatic context is created by the shifting distance between narrator/author and the characters. Mostly, this distance is aesthetic and intellectual. Only on one occasion does Browning use the unreliable narrator technique ("Parleying with George Dubb Dodington") and here the distance lies between the moral norms of the narrator and the reader/ author. The shifts in response from sympathy and identification on the one hand and detachment and overt satire on the other make for dramatic tension. The intellectual pattern of thoughts, ideas, speculations is superimposed upon the emotional pattern of hopes, perplexities and affirmations, further enhancing the richness of the texture.

The language of the *Parleyings* is in the "difficult" style that Robert Preyer says "appears regularly in association with a particular subject-matter: the mind's confrontation with perceptions that resist rational analysis" and "convey the 'feel' of the experience that baffle perception and remain portentous, tantalizing."[34] The problem of giving form to this sense of flux is met by the structure of the *Parleyings* which is such as to allow the speaker to transcend time-bound perspectives. The past and the future coalesce in the present as Browning searches for really enduring patterns in human existence. And it is the creative, synthesizing faculty to which the romanticists gave the name of imagination that becomes the focal idea of the *Parleyings*, for Browning is of the opinion that with the help of his imaginative vision man could give meaning to his world. But Browning does not use his narrative methods to present any ideal truth. At the most he shows how the imagination may be used by the artist to evolve and apprehend truth. In the shorter narrative poems that will be examined in the next chapter, Browning shows how the imaginative rendering of factual matter can invest it with richness of texture and meaning.

NOTES

1. Robert Scholes and Robert Kellogg, *The Nature of Narrative* (Oxford University Press, 1978), pp. 274-75.
2. Robert Langbaum, *The Poetry of Experience*, p. 154.
3. Wayne Booth, *The Rhetoric of Fiction* (Chicago: The University of Chicago Press, 1961), p. 86.
4. John Killham, "Browning's Modernity" in *The Major Victorian Poets: Reconsiderations*, ed. Isobel Armstrong (London: Routledge and Kegan Paul, 1969), p. 170.
5. Henry James, "The Art of Fiction." Quoted in Scholes and Kellogg, p. 161.
6. J. Hillis Miller, *The Disappearance of God*, (Cambridge Mass: Harvard University Press, 1963), p. 132.
7. Robert Langbaum, *The Poetry of Experience*, p. 154.
8. Joseph Conrad, *Lord Jim* (Penguin Edition, 1957), p. 65.
9. *Ibid.*, p. 75.
10. *Ibid.*, p. 101.
11. Quoted in Gilbert Phelps, *The Russian Novel in English Fiction* (London: Hutchinson's University Library, 1956), p. 44.
12. *Ibid.*, p. 55.
13. Robert Felgar, "Browning's Narrative Art," *Studies in Browning and His Circle*, Vol. 3, No. 2 (1975), p. 93.
14. Roma A. King, *The Focusing Artifice*, p. 193.
15. Robert Felgar, p. 91.
16. *The Poetry of Browning*, p. 335.
17. Quoted in Miriam Allott, p. 84.
18. *Ibid.*, p. 287.
19. See *The Bodley Head Henry James*, V, p. 15.
20. *Browning's Later Poetry*, p. 130.
21. Henry James, "The Art of Fiction" in *Henry James: Selected Literary Criticism*, ed. Morris Shapira (London and Toronto: Heinemann, 1963), p. 64.

22. Robert Langbaum, *The Poetry of Experience*, p. 83.
23. J.W. Beach, *The Twentieth Century Novel: A Study in Technique* (New York: Appleton Century Crofts, 1932, Rep; Ludhiana: Lyall Book Depot, 1965), p. 197.
24. *The Focusing Artifice*, p. 199.
25. *The Poetry of Browning*, p. 335.
26. *Ibid.*, p. 21.
27. Francois Mauriac, *God and Mammon*, quoted in Miriam Allott, p. 133.
28. Henry James, "Honore de Balzac," *Notes on Novelists*, 1914, rep. in *Henry James: Selected Literary Criticism*, p. 200.
29. Cf. "I entirely agree with you in your estimate of the comparitive value of French and English Romance-writers. I bade the completest adieu to the latter on my first introduction to Balzac, whom I greatly admire for his faculty, whatever he may choose to do with it." *RB and EBB Letters*, II, p. 658; Letter of April 27, 1846. Also, to Isa Blagden: "make your incidents as simple as you can, put out your strength in the analysis of *character*, keeping in mind the immeasurable superiority (to my mind) of French models than English." Letter of May 22, 1867, *Dearest Isa*, p. 266.
30. Quoted in Miriam Allott, Novelists on the Novel, p. 103.
31. Gilbert Phelps, p. 44.
32. *Selected Literary Criticims*, p. 194.
33. *The Focusing Artifice*, p. 243.
34. Robert Preyer, "Two Styles in the Verse of Robert Browning," *E.L.H.* XXXII, 1965, p. 81.

NARRATIVE ART – THE SHORTER POEMS

Browning's narrative method in *Dramatic Idylls* is to take a character who is morally interesting and to put that character into situations that will best reveal his moral qualities. The object is to isolate the truth of the human condition, not through the oblique view where the reader has to "discover" the meaning, but through a more objective delineation of what men and women did, their manifest actions as being avenues to their secret centres. Thus the idylls display not so much "action in character" that may be said of the interior method of the dramatic monologue, but rather character and motive revealed through action, i.e. the accent is on the "succint little story" (as Browning described a dramatic idyll)[1] rendered in all its totality by a disinterested narrator.

Browning's technique in these shorter poems is varied. In *Red Cotton Night-Cap Country* the narrator was an important means of controlling our responses and his judgements were a refined and restrained projection of the author's own sensibility. In *Dramatic Idylls* there is hardly any emphasis on the personality of the narrator, in order to lend such commentary as he makes (which is sparingly made, but is crucial), the air of authority and impartiality. Important exceptions are "Clive" (Second Series) where the personality of the narrator is explicitly delineated in the interests of thematic significance, and "Ned Bratts" which uses an unreliable narrator for satiric purposes. Though the narrator does not participate in the action, by his resuscitation of the event he shares imaginatively in the experience. In any living event, the pressures of the experience prevent any immediate perception of the truth behind it. Thus, in the *Idylls*, Browning sets out to chart the complexities of human motivation by distancing the event through the use of the narrator, who presents the action as told by the protagonists themselves. This is all the more important in the light of the extreme situations depicted.

Browning's aim is to get the truth about human nature in a very concentrated form, so he dramatizes those moments which make the inherent meaning of a life visible. The emotions depicted are basic ones like fear, anger, jealousy, joy, apathy, but Browning reveals the complexities and contradictions inherent in them.

Unlike the monologuists, the characters in a dramatic idyll talk neither to defend themselves nor to persuade an auditor. Their aim is to recreate the original moment of choice; any insights which emerge are generally hidden from them. It is the narrator's function, either by direct comment or by the presentation of relevant subsidiary material to elucidate them for the reader.

The *First Series* reveals Browning's subtle technique of conditioning the reader's response. Having relegated the narrator to the background in these narratives, he achieves depth through a different method – focusing a double perspective on each event, sometimes external to the main character, sometimes as a part of his own consciousness.

"Martin Relph" depicts the tragic irony of a man who is forced to retreat behind conventional assumptions to escape from his own conscience. To foil "a worm inside which bores at the brain for food" (l.14) Martin prefers to call himself a coward, rather than acknowledge the enormity of the crime which he has committed, and which has been little short of cold-blooded murder. The narrative describes not only Martin's excited state of mind, but effectively presents the tensions of the story's central event – the arrival of Vincent Parkes with the letter which would rescue Rosamund Page from the firing squad, and Martin's deliberate failure to act "When a word, cry, gasp would have rescued both." (l. 137) The sudden shift to the present tense at the climax enhances the dramatic vividness of the action, and aids the simultaneous presentation of action and emotion. The crisis is ostensibly an external one, but its repercussions take place deep within a man's soul. The action is important, but Browning's concern is equally with what the event meant to the main character, what difference it made in him. Martin Relph is led to insights from which he ordinarily shields himself – namely that his action has had quite the reverse effect from what he had intended it to have: "I helped you; thus were you dead and wed." (p. 113) The narrative tension is slackened at this point by presenting the scene through a hubbub of spectator voices, before the final climatic revelation. Browning secures maximum shock effect by withholding the true cause of Martin's heinous crime till almost the end – his love for the girl and his jealousy of her lover; so that the last two verses in which Martin tries to gloss over his real motivations are not only ironical but splendid examples of psychological realism.

In "Pheidippides" we start immediately inside the particular situation, at a particular moment, as it presents itself to the person involved. We gather the facts through Pheidippides' allusion to them in the course of his speech – Athens at war with Persia, Sparta's refusal to come to its aid, Pan's timely promise of help. The account of his triumph, however, has a better chance of being appreciated as factual if it does not seem too personal. Thus, its authenticity is emphasized by the shift in the point of view from protagonist to narrator. This shift also helps the reader to stand back from the action and to assess the moral value of the character. The heroism of Pheidippides, contrasted with the selfishness of those in power, creates the perspective from which emerges the moral implications of the idyll, and it is the narrator who is entrusted with the task of elucidation: "yet never decline, but, gloriously as he began,/ So to end gloriously–." (l. 114)

In "Halbert and Hob," which enacts the mythic rite of initiation inexplicably gone awry, Browning exposes the strangeness of the sudden transformation that weakens the brute force of the father and son, so that time almost stops and their lives begin to weaken and fade away. Animality is destroyed by the expression of civilized restraint. Civilization has broken down savagery. Old Halbert recognizes in this "the finger of God." (l. 50) The quotation from *King Lear* ("Is there a reason in nature for these hard hearts") leads to direct comment by the narrator on the mystery of the forces within and without man. As with the image of the "worm" in Martin Relph and that of fire in "Pheidippides" the implications of the tale are dramatically embodied in the vivid image of the son "crouched all a-tremble like any lamb new-yeaned." (l.39)

In "Ivan Ivanovitch" the action is set in times past to enhance its significance: "We place it in Peter's time when hearts were great not small." (l.13) Further, the contrasted images of hatchet and tool-box create a double frame of reference (elemental innocence versus artificial codes) which will be needed to judge the implications of the action. The narrator's voice vouching for its authenticity and speaking of "a moral that's behind," (l.13) solidly discounts any air of unreality that the tale might bear. Roma A. King sees the setting as symbolic: "The little village, an oasis of semi-civilization is surrounded by the wolf-infested forest," so that in the idyll the conflict is between the "clearing and the wilderness, the rational and the irrational, the conscious and the unconscious."[2]

The actual tale is told by the woman herself, the sharply limited point of view being superbly employed, as in Conrad's tales, for securing an effect of nightmare vividness. The carefully controlled tempo of the narrative, the fragmented jerkiness of the language objectifying the terrified reactions of the woman, the building up of suspense and cumulative heightening of tension make this idyll unique. The dramatic compression that gives simultaneously, action, emotion and the material to judge both is here impressively employed, as in: "Flings? I flung? Never! But think! – a woman, after all/ contending with a wolf!" (l.173) Emotion is dramatically externalized in one poignant image:

> . . . how feels
> The onion bulb your knife parts, pushing through its peels,
> Till out you scoop its clove wherein lie its stalk and leaf
> And bloom and seed unborn? (ll.234-37)

Roma A. King is correct when he says that the woman's monologue reveals "the cruelty beneath the tenderness, the selfishness beneath the love." But one cannot agree with him when he says that the woman "sees herself from a new perspective,"[3] for the experience has brought her no spiritual regeneration. She remains ensconced in her selfishness – "Life's sweet, and all its after-years." (l.253)

The very violence of Ivan's act of beheading the woman, matched as it is with the violence of the woman's act of throwing her babies at the wolves, creates a moral dilemma. No single judgement would suffice to explain completely the paradoxical nature of each act. Browning thus crosses three viewpoints: Ivan's ("God bade me act for him; I dared not disobey"; [l.297]) the judge's ("Ivan Ivanovitch has done a deed that's named/ Murder by law and me"; [ll.315-16]) and the old Pope's ("I proclaim/ Ivan Ivanovitch God's servant." [ll.389-90]) Thus, there is truth as the world sees it, and the inner truth revealed by an imaginative leap made possible by experience and an enlarged consciousness, and these tiered judgements form the base of the poem's moral significance. Ultimately, what emerges as praiseworthy is the courage and vigour of Ivan's convictions, which stand out in sharp contrast to the contradictions in the woman's attitude as a woman and a mother.

In "Tray" Browning shows how the so-called rational, scientific frame of mind may be perverted and grotesque in contrast to simple impulses. His technique here is that of dissociation, the action being set first, against the past concepts of heroism, which lends a comic irony to the modern situation; and secondly, against the inconsequential babble of mildly curious, essentially indifferent onlookers, all ready to discern the irony of Tray's instinctive rescue of not only the child, but of the child's doll as well, speaking off-handedly of the cruelty of vivisection, and thus highlighting the aberrations of their own outlook that works against common humanity.

The essential concern in the *Dramatic Idylls* with the unpredictability of human nature is once again the theme of "Ned Bratts." Instead of using the story to highlight the moral complexities of a single crucial moment, Browning in this poem seems to use the story to emphasize the complexities inherent in religious feeling. There is an aura of melodrama about Ned Bratts and his wife and a savage comedy inherent in their viciousness which reveals itself so uninhibitedly. Yet, even while they are depicted as monstrous, there is an underlying sympathy, for their intuitive reactions to their particular testing moment have been for them a means of salvation. The keynote to their portrayal is "Take the will, not the deed." (l.449) External manifestations are deceptive:

> So many some stricken tree look blasted, bough and bole,
> Champed by the fire-tooth, charred without, yet, thrice-bound
> With detriment about, within life may be found,
> A prisoned power to branch and blossom as before,
> Could but the gardener cleave the cloister, reach the core . . . .
> (ll.365-69)

The essential flatness of the character of the two protagonists is emphasized to reveal the distortions that a simplistic interpretation of salvation may bring about. Browning here uses an unreliable narrator to reinforce the ironic intention of the poem. The coarseness of the speaker matches the obtuseness of the judges; and their inability to comprehend the true significance of Bunyan's teachings allows Browning to subtly imply the ironies behind the "happy hanging." The poem is also an indictment of a society that has no compunctions about jailing a man and then erecting him a statue. Browning's satire is directed against the legal profession:

> What if I had my doubts? Suppose I gave them breath,
> Brought you to bar: what work to do, ere 'Guilty, Death'
> Had paid our pains! What heaps of witnesses to drag
> From holes and corners, paid from out the country's bag!
> Trial three dog-days long! (ll.502-6)

This satire becomes all the more trenchant because of the approval which this manner of thinking receives from the narrator. The complacent, self-satisfied attitude of the narrator and the judge contrasts tellingly with the fervour of feeling, however grotesque, that motivates Ned Bratts to insist on a quick hanging to speed him on his way to heaven. This is in keeping with Browning's emphasis in the *Idylls* on the moral superiority of decisive action as against lethargy or excessive ratiocination.

Browning's narrative technique in the *Dramatic Idylls, Second Series* aims at reinforcing the main theme of the volume – the virtual impossibility of being "sage and certain" about man's innermost being. The increased emphasis on the narrator, whether as a reliable or unreliable spokesman, points to an increased sophistication in narrative presentation.

"Echetlos" is structured upon contrasts, both visual and moral – the men in the "tribe and file" (l.5) contrasted with the one "who kept no rank," (l.7) the "helmed and shielded" (l.10) set against the "clown's limbs broad and bare." (l.11) Though the significance of Echetlos' action is explicitly given by the oracle who pronounces: "The great deed ne'er grows small," (l.27) its moral implications are enlarged through the narrator's setting the "great deed" against the "great name" – that of the Greek heroes, Miltiades and Themistokles who came to ignoble ends.

It is generally accepted among critics that "Clive" has a place among the best of Browning's works. In fact, Browning himself chose the poem as his best in the idyllic mode.[4] Mark Siegchrist in his study of the poem, refers to it as a subtle study of "a subtle moral quandry" and sees "Clive" both "as a dramatic idyll with respect to its title role, displaying the impact of a single crucial event on an individual's insight into his own behaviour, and as a dramatic monologue with respect to its narrator, displaying a more profound self-revealment of his character than he consciously intends."[5]

Browning's technique of narration in this poem is unique. The characterization of the hero is made significant and effective by the subjective background against which it is portrayed. The narrator is here cast in the role of the unreliable eye-witness, so that the poet lays on the reader a special burden of enjoyable ratiocination as he understands and interprets what the character telling the story cannot himself comprehend. The narrator here tries to explain Clive's thoughts and actions, but he does so in the light of his own mental states, his preconceived notions of heroism. The poem's interest lies in the subtlety with which it protrays the difference between the sensitive, tortured Clive and the self-satisfied narrator, for whom the world holds no ambiguities. Its significance lies in the "moral discovery" to which these contrasted character-sketches point. Man is betrayed by what is false and weak within him. And it is, paradoxically, the imaginative, idealistic soul that is most prone to betrayal. The image of the castle is a significant one: "Such a castle seldom crumbles by sheer of cannonade." (l.56) The implication is that forces from within contribute to its decay.

The juxtaposition between appearance and reality – the romantic estimate held by the narrator of the gallant warrior "every whit/ Worth your Alexanders, Caesars, Marlboroughs" (l.72) and the reality of the decaying figure of Clive – "I saw his head sink heavy, guessed the soul's extinguishment/ By the glazing eyeball, noticed how the furtive fingers went/ Where drug-box skulked behind the honest liquor," (ll.65-67), or, in other words, the contrast between what might be termed the public view and the private view creates the ironic tension that sustains the poem.

Through the further contrast that is presented between Clive's tale of the occasion when he felt "most fear," (l.84) and the narrator's obtuse refusal to accept the fact that his hero could feel fear, Browning probes the ambiguities behind ostensibly heroic action. We are made to realize that what Clive feared was not the matter of dying but the matter of living. Mark Siegchrist notes: "As in Conrad's fiction, people in these idylls find themselves suddenly alone confronting the heart of moral darkness, with no support other than their own strength of character, if they have any."[6] For Clive, life without the protective aura of heroic gesture and public accolade appears to be unsupportable. His opponent's reaction in admitting that he had cheated at cards provided him with the opportunity for the grand gesture of magnanimity: "Whosoever, all or each,/ To the disadvantage of the man who spared me, utters speech/ To his face, behind his back, – that speaker has to do with me," (ll.190-192) But Clive is also aware of the fact that had his opponent adopted a different stance, made the heroic gesture himself by sayings:

> . . . There!
> Keep your life, caluminator! – worthless life I freely spare:
> Mine you freely would have taken – murdered me and my good fame
> Both at once – and all the better! Go, and thank your own bad aim
> Which permits me to forgive you! (ll.226-30)

nothing would have remained for him but to take his own life on the spot.

In typical Browning fashion, language becomes an important means of evaluating character. Clive's words – "I passed each speaker severally in review./ When I had precise their number, names and styles, and fully knew/ Over whom my supervision thenceforth must extend, why, then" (ll.178-80) – reveal the extent to which Clive enjoys his position of superiority over people. Once deprived of that, his fall is inevitable.

The narrator, even while he is too obtuse to understand the real implications of Clive's confession, nevertheless unwittingly provides towards the end the moral norms against which Clive's final act of suicide must be judged. His comfortable assumptions are shaken by Clive's acceptance of suicide as an easy way out of difficulties. Though his essential faith in Clive's heroism remains, he attempts mildly to remonstrate: "True, disgrace were hard to bear: but such a rush against God's face/ – None of that for me, Lord Plassy." (ll. 241-42) This does not represent the superficial standards of the narrator any longer, but constitutes the unshakeable norms of morality. The narrator's ambivalence is even more pronounced in his reactions to the news of Clive's suicide; on the one hand are his habitual assumptions that Clive has been "fearfully courageous"; on the other, a nagging suspicion that this is Clive's "worst deed." The conclusion is a masterpiece of understatement. By describing the surface reactions of the narrator, Browning leaves the reader to infer the tumult within the mind of the protagonist that may have led him to take the extreme step. It is the subtlety and suggestiveness that renders all elaboration superfluous that is Browning's most significant contribution to modern narrative art.[7]

In "Muleykeh" the narrator functions not so much as an investigator or even commentator, but as a recounter. Nevertheless, his role as eye-witness helps to lend excitement and urgency to his narrative. His initial reaction to Hoseyn's unexpected gesture in letting his enemy into the secret of the horse Muleykeh's speed is that of surprise: "What folly makes Hoseyn shout." (l.95) Whether he himself understands the implications of Hoseyn's explanatory "'And the beaten in speed!' .. 'you have never loved my Pearl'," (ll.114) is uncertain. The narrator's obtuseness serves the important function of emphasizing the contradictory nature of human responses. The line of action that Hoseyn has taken seems, on face value, to be utterly opposed to the whole line of his disposition as the narrator understands it. Yet, there is a psychological consistency in Hoseyn's willingness to suffer deprivation rather than accept in the object of his love anything less than complete perfection. For him, as for Browning himself, there is no place in love for compromise or selfishness; and Browning achieves dramatic intensity of effect by refraining from any attempt to explain or to justify.

In "Pietro of Abano" the narrator is once again used to point out the moral significance of the tale. The action is set well back in the past so that the tradition itself carries its own authority. This was a necessary device, for the implications of the story were such as to touch a raw spot in the poet himself—the public lack of recognition or adulation. The narrator's mask barely hides Browning's own voice: "Prophets pay with Christians, now as in the Jew's age/ Still is—stoning" (p. 614) and also the bitterly ironical: "Certain, with but these two gifts, to gain earth's prize in time!/ Cleverness uncurbed by conscience." (p.622) Much of the pleasure lies in applying the implications of the poem to the poet's own situation. The poem ends with Browning ruefully commenting through his narrative persona: "Scarce the sportive fancy-dice I fling show 'Venus'" (p. 623) that is, love of the reading public.

"Doctor — " follows a familiar narrative pattern—a story recounted by a narrator, who in turn has heard it from somebody else. This distancing is particularly effective when the story is somewhat far-fetched, as in this tale of the powers of Satan being routed by the powers of a "bad wife." This technique allows for only that much willing suspension of disbelief as the narrator and the reader is willing to give. The grotesque tale nevertheless gives an inkling into the inherent potentialities of the human soul for either good or evil. With the last line—"I tell it, as the Rabbi told me," the narrator disowns any responsibility for the sentiments expressed in the tale.

Apart from the *Dramatic Idylls*, the shorter narrative poems of Browning's later period are spread over the *Pacchiarotto* volume (1876) – "Herve Riel," "A Forgiveness," "Cenciaja," "Fillippo Baldinucci on the Privilege of Burial"; the *Jocoseria* volume (1883) – "Donald," "Solomon and Balkis," "Cristina and Monaldeschi," "Adam, Lilith and Eve": and the *Asolando* volume (1889) – "Rosny," "The Pope and the Net," "The Bean-Feast," "Muckle-Mouth Meg," "Arcades Ambo," "The Lady and the Painter," "Ponte Dell 'Angelo, Venice," "Beatrice Signorini," "Imperanto Augusto Natus est –." Some of these poems are satirical in intention and so have been discussed earlier. In general, these later poems reveal the astonishing fertility of Browning's mind even in his later years. In out-of-the-way stories, anecdotes, historical titbits, he found revealing indications of man's nature and insights into the possibilities of the mind and the imagination. Browning here may be said to reveal the same "passion for exactitude, an appetite, the appetite of an ogre, for *all* kinds of facts" that Henry James noticed in Balzac,[8] who incidentally, was a great favourite with Browning himself, as his letters amply show.

"Herve Riel" is in the tradition of "How They Brought Good News from Ghent to Aix" and "Incident of the French Camp," a celebration of the valour of unsung, unknown heroes. Irvine and Honan note: "'Herve Riel". . . romanticizes and sentimentalizes history. . . . One also sees impressively how many of his doctrines he [Browning] could squeeze into a ballad that is simple and colourful enough to appeal to a child: the helplessness of institutions, the necessity of self-reliance, the redemptive value of decisive action, the supremacy of love, even the 'infinite moment' that transcends time and makes human history significant."[9]

"A Forgiveness" was chosen by Browning as most representative of his narrative poetry.[10] It has all those features that make a good short story – shock, surprise, climax, excitement. The first section, which describes the nobleman's intense love for his wife and his discovery of her guilt, ends with the marvellously laconic "We went in." (l.92) Following the breathless urgency of the lady's confession, it speaks of the traumatic experience more tellingly than an analysis. The section that follows shows the man trying to evade the threat of a personal catastrophe by building a bulwark of an outwardly normal life style. But the sense of compulsively obsessive behaviour masquerading under the guise of normality, though underplayed with striking effect, is very strong. One feels it need but a touch to burst out horrifying into the open.

The seemingly irrelevant digressions at crucial points of the narrative not only enhance the suspense, they serve to reveal the psychology of a frustrated, hate-filled mind operating under a rigid, self-imposed code of conduct. The nobleman's morbid tendencies are revealed in his taste for "things that rend and rip,/ Gash rough, slash smooth, help hate in so many ways." (ll.259-60) The poem is a study of obsessional neurosis no less than that of the Duke in "My Last Duchess." Even at the moment in which he is about to murder his wife, he is able to admire with the precision of a connoisseur the beauty of the dagger he is using. The sense of shock produced by—"She sleeps, as erst/Belovèd, in this your church" (ll.407-8) corresponds to that produced by the Duke in "My Last Duchess," when, as Robert Langbaum describes it, "having boasted how at his command the duchess' life was extinguished, he turns lack to the portrait to admire of all things its life-likeness."[11]

The climax in which the nobleman reveals to the priest that he has recognized him as his wife's lover and then kills him is not as unexpected as it appears. As with a successful detective story, the germ of the resolution is there in the story from the beginning. In this particular poem, Browning has carefully paved the way for the denouement through the very unexpectedness of the preliminary lines: "The monk half spoke, half ground through his clenched teeth,/ At the confession-grate I knelt beneath." (l.6-7) We remember Henry James' demand that the novelist should practice a technique of "continuous relevance,"[12] and Ford Madox Ford's assertion: "Before everything a story must convey a sense of inevitability: that which happens in it must be seen to be the only thing that could have happened."[13] In "A Forgiveness" the atmosphere of suppressed violence leads to the only conclusion possible, the killing of both wife and lover. The ironies inherent in the title of the poem are thus revealed. Ostensibly, the nobleman is asking for forgiveness at the confessional, but in reality he is out for vengeance; ostensibly, he has forgiven his wife for her unfaithfulness, but his hate has passed away only after killing her.

In "Donald" in the *Jocoseria* volume, Browning once again uses a narrator whose reactions focus very clearly the meaning of the tale. The narrator is the sensitive, unbiased perceiver whose opinions cut across the conventional assumptions to the central truth. As in the dramatic idylls, a sudden critical moment of choice reveals in a character hitherto unsuspected traits. The moral value of his response judges the character. Browning here appears to modify the emphasis of swift, instinctive behaviour as the hall-mark of right and truth that had characterized poems like "Ivan Ivanovich." The motive behind the act is now seen as the crucial test. Donald's instincts are those of a hunter, not a man. He is more akin to the predatory beast than a human being. As in "Tray," the sensitive instinct of the animal is superior to the calculating motives of the man. The contrast between the run-of-the-mill belief that "where there is keenness/ For sport, there's little likelihood/ Of a man's displaying meanness!" (ll.46-48) and the sordidness of tale in which a sportsman reveals his lack of honour and humanity, is sharply ironical. But the reactions of the listeners to the both heightens the irony even further. Their obtuseness is of a piece with the general unwillingness of men to accept any radical change in their way of thinking.

"Solomon and Balkis" shows Browning using an anecdote from rabbinical lore to illustrate not the philosophy of a religious tradition, but the nature of individuals within the tradition. The theme – the weakness of the idealized – is a favourite one with Browning. A parallel theme is the necessity of honestly admitting the descendental thrust in one's nature. To spurn the body and the senses in this world is hypocrisy. Even the wise Solomon and the sublime Balkis at last admit to vanity and lust.

"Cristina and Monaldeschi" treats a "crime of passion," as DeVane calls,[14] in a truly dramatic way, in that it is told by one of the actors in the story and told at a moment of crisis in the action, and not as a recapitulation. This at once involves the reader in the emotional movements of the narrative – a swift-paced progression in revealment of guilt and the climatic vengeance. The highlight of this tense, macabre drama is the character of the proud, implacable Cristina. The imagery of the peak "bare and bleak" (l.55) from which there is no retreat, and of "Yawning death in yon abyss/ Where the waters whirl and hiss" (ll.70-71) indicate the relentless fury of a woman crossed in love. The elaborate ritual that she conducts in taking her faithless lover for a walk down the gallery in which hang the portraits of King Francis and his adored Diane, who, she observes with cutting sarasm, are "Prototypes of you and me" (l.12) reveals a mind obsessed, almost like that of the lady in "The Laboratory." Her inscrutability, sadistic calm and complete absorption in her own point of view heightens the tension of the narrative. The manner in which Browning is able to suggest the state of the lover's mind comments both on the nature of the action and the character of the protagonist. The controlled violence of both the lady in "The Laboratory" and Cristina in the present poem, is noteworthy; the former takes sadistic pleasure in visualizing her rival's death-throes – "Let death be felt and the proof remain,/ Brand, burn up, bite into its grace" (ll. 38-39); Cristina orders her hired assassins to kill her lover; "You three, stab thick and fast,/ Deep and deeper." (ll.134-35) DeVane's assessment of "The Laboratory" as "an economical statement of an intricate and tense situation"[15] may be regarded as pertinent to "Cristina and Monaldeschi" also.

In "Rosny" Browning uses the characteristically tragic situation of the ballad form to highlight the peculiar psychology of a woman who values honour more than love. The form of the ballad is an apt medium for the compression and suggestiveness that is the finest feature of Browning's narrative art, – the focusing of the action on a single episode and permitting it to interpret itself with a minimum of comment and descriptive setting. The impersonal manner of the narration, nevertheless, does not preclude the evocation of sympathy for the hero, while the judgement passed on the woman who regards "death and fame" as "love's guerdon" is encompassed in the response evoked by the single word "simpler," used with reference to her. The feelings portrayed in this poem have a complexity however, that go far beyond the elemental, unshaded passions of the traditional ballad.

"Muckle-Mouth Meg" is a dramatization of a Scottish legend, written with Browning's typical zest and whole-hearted appreciation of a man who has the courage of his convictions and who opts for death rather than a loveless marriage. It has the simplicity and clarity of the traditional folk-tale.

Browning called "Beatrice Signorini" his best poem in the *Asolando* volume, and though we may question his choice, it is easy to see why Browning felt as he did. The poem embodies two of his most frequently recurring interests – his love of painting and his fondness for exploring the unsuspected facets of human personality, in this case, with reference to love. The love that he treats here is of two kinds: one that passes from mere physical attraction to a spiritual union, and the other kind, more earthy, more instinctive, but none the less potent. Romanelli is in the long line of Browning lovers whose pride in their beloved's perfection persists despite unfulfilment in love. In this poem Browning once again asserts the essential "rightness" of impulsive action. Beatrice, in whom her husband found "milk for blood" (echoing Guido's words for Pompilia) proves her passionate nature in a most unsuspected fashion and wins her husband's love "Past power to change." (l.351)

"The Bean-Feast" and "Imperante Augusto Natus Est – " may be taken together as complementary poems illustrating opposed ways of regarding Divine power. In the former, which is straightforward narrative, the Pope's humility in acknowledging himself as merely an instrument of God: "earth obeys/ Thy word in mine, that through me people know thy ways" (ll.41-42) and his grateful acceptance of God's beneficence: "Thy goodness nowise scants/ Man's body of its comforts" (ll.44-45) contrasts tellingly with the deification accorded to and accepted by the Emperor Augustus. A further contrast is presented by the Pope's joyous relationship with his God, and the Emperor's superstitious fear of "Fate's envy, the dread chance of things." (l. 130)

In "Imperante Augusto Natus Est – " Browning's narrative art attains a high degree of sophistication. The pivotal feature of this poem is the consistently maintained tension between Caesar's assumed divinity and the reality of his being born of "flesh and blood." (l.81) Browning's use of the narrator to highlight this tension is parallelled by the corresponding tension within the narrator himself, who is torn by conflicting feelings embodied in the telling line: "where was escape from his prepotency?" (l.32) On the one hand, the narrator is part of the society that raves "Be Caesar God!"; on the other, the stifling atmosphere of this mindless adulation leads him to seek relief – "Jove thus dethroned, I somehow wanted air." (l.23) The juxtaposition between the narrator's concept of Caesar as "Our Holy and Inviolable One" (l.100) and his almost unconscious thought of the prophecy of the grey Sibyl – "Caesar Augustus regnant, shall be born/ In blind Judea – one to master him," (ll.158-59) highlights the ambivalence within the man, as also his exclamation, "Crown, now – Cross, when?" (l.151) But the fear that these subversive thoughts arouse in the narrator is tellingly embodied in his query, "Him and the universe?" (l.160) and this, in turn, leads him to hastily "regain his equilibrium" (David Shaw's term) by dismissing the prophecy as "An old wife's tale?" (l.160) The question mark, once again expressing his mental conflicts, is very apt. The manner in which he turns furiously upon the bath drudge is not merely a "revealing disclosure of pagan pride" as Shaw puts it,[16] it is also a masterpiece of psychological realism, for it shows him masking his inner fears by being violent. Like "An Epistle of Karshish" the poem dramatizes a psychological conflict and the subtly held interplay of contrary ideas reveals a poet who even in his very last phase has not lost his skilful touch.

NOTES

1. Se DeVane, *Handbook*, p. 430.
2. *The Focusing Artifice*, p. 219.
3. *Ibid.*, p. 221.
4. See DeVane, *Handbook*, p. 430.
5. Mark Siegchrist, "Narrative Obtuseness in Browning's 'Clive'," *Studies in Browning and His Circle*, 3 (Spring 1975), pp. 53-60.
6. Mark Siegchrist, "Thematic Coherence in Browning's *Dramatic Idylls*," *Victorian Poetry*, 15, 3 (1977), p. 232.
7. Conrad's view on the craft of writing is interesting in this connection: "I beg leave to illustrate my meaning from extracts. . . . 'When the whole horror of his position forced itself with an agony of apprehension upon his frightened mind Pa Tua for a space lost his reason'. . . . In this sentence the reader is borne down by the full expression. The words: *with an agony of apprehension* completely destroy the effect therefore interfere with the truth of the statement. . . . The imagination of the reader should be left free to rouse his feeling.

'When the whole horror of his position forced itself upon his mind, pa Tua for a space lost his reason. . . .' This is truth, this it is which, thus stated, caries conviction because it is a picture of a mental state."
Quoted in Miriam Allott, pp. 319-20.

8. Henry James, "Honore de Balzac" in *Henry James: Selected Literary Criticism*, ed. Morris Shapira, p. 192.
9. Irvine and Honan, *The Book, the Ring and the Poet*, p. 421.
10. See DeVane, *Handbook*, pp. 409-10.
11. *The Poetry of Experience*, p. 78.
12. Cf. Henry James' opinion in "The Art of Fiction": "I cannot imagine composition existing in a series of books, nor conceive, in any novel worth discussing at all, a passage of description that is not in its intention narrative, a passage of dialogue that is not in its intention descriptive, a touch of truth of any sort that does not partake of the nature of incident, and an incident that derives its interest from any other source than the general and only source of the success of a work of art—that of being illustrative."
13. Quoted in Miriam Allott, p. 245.
14. See DeVane, *Handbook*, p. 466.
15. DeVane, *Handbook*, pp. 170-71.
16. W. David Shaw, *The Dialectical Temper; The Rhetorical Art of Robert Browning* (Ithaca: Cornell University Press, 1968), p. 170.

CONCLUSION

On October 18, 1862, Browning wrote to Isa Blagden; "life is, as you describe Mr. Landor's dressing gown, 'all the colour washed out of it' – but, with the particular incentives I retain, I hope to fight a good fight and finish my course."[1] This is expressive of the dual strain in Browning's temperament in his later years, of his awareness, on the one hand, of pain and frustration, and the vigorous resolve, on the other hand, not to be overcome by life's difficulties. While a poet like Matthew Arnold wilted and withdrew in the face of the pressures of existence, Browning was impelled to conduct an exploration in order to discover meaning in life, using all the means at his disposal, intellectual as well as intuitional.

The duality finds expression in all aspects of his later art. The thought embodied in them veers between the poles of affirmation and doubt. For while Browning held the view that "the world is not to be learned and thrown aside but reverted to and relearned,"[2] his own course of relearning his world brought with it an accompanying realization of the gap between the ideal that is imagined and the actual that is realized. Poem after poem in the later period records this awareness. On the one hand it leads to satire, when the aberrations from the ideal are too glaring to be exculpated, and to an exposure of the casuistry that attempts to bridge the gap solely through the reasoning faculty. Conversely, it leads to an emphasis on love as a means of transcending limitation and as a mediator between the real and the ideal.

When Browning treats the theme of love in his later poetry, there is on the one side an affirmation of its supreme value as the ultimate reality, the idea of love as a bulwark against negation, and of its creative powers in positing the ideal in the real. On the other side, there is a keenly-felt realization of the difficulties that beset love, the fleeting nature of true communion, of time and death as realities that serve to separate lovers in the flesh. Thus Browning stresses the need for accepting love in its human, physical aspect (with its imperfections and partial fulfilments) as well as its spiritual aspect embodying completion and perfection.

In his treatment of philosophical questions, Browning emphasizes that God is an essentially unknowable entity and that man's attempts to gain complete knowledge can only lead to frustration. But this does not occasion despair, for Browning presents a two-fold way of coming to terms with this limitation: the exercise of love, which repeats God's love on earth and through which the ideal may be discerned in the real; and the exercise of the imagination, in which the symbolic method is used to encompass the infinite within the finite. Thus belief, for Browning, becomes an intuitive process, based on the facts of personal experience, whose validity lies in its response to personal needs.

In the face of his awareness of flux, change and dissolution, Browning found hope in the creative capacities of man's imagination. The importance of the imagination for the poets and painters is particularly stressed. The imagination allows them to view themselves as part of an evolving tradition, but also to cut across the superficial accretion of that tradition to its central core of truth and to shape it anew in a more meaningful way. Browning's own imaginative rendering of Greek myths and legends is an illustration of this principle. It is seen as particularly necessary to the artist in his role as interpreter of the higher reality that he envisions. As Browning demonstrates in the *Parleyings,* symbolic art is the appropriate vehicle for the imaginative experience, in that it represents a coalescence of the duality that is the artist's concern to resolve. This suggests his affinities with romanticism, which in the words of Robert Langbaum, is "both idealistic and realistic, in that it conceives of the ideal as existing only in conjunction with the real and the real as existing only in conjunction with the ideal. The two are brought into conjunction only in the act of perception when the higher or imaginative rationality brings the ideal into the real by penetrating the external world as a way of knowing both itself and the external world."[3] In Browning's later poetry, whether it deals with philosophic questions, love, art, or the everyday business of living, the imagination becomes the shaping power whereby man is impelled through his personal experience towards self-realization, self-discovery and self-development.

Nevertheless, as we have seen in our study of the poems, Browning presents his affirmations, not in a positive and authoritarian manner, but in terms of a "sustained query."[4] In *La Saisiaz* he explicitly rejects the passive acceptance of formulated beliefs, and in the "Epilogue" to *Ferishtah's Fancies* throws doubt on the concept of absolute truth. Thus it is not so much that "the answer of goodness and greatness is dying away"[5] in the later poetry, but that Browning refuses to provide any answers that encourage inert acquiescence. If, in a sense, Browning may be called a Romantic – that is, in his assertion of the importance of the self as a creator of value, he may also be seen as a modern, keenly aware of ambiguity, uncertainty and impermanence. Few poems embody this aspect of his mind as subtly as *Fifine at the Fair* does. This realization of the relativity of points of view, of the subjective nature of all apprehensions and of the multiplicity of reality leads Browning to the view that there is no one truth that can be held valid for all. Truth is to be evolved by each one out of his own experience in response to his own needs.

This attitude is reflected in the longer poems of this period (e.g. *Red Cotton Night-Cap Country*) where the concern is not just with a point of view, but with the manifold forces that operate within that view, thus creating multiple levels of significance. The aim is to evoke the "feel" of an experience in much the same way as the novel does, by juxtaposing different perspectives and thereby creating a pattern of meaning. In *The Inn Album* Browning discards the stance of the omniscient narrator, preferring to let meaning emerge through the inter-play of dramatized situations and consciousness. But this is more than a technical device. It is a choice grounded on moral conviction that the right or wrong of any episode depends on our awareness of it in its full intensity, there being no truths apart from those that emerge from experience. This results in an increased use of the narrator as an imaginative participant or imaginative recreator of the event, to focus our attention not so much on the things that happened as on their meaning. The ultimate emphasis is not on the objective reconstruction of fact but on the subjective, imaginative leap to the truth. The "fancies" are as important as the "facts." In each of the longer narrative poems that we have examined, the truth created by the ordering of significant detail is far above the empirical facts which, in themselves, may be merely sordid, grotesque or mundane.

Browning's art in the later period represents a growth and an advancement, for his wider range allows for a more complex treatment of his subject-matter. From *Balaustion's Adventure,* with its dual interpretation of a single story; *Prince Hohenstiel-Schwangau,* where multiple points of view operate more or less simultaneously within a dramatic monologue; *Fifine at the Fair,* in which what has been termed its "shifting perspectives in time and space"[6] are used to explore the protean nature of reality, through the novelistic techniques of *Red Cotton Night-Cap Country* and *The Inn Album* to the wide-ranging, three-tiered viewpoints of the *Parleyings* – we may discern an increasing technical maturity.

The form, however, represents the poet's mind in the later period. For while the later poetry has links with the earlier in its realization that man lacks direct access to absolutes and that his resolutions are, of necessity, partial, it goes beyond this awareness in its attempts to chart a way by which man may achieve fulfilment and a sense of unity and wholeness despite his limitations. But Browning appears to have moved beyond the basic assumption of the dramatic monologue, the notion, as J. Hillis Miller puts it, that one "can approach an absolute vision only by attempting to relive, one by one, all the possible attitudes of the human spirit."[7] The later poetry takes a wider view, positing further ways of achieving this absolute vision to the extent allowed to man in this world – the process of seeing in each facet of life a multiplicity of aspects which need to be viewed with a corresponding comprehensiveness of vision; and the process of creating value from within one's own self, from the facts of one's own experience operating on the external world. It establishes an inseparable link between the inner self and the outer world, each being necessary for the total experience.

Browning's own pursuit of the total experience continued with unabated vigour through his later years, and produced a body of work which disturbs and challenges conventional assumptions about poetry even as it illuminates and extends the range of poetic experience. It reveals a poet rooted in his age, but also ahead of it in many ways, whose attitudes foreshadow the more radical literary innovations of the coming generation.

NOTES

1. *Dearest Isa*, p. 160.
2. *Essay on Shelley*, in *Browning: Poetry and Prose*, selected by Simon Nowell-Smith, pp. 674-75.
3. *The Poetry of Experience*, p. 16.
4. Patricia M. Ball, "Browing's Godot" in *Browning: A Casebook*, ed. J.R. Watson, p. 180.
5. Maisie Ward, *Robert Browning and His World: Two Robert Brownings?*, p. 215.
6. Clyde de L. Ryals, *Browning's Later Poetry*, p. 60.
7. *The Disappearance of God*, p. 107.

SELECT BIBLIOGRAPHY

EDITIONS

The Poetical Works of Robert Browning. 2 vols. London: Smith Elder, 1904.

The Poems and Plays of Robert Browning. New York: The Modern Library, 1934.

Browning: Poetry and Prose. Selected by Simon Nowell-Smith. London: Rupert Hart-Davis, 1967.

Browning: Poetical Works, 1833-1864. Ed. Ian Jack. London: Oxford University Press, 1970.

Browning: Poems and Plays. 5 vols. Everyman's Library. London: J.M. Dent, 1919. Reprinted, 1970.

LETTERS

Letters of Robert Browning, Collected by Thomas J. Wise. Ed. Thurman L. Hood. London: John Murray, 1933.

Robert Browning and Julia Wedgewood: A Broken Friendship as Revealed by Their Letters. Ed. Richard Curle. London: John Murray and Jonathan Cape, 1937.

Dearest Isa: Robert Browning's Letters to Isabella Blagden. Ed. Edward C. McAleer. Austin: University of Texas Press, 1951.

New Letters of Robert Browning. Ed. William Clyde DeVane and Kenneth L. Knickerbocker. London: John Murray, 1951.

Browning to His American Friends: Letters between the Brownings, the Story's and James Russell Lowell. Ed. Gertrude Reese Hudson. London: Bowes and Bowes, 1965.

Learned Lady: Letters from Robert Browning to Mrs. Thomas Fitzgerald. Ed. Edward C. McAleer. Cambridge: Harvard University Press, 1966.

The Letters of Robert Browning and Elizabeth Barrett, 1845-1846. Ed. Elvan Kintner. 2 vols. Cambridge, Mass.: The Belknap Press of Harvard University Press, 1969.

BOOKS (BIOGRAPHY AND CRITICISM)

Allingham, William. *A Diary.* Ed. H. Allingham and D. Radford. London: Macmillan, 1907.

Armstrong, Isabel, ed. *The Major Victorian Poets: Reconsiderations.* London: Routledge and Kegan Paul, 1970.

Brockington, A. Allen. *Browning and the Twentieth Century: A Study of Robert Browning's Influence and Reputation.* London, 1932.

Broughton, Leslie N., and B.P. Stelter. *A Concordance to the Poems of Robert Browning.* 2 vols. New York: G.E. Stechart, 1924-25.

__________, Clarke Sutherland Northrup, and Robert Pearsall, Comps. *Robert Browning: A Bibliography, 1830-1950.* Ithaca: Cornell University Press, 1953.

Bush, Douglas. *Mythology and the Romantic Tradition in English Poetry.* Cambridge, Mass.: Harvard University Press, 1937. Re-issued, with new preface, 1969.

Chesterton, G.K. *Robert Browning.* New York and London: Macmillan, 1903.

Collins, Thomas J. *Robert Browning's Moral-Aesthetic Theory, 1833-1855.* Nebraska: The University of Nebraska Press, 1967.

Davies, Hugh Sykes. *Browning and the Modern Novel.* The St. John's College, Cambridge Lecture, 1960-62, Hull, 1962.

DeVane, William Clyde. *Browning's Parleyings: The Autobiography of a Mind.* New Haven: Yale University Press, 1927.

__________. *A Browning Handbook.* 2nd. ed. New York: Appleton Century Crofts, 1955.

Domett, Alfred. *The Diary of Alfred Domett*, 1872-1885. Ed. E.A. Horsman. London: Oxford University Press, 1953.

Drew, Philip. *The Poetry of Browning: A Critical Introduction.* London: Methuen, 1970.

__________, ed. *Robert Browning: A Collection of Critical Essays.* London: Methuen, 1966.

__________, ed. *Annotated Critical Bibliography of Robert Browning.* Harvester Wheatsheaf, 1989.

Duckworth, Francis R.G. *Browning: Background and Conflict.* London: Ernest Benn, 1931.

Duffin, Henry Charles. *Amphibian: A Reconsideration of Browning.* London: Bowes and Bowes, 1956.

Faverty, Frederic E. *The Victorian Poets: A Guide to Research.* Cambridge, Mass, 1956

Flowers, Betty S. *Browning and the Modern Tradition.* London: Macmillan, 1976.

Govil, O.P. *Browning's Poetics.* Aligarh: The Raleigh Literary Society, Aligarh Muslim University, 1955.

Gridley, Roy E. *Browning.* London: Routledge and Kegan Paul, 1972.

Griffin, W. Hall and Harry Christopher Minchin. *The Life of Robert Browning.* Revised ed. London: Methuen, 1910; rpt. Hamden, Conn: Archon, 1966.

Hair, Donald S. *Browning's Experiments with Genre.* Toronto: University of Toronto Press, 1972.

Harrold, William E. *The Variance and the Unity.* Athens: Ohio University Press, 1973.

Hintner, John Meigs. *Browning's Analysis of a Murder: A Case for The Inn Album.* Marquette: Northern Michigan University, 1969.

Honan, Park. *Browning's Characters: A Study in Poetic Technique.* New Haven and London: Yale University Press, 1961.

Irvine, William and Park Honan. *The Book, the Ring, and the Poet: A Biography of Robert Browning.* London: The Bodley Head, 1974.

Jack, Ian. *Browning's Major Poetry.* Oxford: Oxford University Press, 1973.

James, Henry. "The Novel in *The Ring and the Book.*" *Notes on Novelists with Some Other Notes.* London: Dent, 1914.

Faverty, Frederic E. *The Victorian Poets: A Guide to Research.* Cambridge, Mass., 1956.

Johnson, E.D.H. *The Alien Vision of Victorian Poetry: Sources of the Poetic Imagination in Tennyson, Browning and Arnold.* Princeton: Princeton University Press, 1952.

Jones, Sir Henry. *Browning as a Philosophical and Religious Teacher.* London: Macmillan, 1899.

Kenmare, Dallas. *Browning and Modern Thought.* London: Williams and Norgate, 1939.

King, Roma A., Jr. *The Bow and the Lyre: The Art of Browning.* Ann Arbor; The University of Michigan Press, 1957.

__________. *The Focusing Artifice.* Athens: Ohio University Press, 1968.

Langbaum, Robert. *The Poetry of Experience: The Dramatic Monologue in Modern Literary Tradition.* London: Chatto and Windus, 1957; rpt. Penguin University Books, 1974.

__________: *The Modern Spirit: Essays on the Continuity of Nineteenth and Twentieth Century Literature.* New York: Oxford University Press, 1970.

Litzinger, Boyd and K.L. Knickerbocker, eds. *The Browning Critics.* Lexington: The University of Kentucky Press, 1965.

Litzinger, Boyd and Donald Smalley, eds. *Browning: The Critical Heritage.* London: Routledge and Kegan Paul, 1970.

Maynard, John. *Browning's Youth.* Cambridge, Mass.: Harvard University Press, 1977.

Melchiori, Barbara. *Browning's Poetry of Reticence.* London: Oliver and Boyd, 1968.

Miller, Betty. *Robert Browning. A Portrait.* London: John Murray, 1952.

Miller, J. Hillis. *The Disappearance of God: Five Nineteenth Century Writers.* Cambridge, Mass.: Harvard University Press, 1963.

Orr, Mrs. Sutherland. *Life and Letters of Robert Browning* (1891). New Edition, revised and in part written by Frederic G. Kenyon. London: John Murray, 1908.

________. *A Handbook to the Works of Robert Browning.* 6th ed. London: Geoge Bell, 1927.

Raymond, W.O. *The Infinite Moment, and Other Essays in Robert Browning.* 2nd. ed. Toronto: University of Toronto Press, 1965.

Ryals, Clyde de L. *Browning's Later Poetry (1871-1889).* Ithaca: Cornell University Press, 1975.

Seigchrist, Mark. *Rough in Brutal Print: Legal Sources of Browning's Red Cotton Night-Cap Country.* Ohio State Univ. Press, 1986.

Shaw, W. David. *The Dialectical Temper: The Rhetorical Art of Robert Browning.* Ithaca: Cornell University Press, 1968.

Smalley, Donald, ed. *Browning's Essay on Chatterton.* Cambridge: Harvard University Press, 1948.

Tillotson, Geoffrey and Kathleen. *Mid-Victorian Studies.* University of London: Athlone Press, 1965.

Tracy, Clarence, ed. *Browning's Mind and Art: Essays Old and New.* Edinburgh and London: Oliver and Boyd, 1968.

Walker, Hugh. *The Literature of the Victorian Era.* Cambridge University Press, 1910. Reprinted, Delhi: S. Chand, 1955.

Ward, Maisie. *Robert Browning and His World.* 2 vols. *The Private Face 1812-1861.* London: Cassell, 1967.

________. *Two Robert Brownings 1861-1889.* London: Cassell, 1969.

Wiley, Basil. *Nineteenth Century Studies.* London: Chatto and Windus, 1949.

ARTICLES

DeVane, William Clyde. "The Harlot and the Thoughtful Young Man: A Study of the Relation between Rossetti's *Jenny* and Browning's *Fifine at the Fair.*" *Studies in Philology*, 29 (1932), 463-84.

________. "Browning and the Spirit of Greece." *Nineteenth Century Studies*, ed. H. Davis, W.C. DeVane, and R.C. Bald. Ithaca: Cornell University Press, 1940.

________. "The Virgin and the Dragon." *Yale Review,* 37 (1947), 33-46.

Columbus, Claudette Kemper. "*Fifine at the Fair.* A Masque of Sexuality and Death Seeking Figures of Expression." *Studies in Browning and His Circle*, 2, No. 1, Spring 1974, 21-38.

Crowder, Ashby Bland. "A Note on Section VIII of Browning's *The Inn Album*." *Studies in Browning and His Circle,* 1, No. 1, Spring 1973, 21-23.

__________. "Browning's Case for the Elder Man." *Studies in Browning and His Circle,* 2, No. 2, Fall 1974, 21-31.

Davis, Cory Biemann. "From Knowledge to Belief in *La Saisiaz: The Two Poets of Croisic*." *Studies in Browning and His Circle*, 6, No. 1, Spring 1978, 7-24.

Fairchild, Hoxie Neale. "Browning, the Simple-Hearted Casuist." *University of Toronto Quarterly.* April 1949, 234-40.

Felgor, Robert. "Browning's Narrative Art." *Studies in Browning and His Circle*, 3, No. 2, Fall 1975, 81-94.

Friend, Joseph H. "Euripides Browningized: The Meaning of *Balaustion's Adventures*." *Victorian Poetry,* 2 (1964), 179-86.

Govil, O.P. "Satire in Browning's *Fifine at the Fair*." *Nineteenth Century Studies: Essays Presented to Dr. A. Bose.* Calcutta: The World Press, 1973, 143-61.

Hetzler, Leo A. "The Case of *Prince Hohenstiel-Schwangau:* Browning and Napoleon III." *Victorian Poetry*, 15, No. 4, Winter 1977, 335-50.

Hicks, M.A. "Browning's *The Inn Album*: Conclusions beyond the Curtain Call." *Studies in Browning and His Circle*, 3, No. 1, Spring 1975, 120-23.

Hintner, John Meigs. "Browning's Grotesque Period." *Victorian Poetry*, 4 (1966), 1-13.

Kendall, J.L. "Browning's *Fifine*: Meaning and Method." *Victorian Newsletter*, No. 22, Fall 1962, 16-18.

King, Roma A., Jr. "The Necessary Surmise: The Shaping Spirit of Robert Browning's Poetry." *Romantic and Victorian: Studies in Memory of William H. Marshall*, ed. W. Paul Elledge and Richard L. Hoffman. Rutherford: Fairleigh Dickinson University Press, 1971, 346-61.

Knickerbocker, Kenneth L. "Browning and His Critics." *Sewanee Review*, 43 (1933), 283-91.

Langbaum, Robert. "Browning and the Question of Myth." *PMLA,* 81 (1966), 575-84.

Melchiori, Barbara. "Browning's Don Juan." *Essays in Criticism*, XVI (1966), 416-40.

Preyer, Robert. "Two Styles in the Verse of Robert Browning." *ELH,* 32 (1965), 47-59.

Priestley, F.E.L. "A Reading of *La Saisiaz*." *University of Toronto Quarterly*, 25, No. 1, October 1955, 47-59.

Siegchrist, Mark. "Browning's *Red Cotton Night-Cap Country:* The Process of Imagination." *Victorian Poetry*, 12, 1974, 137-52.

_________. "Narrative obtuseness in Browning's 'Clive'." *Studies in Browning and His Circle*, 3, No. 1, Spring 1975, 53-60.

_________. "Type needs Antitype: The Structure of Browning's *Parleyings.*" *Victorian Newsletter*, No. 50, Fall 1976, 1-10.

_________. "Thematic Coherence in Browning's *Dramatic Idylls.*" *Victorian Poetry*, 15, No. 3, Autumn 1977, 227-39.

Slim, E. Warwick. "Judgement and Justice in 'Ivan Ivanovitch'." *Browning Society Notes*, 4, No. 1, March 1974, 3-9.

Watkins, Charlotte Crawford. "The Abstruser Themes of Browning's *Fifine at the Fair.*" *PMLA,* 74 (1959), 426-37.

_________. Browning's *Red Cotton Night-Cap Country* and Carlyle." *Victorian Studies,* 7 (1964), 359-74.

_________. "Form and Sense in Browning's *The Inn Album.*" *Browning Institute Studies*, 2, January-July 1974, 65-76.

ANCILLARY STUDIES

Allott, Miriam. *Novelists on the Novel.* London: Routledge and Kegan Paul, 1962.

Beach, J.W. *The Twentieth Century Novel: A Study in Technique.* New York: Appleton Century Crofts, 1932. Rep., Ludhiana: Lyall, 1965.

Booth, Wayne. *The Rhetoric of Fiction.* Chicago: The University of Chicago Press, 1961.

Leavis, F.R. *The Great Tradition.* London: Chattto and Windus, 1962.

_________. *New Bearings in English Poetry.* London: Chatto and Windus, 1935. Revised edition, 1950.

O'Connor, William Van. *Forms of Modern Fiction: Essays Collected in Honour of Joseph Warren Beach.* Bloomington: Indiana University Press, 1962.

Phelps, Gilbert. *The Russian Novel in English Fiction.* London: Hutchinson's University Library, 1956.

Raban, Jonathan. *The Technique of Modern Fiction: Essays in Practical Criticism.* London: Edward Arnold, 1968.

Scholes, Robert and Robert Kellogg. *The Nature of Narrative.* London: and Oxford: Oxford University Press, 1966. Reprinted, 1978.

Shapira, Morris, ed. *Henry James: Selected Literary Criticism.* London: Heinemann, 1963.

Sutherland, James. *English Satire.* The Clark Lectures. Cambridge: At the University Press, 1956.

INDEX